Administration of Schools
for
Young Children
Second Edition

Administration of Schools for Young Children

Second Edition

PHYLLIS CLICK

10   9   8   7

LIBRARY OF CONGRESS CATALOG CARD NUMBER: 79-55285
ISBN: 0-8273-1575-9

Printed in the United States of America
Published simultaneously in Canada
by Nelson Canada,
A Division of International Thomson Limited

DELMAR PUBLISHERS INC.
2 COMPUTER DRIVE, WEST — BOX 15-015
ALBANY, NEW YORK 12212

PREFACE

Administration of Schools for Young Children is based on more than thirty years of experience in early childhood education. The book covers areas dealing with the duties and responsibilities of an administrator, including preparation, implementation, and evaluation of educational goals. Units dealing with the selection, supervision, and evaluation of staff members; budgeting processes; food and health services; and discussion of laws and regulations with which the administrator should be familiar all provide the director with pertinent data. A section on the value of professional organizations and agencies and of their publications serves as an excellent resource aid for additional information and professional growth. The units on working with parents describe the development of parent education and community participation.

The student of childhood programs and the beginning director will be able to gain understanding of the administrator in the roles of director and teacher; the director with experience may be challenged by some of the ideas presented in the text.

Administration of Schools for Young Children is highly illustrated and has suggested activities and unit-end reviews based on the objectives which introduce each unit. Interaction with people is emphasized. Practical guides are given.

Traditionally, early childhood programs have been staffed almost exclusively by women. Although this situation is presently changing, this text still refers to the director as a woman — but only for the sake of clarity. The child is consistently referred to as male.

Phyllis Click has vast experience in early childhood education and elementary school settings. She has served as designer and director of federally funded projects for training administrators and teachers of child care. As chief administrative officer of a private junior college which provided students with theory and practice in child care programs, she became familiar with problems of administration and education. She is currently teaching Early Childhood Education at Moorpark College in California.

Other books in the Early Childhood Education series are:

Early Childhood Experiences in Language Arts — J. Machado
Creative Activities for Young Children — Mayesky, Neuman, and Wlodkowski
Early Childhood Development and Education — J. Gilley
Home and Community Influences on Young Children — K. VanderVen
Experiences in Music for Young Children — M.C. Weller Pugmire
Experiences in Science for Young Children — D. Neuman
Experiences in Math for Young Children — R. Charlesworth and D. Radeloff
Mainstreaming in Early Childhood Education — E. Allen
A Practical Guide to Solving Preschool Behavior Problems — E. Essa
Understanding Child Development — For Adults Who Work With Young Children — R. Charlesworth

CONTENTS

Section 1
ADMINISTERING THE PROGRAM

Unit 1 Responsibilities of the Director

OBJECTIVES

After studying this unit, the student should be able to

- State the responsibilities of a director
- Identify the three roles of a director
- Devise and use a self-evaluation instrument

Directing a school for young children means taking part in a wide variety of activities. During a given day, a typical director may perform any or all of the following tasks:

- Greet parents and children
- Help some children part with parents for the day

- Find a substitute for an ill teacher
- Review the rainy day schedule with teachers
- Prepare a monthly financial report
- Arrange for repair of a leaking roof

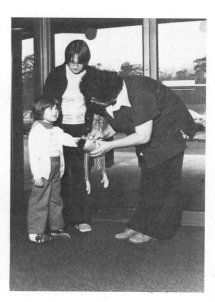

Fig. 1-1 Transition from Home to School

| | DAY CARE CENTER | | FAMILY DAY CARE |
	DIRECTOR	TEACHER	HOME OPERATOR
ALABAMA	+	HS	NS
ALASKA	HS	NS	(NS)
ARIZONA*	NS	NS	NS
ARKANSAS	HS	NS	(NS)
CALIFORNIA	+	+	NS
COLORADO	+	HS	NS
CONNECTICUT	+	HS	NS
DELAWARE	+	+	(NS)
FLORIDA	NS	NS	NS
GEORGIA	HS	HS	NS
HAWAII	+	+	NS
IDAHO**	NS	NS	NS
ILLINOIS	+	+	NS
INDIANA	+	+	NS
IOWA	+	+	NS
KANSAS	+	NS	NS
KENTUCKY	NS	NS	NS
LOUISIANA*	NS	NS	NS
MAINE	+	HS	(NS)
MARYLAND	NS	NS	NS
MASSACHUSETTS*	+		NS
MICHIGAN	+	+	NS
MINNESOTA	NS	NS	NS
MISSISSIPPI**	+	+	NS
MISSOURI	+	NS	(NS)
MONTANA	NS	NS	NS
NEBRASKA	+	+	NS
NEVADA	+	NS	N/AP
NEW HAMPSHIRE	HS	HS	NS
NEW JERSEY*	+	+	N/AP
NEW MEXICO	NS	NS	NS
NEW YORK	NS	NS	NS
NORTH CAROLINA*	NS	NS	(NS)
NORTH DAKOTA	HS	NS	(NS)
OHIO*	+	HS	NS
OKLAHOMA	HS	HS	NS
OREGON*	NS	NS	N/AP
PENNSYLVANIA	+	+	NS
RHODE ISLAND	+	+	NS
SOUTH CAROLINA	NS	NS	(NS)
SOUTH DAKOTA	+	+	NS
TENNESSEE	+	+	NS
TEXAS	HS	NS	NS
UTAH	NS	NS	NS
VERMONT	NS	NS	
VIRGINIA	+	HS	NS
WASHINGTON	+	NS	NS
WEST VIRGINIA*	HS	NS	NS
WISCONSIN	+	+	N/AP
WYOMING	+	+	NS
DISTRICT OF COLUMBIA	NS	NS	NS

+	Some college or equivalent experience	*	No mandatory licensing requirement for family day care homes
HS	High school	**	No mandatory licensing requirement for day care centers
NS	Not specified		No licensing law for homes
N/AP	Not applicable	( )	Also a requirement for group day care homes

Fig. 1-2 Education and Training Requirements For Day Care Center and Family Day Care

(State and Local Day Care Licensing Requirements, U.S. Dept. Health, Education, and Welfare. (OCD) 73-1006, p G-1)

- Hire a new cook

- Outline an agenda for a staff meeting

- Arrange a conference with a parent to discuss a problem

- Resolve a dispute between two teachers

- Show a new parent and child around the school

- Confer with the cook about menus for the following week

- Order a supply of canned goods

- Schedule a trip for the five-year-old group

Also, in some schools the director must assume part or total responsibility for teaching a group of children. In a small proprietary school or in a family day care home, the director-operator may be the only staff member. Administrative tasks must be done before or after class time. In a larger school, teaching may take only a portion of the director's time; the remainder can be used for administrative jobs.

Thus, to perform these many tasks effectively, the director or director-teacher must make use of a wide range of skills acquired from a variety of experiences. As shown in figure 1-2, some states require completion of college courses before licensing a day care owner. These courses may include child development, program planning, and administration. It is helpful if a director has a knowledge of management principles either from academic work or from job experience.

In addition to management and teaching skills, a director must have the ability to organize the many resources of the school. She also fosters good human relations through use

Fig. 1-3 **The director is manager, organizer, and communicator.**

of effective and clear communication with children, teachers, and parents.

THE DIRECTOR AS MANAGER

Because the director of a school for young children is often the only person responsible for the day-to-day operation of the school, the management style and management skills of the director are extremely important to its success. The director's style of management should provide an atmosphere in which staff, parents, and children are happy; her methods of management should provide for the smooth functioning of all parts of the school operation.

Management Style

Management style may be classed as democratic, authoritarian, or laissez-faire. The *democratic manager* involves others in decisions and policy-making processes. She provides opportunities for them to share in making choices and accepting responsibility for those choices.   She involves them in the formulation of policies that affect them.   The *authoritarian manager* makes the decisions and determines policies.   She tells others what is to be done and allows no choices.   The *laissez-faire manager* remains passive, leaving decisions and policy-making to others.   She may give suggestions, but does not participate nor provide leadership.

The democratic manager sets up a school in which staff members are involved in many aspects of the operation.   They may take part in developing objectives, program planning, equipment purchases, and parent education activities.   The director provides leadership and support and sometimes acts as arbiter, but decisions are made and policies are formulated by the entire staff.

The authoritarian manager usually believes she has greater knowledge and experience and, therefore, has the responsibility for making decisions for others.   She sets objectives for the school, indicates ways in which these objectives will be implemented, purchases equipment to support objectives, and conducts all parent education activities.

The laissez-faire manager takes a less active role than either of the other types.   This kind of manager may allow teachers to set objectives for their own classrooms and to implement those objectives however they wish.   Suggestions may be made for purchases, but decisions are left to teachers or a governing board.   Parent education activities may be done by teachers or by the director.

Strong, experienced teachers usually can function well and be quite happy under a laissez-faire manager.   Inexperienced or unsure teachers may find they need the kind of direction and support offered by a democratic or an authoritarian manager. The authoritarian director tells them what to do; the democratic director involves them in decision making only as they are ready to accept the responsibility.

In practice, few directors can be classed strictly as one kind of manager or another. Most will probably find that a certain approach is effective at times but that a different approach is needed at other times.   It is necessary to be authoritarian with some teachers. Other staff members can be allowed more freedom of action.

Methods of Management

Methods of management include the tools, procedures, and techniques that ensure the smooth operation of all aspects of a school.   Records, schedules, budgets, inventories, personnel policies, and hiring practices are examples.   The director must be aware of all the areas of her responsibility and develop ways to fulfill each of these effectively and without wasted time and energy.

This unit points out the responsibilities of a director.   The following units help in acquiring the tools, procedures, and techniques a director needs.   Some **general responsibilities of a director are listed**:

- She determines the state and local regulatory agencies and the requirements that must be met regarding licensing, health, and safety regulations.

- She serves as an ex-officio member of the board of directors and attends committee meetings as necessary.

- She provides leadership for setting overall goals for the school — to be used as a basis for curriculum objectives.

- She evaluates her own work as a director and plans for continuing professional growth.

The director has enrollment duties:

- She enrolls children and keeps an accurate waiting list.

- She interviews prospective parents, giving information about the school.

- She plans orientation for new parents.
- She knows the changing needs of the community in order to maintain full enrollment.

The director works with curriculum:

- She provides direction to staff in setting curriculum objectives appropriate to the school.
- She works with staff to implement and maintain objectives.
- She provides leadership in evaluating the curriculum.

The director is responsible for the physical plant and equipment:

- She plans, allocates, and uses space effectively.
- She maintains the physical plant by providing custodial care and repair services.
- She plans for the future needs of the school for space and equipment.
- She keeps records such as inventories, repair schedules, and purchase information.
- She manages supplies – reordering as needed.

The director is in charge of finances:

- She sets up a budget.
- She controls budget expenditures.
- She collects fees and tuition.
- She keeps adequate records of income and expenditures.
- She handles petty cash disbursements.
- She prepares monthly reports on expenditures to date.
- She prepares a year-end analysis of budget and expenditures.

The director is concerned with staff relationships:

- She recruits and hires staff.

- She prepares job descriptions for each position.
- She formulates and implements personnel policies.
- She assists staff in implementation of school objectives.
- She provides a continuing assessment of staff development needs.
- She plans with staff for in-service training.
- She encourages staff involvement in community activities.
- She meets with staff members to resolve problems.
- She prepares a staff handbook and keeps it current.
- She keeps personnel records.

The director provides leadership in parent involvement and education:

- She communicates objectives of the school to parents.
- She plans and implements parent education activities.
- She confers with parents regarding their child's progress.
- She encourages a variety of ways for parents to be involved in school activities.
- She keeps adequate records of parent involvement and education activities.

The director must plan for health and safety:

- She maintains an adequate health program for the school.
- She keeps health records on all children enrolled.
- She keeps staff informed concerning the health status of each child.
- She confers with parents as needed about child's health status.

- She refers families to community agencies for special help when necessary.
- She continues to be informed regarding legal responsibilities of the school in relation to safety.
- She plans activities for staff and children to teach safety.

The director builds and maintains good community relations:

- She interprets the school and its objectives to visitors.
- She represents the school at community functions.
- She establishes contacts with community agencies.
- She involves self and staff in professional and legislative activities.

THE DIRECTOR AS ORGANIZER

In order for the many parts of any institution to work together as a unit, the director must be able to organize the use of its resources. Institutional resources include people, time, and materials. Organization of the use of these resources enables those involved to accomplish their tasks more effectively. Lack of organization usually results in an inefficient use of time.

People

The people in a school are its most important resource. Without them the school cannot operate. The manner in which people work together determines the success or failure of the program.

The director must create and foster the feeling that each staff member is important as an individual and as a member of the group. This requires a sensitive balancing of group needs and individual needs. Scheduling of time, allocation of space, and assignment of

Fig. 1-4 **Director and Parent: A Partnership for the Care and Education of the Child**

duties are all areas in which group and individual needs may have to be resolved.

Time

Adequate time must be allowed for all essential functions. Schedules must be flexible enough to allow time for unexpected and unplanned activities.

Within the time span of a school day certain essential activities take place. These activities are dictated by the program type or program objectives. The director must allow time for each within a schedule that is flexible enough to allow an extension of an activity when necessary. For example, a day care center allows time for personal care activities such as toileting, hand washing, teeth brushing, eating, and resting. A half-day school, whose objectives emphasize the development of cognitive skills, allows time for a variety of learning activities. In each of these cases, teachers and children should have enough time to satisfactorily complete the activity and, whenever possible, extend it if it seems to be called for.

The director can organize time into small units for each activity or she can schedule blocks of time during which choices of several activities are available. A schedule that is organized into small blocks tends to be fragmented and may prevent a child from getting intensely involved because he knows he has only a limited amount of time. On the other hand, a schedule organized into larger blocks of time allows a child to make choices. He can spend a large amount of time on one activity, or he has time to explore several activities for shorter periods of time. Figure 1-5 shows examples of these two methods of scheduling.

Tight organization of time may affect the way in which teachers function as well as the way children respond. If a teacher must constantly be aware of the clock, she can hardly concentrate on her interactions with children. Close organization of time may not allow for differences in how people function. Some move at a slow pace; others at a fast pace. A rigid schedule may allow adequate time for one teacher, but too little for another. It is the responsibility of the director to assess, use, and organize time well and still satisfy as many needs as possible.

Materials

Equipment and supplies are the materials used to achieve the given objectives of a childhood center. How materials are distributed — how much is given and when — is an issue that affects the atmosphere of a school.

The director must be able to organize distribution of materials in such a way that each person is adequately supplied. Each staff member should have the materials necessary to carry out her or his job. Each should feel that the supplies were given out fairly.

On the other hand, the director must be able to dispense materials in such a way that waste is minimized. The staff should realize that the supply is not endless and should be encouraged to use materials wisely.

Each director must decide if an open central supply area will be successful or if supplies

TIGHT ORGANIZATION OF TIME	
9:00 - 9:15	Group time - sharing, songs, etc.
9:15 - 9:45	Learning center choices
9:45 - 10:00	Cleanup and toileting
10:00 - 10:15	Snack time
10:15 - 10:30	Music activities
10:30 - 11:15	Outdoor play
11:15 - 11:30	Inside for story time
11:30	Go home

LOOSE ORGANIZATION OF TIME	
9:00 - 10:15	Inside time - group activities, learning centers, cleanup and toileting.
10:15 - 10:40	Snack time and motor coordination activities
10:40 - 11:20	Outdoor play
11:20 - 11:30	Inside for story, music, etc. (Outdoors in good weather)
11:30	Go home

Fig. 1-5 Sample Schedules to Illustrate Ways to Organize Time

must be given out at intervals as needed. The decision has an important effect on staff morale. The manner in which the decision is carried out is even more important in determining how the staff works together.

THE DIRECTOR AS COMMUNICATOR

Much of the work of early childhood education is based on communication between adults and between adults and children. Teachers talk to each other about schedules or exchange ideas for the curriculum. Parents like to know what their children have done while at the center. They talk to the teacher about home events that may be important to the child. Young children talk a great deal as they develop speech. They ask endless questions in order to satisfy their curiosity. The director spends much of her day talking to staff, parents, and children in order to carry out her duties.

The ability to talk sets human beings apart from all other animals. People have learned to use this ability to communicate with one another for many purposes. Communication often brings about closer relationships among people. It may provide the solution to a problem. It may bring about a change in the behavior of one or more parties to the communication. Communication offers a sharing of experiences not otherwise possible.

The importance of the quality of this communication cannot be underestimated. The director of an early childhood center can set the example for communications throughout her school. If she is clear and direct in her messages to others, she will serve as a model to them. She can help others to develop the ability to speak clearly and effectively by recognizing and using clear and direct communication.

Nearly everyone has experienced difficulty in communicating clearly with another person. Each person knows what she means when she says something and is sure her meaning is clear to the other person. Often, however, what has been said is misunderstood. Something has happened during the sending and receiving process.

In order to understand what goes wrong in the communication process, it is important to recognize that there are two kinds of messages that are being sent and received. There are *verbal messages* — messages based on words, symbols, and ideas. There are also *nonverbal messages,* based on facial expression, movements, posture, and tone of voice.

Verbal Messages

Words are the coding system and the means by which thoughts or ideas are conveyed. Although each word in a language has a specific meaning, coloration of that meaning is acquired by life experiences. When a specific word is chosen, all the speaker's experiences with that word are included in the meaning.

In a similar way, when the listener hears the word, its meaning is sifted through all of the listener's past experiences with the word. If their experiences have been different, the sender and receiver of the verbal message may interpret its meaning quite differently.

Nonverbal Messages

Nonverbal messages are also very much a part of our system of communicating. Certain gestures or expressions are fairly well understood by everyone. A smile usually means the person is happy and a frown may convey anger.

There are many subtle ways of expressing feelings that are not universally understood or recognized. A slight tilt of the head may add a questioning quality to a smile. A relaxed posture may indicate that the anger conveyed by the frown is not intense. Not everyone notices these more subtle nonverbal messages, nor will they interpret nonverbal messages in the same way.

Fig. 1-6 Nonverbal Communication

The director of a center who wishes to establish and maintain clear communication with others must be aware of the effect of both kinds of messages. She must learn to choose her own verbal and nonverbal communications so that others understand what is meant. She must also learn to observe and understand the words and gestures or expressions of others.

Preventing Problems in Communication

To prevent problems in communication, there are some specific steps a director may take. First, she should be certain **what** she wishes the other person to know.

Indecision about the content of the message may cause the receiver to be confused. The words of the communication may say one thing; the facial expression or gestures may say another. If the director is clear about the content, words and expression are more likely to say the same things.

Second, the director should carefully consider **when** to convey her message. An important message should not be related when the listener is otherwise engaged and cannot give full attention. For instance, a teacher cannot give full attention to a message when she is busy with a child.

If the director needs to discuss a problem with a teacher, she should choose a time when the teacher is free and rested. Discussion of problems will be less constructive if they take place at the end of a hectic day.

Allowing **enough time** for the sending-receiving process will also help to eliminate problems in communication. Words said "on the run" are likely to be misunderstood. Topics that may need discussion or clarification should be started only if there is ample time to discuss them.

Where messages are conveyed is also an important issue. Different atmospheres for the communication are created in the office and in a staff lounge when one is available. Selection of the office for the discussion may emphasize its seriousness or confidential nature. The lounge may create a more informal and open atmosphere. The director may choose one over the other, but should be conscious of the location and its probable effect.

How messages are conveyed is a fifth consideration in the prevention of communication problems. A director may choose to write certain messages rather than talk to each person involved. Written messages may be more efficient, but they are somewhat impersonal. Also, they allow no opportunity for immediate feedback.

How messages are conveyed may include the use of expressions or gestures rather than words. Sometimes a smile or a nod of the head conveys as much as is needed in a particular situation; words would not add to the message.

It is often necessary to **follow up** on a message. It may become apparent that distortion or confusion has taken place. If an atmosphere for open dialogue has been encouraged in the school, the person involved will admit any confusion, ask for clarification, and feel free to offer suggestions. The director herself may reopen the issue and further explain her meaning. She may also try to find out why the confusion took place so that she can avoid it in the future.

Although the difficulties involved in communicating ideas and feelings to another person are sometimes frustrating, an effective director will persist in her efforts. Clear and direct lines of communication throughout the school will make the job of director easier and more rewarding.

SELF-EVALUATION

Assessment of her own strengths and weaknesses is an important task for the

DIRECTOR'S SELF-ASSESSMENT			
	Often	Never	Sometimes
• I show consideration for the feelings of my employees.			
• I can admit my mistakes when I am wrong.			
• I try to praise more often than criticize.			
• I let my employees share in decisions that affect them.			
• I welcome suggestions from others.			
• I listen carefully to the problems of others.			

Fig. 1-7 Sample Director's Self-evaluation Sheet

director. Self-evaluation enables her to look at her own performance and see the parts of her job that she wishes to improve upon. It will also enable her to see the things she does well and to feel a sense of accomplishment.

Since the director does many different kinds of tasks, she may want to concentrate on certain parts of her job during any given time period. As an example, she may want to judge her relationship with staff members. The job responsibilities listed earlier show that a variety of tasks are included in staff relationships.   From these, questions for self-assessment can be formulated:

- Have I found the best possible teachers for my school, or could I have explored other recruitment sources?

- Do my job descriptions include all the tasks that I expect staff members to perform?

- Have I created an atmosphere in which teachers see evaluation as a way to help them?

- Do I convey the attitude that I am willing to help others to solve problems?

Another form of assessment is based on a list of desired characteristics and makes use of a rating scale. This list may vary from year to year, again as the director decides to concentrate on parts of her job. Figure 1-7 shows an example of this kind of assessment tool.

Either of these assessment instruments will yield information that the director can use to improve her functioning. A list of specific things to do will help. Ways in which a director might wish to improve staff relationships are listed:

- Remember to spend a few minutes each day with each staff member.

- Remember to praise for work that is well done.

- Try to understand the feelings of others by listening.

- Offer help without being asked.

- Encourage staff members to increase their own abilities by trying out new ideas.

- Really consider the suggestions that are made by others.

SUMMARY

Directing a school for young children requires a variety of skills: the ability to manage, organize, and communicate.

The director's style of management should provide an atmosphere in which staff, parents, and children are happy. Management style may be classed as democratic, authoritarian, or laissez-faire.

The methods of management encompass the tools, procedures, and techniques that ensure smooth operation of all aspects of a school. The job responsibilities of the director are varied and include such diverse areas as licensing and regulations, setting goals, self-evaluation, enrollment, curriculum, physical plant and equipment, finances, staff relationships, parent involvement and education, health and safety, and community relations.

As organizer, the director must be able to use the resources of the school. She must be able to use the abilities of people in ways that are sensitive to group and individual needs. She must be able to set aside specific time for essential functions and still allow time for unexpected activities.

As communicator, the director must establish a climate of clear and direct communication. She sets an example by being clear and direct in her messages to others. She helps others to develop communication skills. She must be able to recognize verbal and nonverbal messages.

To prevent confusion and maintain clear communication with others, the director should

- Know what she wishes the other person to know

- Consider when to convey her message

- Allow enough time for the sending-receiving process

- Choose where messages are conveyed

- Decide how messages are to be conveyed

- Do follow-up when messages are unclear

Assessment of her own strengths and weaknesses is an important task for the director. She can use questions formulated from a list of job responsibilities. She can also use a rating scale based on a list of desired characteristics.

STUDENT ACTIVITIES

- Visit a school for young children. With her permission, follow the activities of the director for an hour or two. Count the number of people she talks to and note what action it was necessary to take regarding each contact.
- Discuss the method used by your center for the distribution of materials. Make suggestions as to how waste can be controlled without denying needed supplies to the staff.
- Discuss an incident in which your communication to another student or teacher was misinterpreted. Why do you think it happened?
- Discuss the problems which might arise in a center regarding allocation of time. How could those problems be prevented?

REVIEW

1. Name three styles of management.
2. Compare authoritarian and democratic managers.
3. What is meant by the term *laissez-faire*?
4. What are the most important resources of a school?
5. What are the director's responsibilities for curriculum, for the physical plant and equipment, and for staff relationships?
6. Give two examples of nonverbal messages.
7. List six ways a director can communicate clearly and effectively.

Unit 2 Types of Schools and Programs

OBJECTIVES

After studying this unit, the student should be able to

- State the differences between a half-day school and one that is in session all day
- State the primary source of income for the two types of schools
- Describe the characteristics of each type of private and publicly funded program

There is a growing trend for women to continue to work after marriage or childbirth. Seventeen million women with children under the age of thirteen work outside the home. Many of these children are cared for in nursery schools, day care centers or family day care homes. More day care services are needed, however, because a large proportion of these children are left to care for themselves before and after school hours. Working women are demanding day care services as part of their job benefits; women's political organizations are making provision for day care an important issue.

Intense concern for the education of the young child is also a product of changes in the last two decades. Education research has pointed to the importance of early learning experiences as a base for later learning. Greater knowledge of how the child perceives, thinks, and learns has led to an awareness of the need for good educational programs at the preschool level.

The student of child development, the potential director, and the person who is already directing a school for young children —

all need to be familiar with the types of programs available. They should all know how each kind of program is funded, the characteristics of each, and any other factors of importance to the director. The student of early childhood education should have an overall understanding of the types of programs in order to choose the one for which he or she is best suited. The experienced teacher accepting a first job as a director must understand the differences in programs in order to meet the problems she will face. Problems successfully solved by other directors in a similar situation may help the new director to deal more effectively with problems that may arise. The person who is already administering a school will gain by understanding the similarities and differences among programs.

It is important to understand the differences in programs based on the length of the school day. There are two basic program types: those that are in session for half a day and those that are open for longer hours. The difference in the number of hours that children attend school influences the purpose, the curriculum, and the characteristics of the staff needed.

HALF-DAY SCHOOLS

Schools that offer daily sessions of four hours or less are usually established for the primary purpose of providing educational experiences to young children. Some schools have added educational programs for parents along with their infants and toddlers. Some offer job training to mothers.

Half-day schools are likely to be organized around groups of children with one or several teachers. The groups vary in size according to the ages of the children. From 6 to 10 two- and three-year-olds may be in one group. As many as 20 or 25 four- and five-year-olds may make up another group. The ratio of adults to children will vary from 1:5 (one adult to five children) up to the higher 1:15 ratio. Some programs have ratios that must conform to federal guidelines, or are dictated by state regulations.

A typical session lasts three hours, although some programs may be scheduled for two-and-one-half or four hours. During the session there are opportunities for the child to participate in a variety of activities such as art, block building, or dramatic play; group activities may include story time, music, and snack or lunch. Individual or group experiences for the development of learning ability may also be planned. Early childhood experiences in language arts and outdoor play with wheel toys, large blocks, climbing equipment, and a sandbox will probably be part of the day's schedule.

The staff and director of a half-day school must be committed to the concept that young children are ready and eager to learn. The teachers, who are the ones who work most closely with the children, must be interested and enthusiastic about learning. They must be aware of the infinite possibilities for planned and spontaneous learning experiences within the school setting. The education of the director and teachers in this type of school should include courses in child development and general curriculum planning as well as work in specific areas such as science, music, math, art, literature, and language.

FULL-DAY SCHOOLS

Schools that offer sessions of more than four hours are established to provide group care while the parent works or for some other reason is not available to care for the child. These schools provide care for the preschool age child and for the school age child before and after his classes. A few offer care for infants and toddlers.

Day care centers, like the half-day schools, are usually organized around groups of children with one or several teachers. During the school day, there will be a change of teachers in each group as the shift ends. The director should try to keep these changes at a minimum because of the undesirable effects that frequent changes in staff have on the children.

The best programs use small groups and maintain a lower teacher/child ratio than is found in many half-day schools. Usually a 1:5 or 1:7 ratio is ideal; infants and toddlers require a lower ratio. Optimum group size ranges from six to fifteen children. Unfortunately,

Fig. 2-1 Day care centers, like half-day schools, are usually organized around groups of children with one or several teachers.

economic constraints in some programs increase the teacher/child ratio and the group size.

Typical sessions in day care are at least ten hours long although all children may not stay throughout that time. In order to allow for differences in parents' working hours, some centers may be open twelve hours or more. A very few schools around the country are open longer hours to accommodate evening work shifts. A few are open on Saturday and Sunday and provide overnight care.

A good program should provide for the total developmental needs of the child because children in day care are in school most of their waking hours. Time is allowed for the same experiences offered by the half-day session. Children participate in activities such as art, block building, puzzles, or dramatic play. Individual or group learning activities are planned for the development of the child's cognitive and perceptual skills. Outdoor play with wheel toys, large blocks, sandbox, and climbing equipment foster the child's motor development. In addition, enough time must be allowed for the child to learn to care for his physical and health needs. He learns to wash his hands, brush his teeth, and use the toilet without adult help. Sufficient time must be scheduled for the child to rest or sleep. Mealtimes and snacktimes are also important times of the day since the school should provide two-thirds of the child's food intake.

A good day-care program allows opportunities for children to be by themselves. Time may be scheduled so that children can be away from the group if they wish; after the nap is an appropriate period. Quiet activities which require limited involvement and stimulation or activities that the child can do alone should be a part of the afternoon schedule.

The director and teachers in a day care program must be physically and emotionally able to withstand the demands of being with young children for long hours each day. In order to conserve their own energy and that of the children, it is helpful if the adults are slow-paced and easygoing. Teachers who can and want to develop close relationships with children are successful in day care. The day care teacher strengthens and at times replaces the mother's role with the child. Children need the kind of nurturing, responsiveness, and physical care that a loving teacher can give. A knowledge of child development is important in order to understand and bring about changes in the child. Toilet training often takes place in school, eating habits are established, and learning patterns developed. In addition, the day care teacher must have the same kind of background in curriculum planning as the teacher in a half-day school needs.

TYPES OF SCHOOLS

Schools may also be classified according to sponsorship and their primary source of income. Although some schools may have

Fig. 2-2 **A child in day care needs to be alone at times.**

several sources of income, the primary source is used here to identify the type of school. The two types according to primary source of income are private schools and public schools.

Private Sponsorship

Private schools are owned by individuals or groups. Their primary source of income is from tuition.

Private proprietary schools. These schools have half-day or full-day programs, are owned by one or more persons, and are operated as profit-making businesses. They are the most numerous and are expected to be financially self-sustaining through tuition charges. Each school is licensed for a specific number of children, thus limiting the potential income.

As the profit margin for this type of school is often small, the owner is likely to be the director; she may possibly even be owner, director, and teacher. Sometimes a couple will operate a school such as this, sharing or interchanging the responsibilities of administering, teaching, and maintenance.

Two factors are important to a director of a private school. First, there is the freedom to initiate a program based on the owner's educational ideas. She may wish to further a particular method of teaching or emphasize one area of curriculum. For example, a Montessori school will have a program built around the ideas and materials of the Montessori method. Another school might use music or art as a vehicle for teaching all parts of the curriculum.

The second factor important to proprietary schools is the limited resources for income. These schools must be self-sustaining through tuitions; the number of children they can enroll is defined by licensing limits, however. When additional income is needed they cannot add more children; they can only raise

Fig. 2-3 A Private Preschool and Primary School

the tuition or cut back on expenses. There is always danger that budget concerns will become more important than the educational program. Often a director must try to find additional ways to add to the income of the school in order to resolve the problems. In a half-day school, she may offer both morning and afternoon sessions. She may institute Saturday classes for older children or evening classes for parents. She may accept some children three days a week or two days a week. Tuition for these two classes can be slightly higher than for one child enrolled five days a week. Although it is doubtful that it is possible to make large profits from a single private proprietary school, it is possible for the owner-operator to earn a reasonable income.

Family Day Care Home. The family day care home is usually a full-day school that provides care for the child of a working parent. It is owned and operated for profit by an individual and is licensed by a state agency. The license limits to six to ten the number of children who can be enrolled including the day care mother's own children.

Tuition is the only source of income and is very limited by the small number of children served. The day care mother does all of the administrative tasks, cleans, cooks, and provides educational activities for the children.

The advantage of this kind of program is that a woman can earn some income while at home with her own children. She also has complete freedom to design a curriculum that she believes in or that meets the needs of the children she serves. The disadvantage is that there is no relief for her during the hours that the children attend. Sometimes other family members may help her, but for the most part, the woman works alone. Also, she is isolated from professional aids and supports that other teachers may have available to them. She has no one to talk to about problems she encounters nor to help her with her own learning. A few colleges or community agencies are beginning to recognize the need for support and training for day care mothers and are developing programs to meet these needs.

Private educational corporations. As a result of the interest in early childhood education, private educational corporations have come into operation. A group of people may set up a corporation to plan and operate several schools for young children. These schools may offer half-day or day care programs. A chief administrator may be hired to coordinate the efforts of all the schools, and will hire and supervise the director of each school.

Financial problems may be lessened when several schools are in a corporation. Purchasing supplies and equipment may be less costly when it can be done in quantity. One building plan may be used for all the schools in the corporation. Maintenance and repair can be done by a rotating crew.

The director of each school in an educational corporation will have some advantages that are not available in a single school. Each

director may be able to obtain help from a shared consultant when planning a program or working on a budget. There may be opportunities for the directors of all the schools to share ideas and problems.

The director of a corporation school will probably not have the freedom to design the program she wants. It is more likely that the curriculum has been planned by the originators of the corporation. The director will be responsible for carrying out their directives.

Private franchise schools. A variation of the educational corporation schools are private franchise schools; they may be half-day or full-day programs. A *franchise* is a contract to provide a variety of services to the purchaser; the franchise is sold to an individual or group by a corporation. Curriculum guides, building plans, or financing may be included in the franchise. It may also have a name that is known and, therefore, have an advantage in recruiting children. The contract may provide for consultant help in finding and hiring staff.

The franchise school is a good method of investing in private enterprise for the person who has limited background or experience in early childhood education. A franchiser who is knowledgeable in early childhood education can supply the expertise needed to plan and operate a good program. As in the corporation school, however, freedom of the owner-director to design and conduct her own kind of school may be limited.

The prospective investor in a franchise school should be sure that the services promised can actually be delivered and that the program is educationally sound. A few franchises have been put together by businesses which have no real knowledge of early childhood education. They use a name and money to sell something that has no substance.

Company or business-owned schools. Another variation of the proprietary school is the company or business-owned school. Companies employing large numbers of women may include a day care center on their premises. Enrollment in these schools is usually limited to children of employees. Many companies have found this to be a way of stabilizing employment.

A related type of school is the early childhood school or day care center in an apartment complex or hospital. Here, too, enrollment will probably be limited to children of residents or employees.

These privately-owned schools may be only partially supported by tuition charges. The balance of the cost per child is shared by the company, hospital, or apartment owner. The cost that is not covered by tuition is considered to be a fringe benefit to the employee. In an apartment complex, the school is an added inducement to prospective tenants.

One of the most important characteristics of this type of school is its location. The company or hospital school is close to the parent's employment. This location makes transporting the child to school easy for the mother. It also makes it possible for the parent and child to visit each other during the day. A parent can have lunch with the child or visit during playtime. The children may take trips to the place where their parents work.

The apartment school is close to home. Often children can walk to school by themselves. This kind of school is truly a part of the community. Parents can work closely with staff to provide a good experience for the children.

Cooperative or playgroup schools. These schools are also privately owned but are operated as nonprofit enterprises. A co-op (as it is usually called) and a playgroup school are organized and owned by a group of parents who

have children in the school. Ownership is passed on when school enrollment ends. These schools may be incorporated and have a board of trustees elected by the parent members.

The co-op may be operated by a director hired by the parents. The director may also be required to function as the teacher. Parents take turns performing administrative functions, purchasing supplies, assisting in the classroom, and managing finances.

Cooperative and playgroup schools may offer half-day or full-day programs. Although these schools are usually sustained by tuitions, they are less costly to operate than other kinds of schools. Salary costs are considerably less than in other schools because of the active participation of the parents. Since they are nonprofit organizations, contributions are solicited and fund-raising activities planned in order to provide scholarships or supplement income.

Important to the director of this kind of school is the fact that all the parents are involved much more intensely than in any other kind of school. Participating parents have an opportunity to learn a great deal about early childhood education as well as the day-to-day details of administering a school. However, a parent working as an aide in the classroom may create problems for her own child. The child finds he must share his mother with other children. He may show his

Fig. 2-4 **Mothers and Children in a Cooperative School**

jealousy by clinging to his mother, crying, hitting, or withdrawing from activities. A sensitive director is needed to help mothers understand and deal with this kind of behavior. Also, parents who perform teaching or administrative functions become co-workers as well as employers. The director must be sensitive to the complexity of this kind of relationship.

The playgroup school may be more loosely organized than the cooperative. A group of mothers decide to meet several days a week to provide a group experience for their children. They may or may not hire a teacher to direct the activities. There is often no need for any kind of administrative structure or tuition. Expenses are shared because the group meets at the home of individual members.

Both the cooperative and the playgroup school can be beneficial to parents. By seeing their own child with other adults and children and by working with children from other families, parents can develop a better understanding of problems and relationships. They can also talk to other parents about the common problems of child rearing. In addition, observation of a teacher's methods of handling situations will add to their understanding of child behavior.

The director or teacher of a co-op or playgroup school must be able to respect and understand parents as well as children. She must be able to get along well with people. She must work with an untrained and volunteer staff.

Laboratory schools. Private colleges or universities may operate another type of private, nonprofit school. These are called laboratory schools and are usually housed on or near the campus. A half-day or full-day program may be offered. Although tuition may be charged, operational expenses are supplemented by one or several departments of the college or university. Sometimes grants for research or special projects add to the school's income.

The director of a "lab school" is expected to design a model program for young children. The school may be used for observations by students in many college classes; the model curriculum may be the basis for various kinds of research. The program of the laboratory school may set standards for other schools in the community.

Another purpose of the laboratory school is to provide practice teaching for students enrolled in teacher education at the sponsoring institution. The director must work closely with the academic department to design learning experiences for the students. She also has the advantage of working with other experts in the field of early childhood education. She, herself, may teach a related course in the college or university. Public colleges and universities may also have lab schools. (See description of day care centers in public colleges and universities.)

Parochial schools. Another type of private, nonprofit school is the parochial or church-sponsored school. These are set up by the church as an extension of its educational pro-

Fig. 2-5 A parochial school is sometimes an extension of the educational program of the sponsoring church.

gram or as a service to its members. Some may be completely financed by the church; others, partially financed. Enrollment may be limited to families of church members. This kind of school may be either full-day or half-day.

Policies for the parochial school are determined by a committee appointed by the church board. When the school is intended to serve as an extension of the church's educational program, it may be considered important that the director belong to the same faith. The director of a parochial school must work cooperatively with the church members in determining the kind of curriculum offered. She probably will have to submit her budget to the church board for approval.

Often, the facilities in a church-sponsored school must be shared with other activities of the church during the week or on weekends. The classroom may be used for Sunday school or social functions. The director and her staff may have to develop creative ways to utilize space and to store equipment at the end of the school day.

Community-sponsored schools. Another type of private, nonprofit school is the community-sponsored school. A women's group, philanthropic organization, or professional group assumes responsibility for financing the school. They conduct fund-raising drives and solicit contributions. Tuition, if any, is minimal. Some schools in this category have been started in order to provide day care for the children of working mothers. Training in child care for the residents of the community might also be included in the community-sponsored school.

Some community-sponsored schools may be classified as special schools. These schools offer half-day programs designed to meet the needs of children who have physical or emotional handicaps. Schools for the blind, deaf, or disabled fit into this group. Children

Fig. 2-6 **A father brings his son to a children's center.**

with behavior disorders or learning disabilities may also benefit from special schools.

The director of the community-sponsored school must be responsive to the needs of the community. Sometimes, the director is required to be a resident of the community. If not a resident, she must learn about the people, the problems, and the resources of the community.

Public Sponsorship

Public preschool programs are administered and funded through public agencies. They may be sponsored by a school district, social services, or a governmental bureau. Money for operation comes from local, state, or federal sources.

Child care centers. Child care centers are sponsored by public agencies and are maintained primarily to meet the needs of working mothers or one-parent families with limited incomes. They are full-day programs, usually open ten or twelve hours a day, five or six days a week. Funding comes from federal, state, county, or city sources — or a combination of these. Tuition may be charged on a sliding scale according to family income. Responsibility for operating the schools usually rests with the local school district, and the centers are often housed on elementary school grounds. They are sometimes referred to as child development centers.

The director of a child care center is hired by the local school board and carries out the policies of the board. Guidelines and regulations for parent fees, curriculum, staff qualifications, salary scales, purchasing, facility plan, and maintenance procedures may all be covered by board policy. Federal or state guidelines may include additional restrictions on administrative procedures and program requirements.

In this type of center, the director functions more as a manager, carrying out the policies handed down to her. The trend by the school districts, however, is now toward broader participation by the director in decision-making activities. In this way, it is possible for the director to have an opportunity to influence and guide policies before they are adopted.

Child care centers are often designed to accommodate a larger number of children than one usually finds in private schools. The funding of child care centers requires that large numbers of children be reached. The director may have to plan for as many as 150 children. She often must plan for a wide range of ages because many of these schools include after-school care for children who are six to twelve years old.

Resources available to a director of a publicly sponsored center are much more extensive than those available to private schools. Curriculum consultants, psychologists, nutritionists, doctors, dentists, and social workers may be available through the school system. These people make it possible for the child care center to provide a wide variety of programs and services to the staff and families.

Head Start. Since the early 1960s, the federal government has appropriated funds to provide preschool programs for children of low-income families. These are called Head Start and are considered one type of compensatory education program. They usually are half-day sessions, but may be full-day. Funds are distributed by a local community action agency to school districts, social agencies, colleges, or universities to operate the centers. Monitoring of Head Start centers is done by the Office of Child Development.

The curriculum is designed to offer early learning experiences to children who might not get these experiences at home. The curriculum is also designed to overcome deficiencies and to help prepare children to meet the academic demands of the elementary school.

Community participation and some community control are written into the program guidelines. The local community action council, whose members represent community groups and interests, serves this purpose. Therefore, the director must be involved in, and sensitive to, the needs of the community. She must be able to listen to and respect the views and values of families in that community. The curriculum that is designed by the director and her staff must reflect the needs of children while also meeting federal guidelines.

Day care centers in public colleges and universities. Many campuses now recognize the need for day care centers on campus. Funding for operation may be shared jointly by the student body association and the college or university board. Minimal tuition may be charged. Enrollment is usually limited to the children of students and, sometimes, faculty members.

The director of this type of program may face some unique challenges. The students see the school as a service. The academic institution may insist that the school be an integral part of the instructional program and that it must be called a laboratory school. Conflicts sometimes arise over the contents of the program.

A director of a student day care center is faced with the challenge of varied schedules. Students are in class for varied periods during the day. Should the director require that the children attend on some kind of regular schedule in order to bring continuity to the program? Can she allow the children to attend only when their parents are in class?

Parent observation classes. School districts sometimes operate another type of program for young children called parent observation classes. These classes are half-day sessions, usually meeting one or two days a week, and are sponsored by the adult education department of the district.

It is the parent who is actually enrolled in the adult education class. Children who accompany their parents must be between the ages of three and five. These programs meet in a local school, park, community center, or church.

The purpose of the parent observation program is the education of the parent. The parents observe as the children engage in typi-

cal nursery school activities. Music, art, blocks, and stories are offered. New approaches to learning may also be shown to the parents.

After the parents have observed for half of the daily session, the remaining time is spent in discussion. The adult education teacher leads the discussion of parents' observations or other topics of interest.

In communities where this type of program exists, there is usually intense interest. This is an indication that many parents want help with the problems of child rearing. Some parents like the program because the child can have a group experience on a limited basis.

Although this kind of school does not have a director, it is included here because it should be of interest to directors and child development students. The techniques for helping parents to develop their own strengths may be easily incorporated in other settings as well. Private and public schools or day care centers may adopt similar parent education programs.

SUMMARY

The chart in figure 2-7 summarizes the contents of this unit.

STUDENT ACTIVITIES

- Visit a half-day school and a full-day school. Observe the similarities and differences in the programs. Report your findings to the class.
- Describe a childhood center or school with which you are familiar, according to length of session, terms of sponsorship, purpose, and sources of income.
- Visit a school that is funded differently from the one described above. Talk to the director about her main responsibilities. Share your findings with the class.

REVIEW

1. How does the teacher/child ratio differ in half-day and full-day programs?
2. Name three factors in administration of the school program which are influenced by the length of the daily sessions.
3. Explain how the curriculum in a full-day care center differs from that of a half-day curriculum.

TYPES OF SCHOOLS			
TYPE	SPONSORSHIP	SOURCE OF INCOME	CHARACTERISTICS
Private			
Proprietary School	One or more individuals	Tuition	Profit-making. Freedom to initiate program. Limited resources for income.
Family Day Care Home	Individual	Tuition	Same as proprietary school.
Educational Corporation	Group of people	Tuition	Shared resources for planning, purchasing, maintenance. Curriculum planned by originators, implemented by director.
Franchise	Corporation	Tuition	Expertise supplied by franchisor if franchisor is knowledgeable.
Company, Hospital or Apartment	Owner(s) of company, hospital, or apartment	Tuition Supplemented by owner(s)	Location close to work or residence.
Cooperative or Playgroup	Member families	Tuition Fund-raising	Intense parent involvement. Less costly to operate. Opportunities for parent education.
Private Laboratory	Private college or university	Tuition Departmental supplements	Model program design. Used for practice teaching placements.
Parochial	Church	Tuition Church supplements	Policies determined by church. Use church facilities. Is part of the church educational program.
Community	Community organizations	Fund-raising and contributions Tuition	May be designed for handicapped children. Requires knowledge of the community.
Public			
Child Care Centers	Local school district	Federal, state, county, city Tuition	Director functions as a manager. Often must accommodate large numbers of children. School district resources available.
Head Start	Public or private nonprofit agencies	Federal funds Tuition (minimal)	Designed to overcome deficiencies and prepare child for school. Community participation and control.
Student Day Care centers (laboratory)	Student body association Public college or university	Student body funds University or college supplements	Conflicts may arise over content of program, student's ideas and college administration. Must be scheduled to meet the student class times.
Parent Observation Classes	School district	Adult education funds	Parent is enrolled, child attends. Purpose: education of parent.

Fig. 2-7 Types of Schools

Unit 3 Opening a New School

OBJECTIVES

After studying this unit, the student should be able to

- Discuss factors affecting the choice of location for a school
- Identify the agencies responsible for licensing requirements
- Discuss additional requirements a school should meet before beginning operation

In a time of rising costs for operating a business, the person interested in opening a school for young children must do some careful preparatory research. The proper location for the school, a well-planned building, carefully thought-out sources of income, a thorough assessment of cost, and extensive advertising for recruitment will increase the possibility of success in the venture.

LOCATION

Requirements set by the local zoning board determine to a great extent where a school can be located. Zoning requirements specify the kind of neighborhood in which a school can be operated, usually in a multiple unit residential or commercial area. Zoning laws may also specify that the lot must be large enough to provide parking spaces and an area for unloading children from a car or bus.

Besides meeting the local zoning requirements, the prospective owner must consider other factors as well. The site of the school should be easily accessible to the families who will use the service. Some parents may need to use public transportation; others do not

want to spend extra time driving to an out-of-the-way location. To some, easy accessibility may mean close proximity to their residence. Other parents prefer to have a school located near their place of business. Many busy mothers like to be able to leave their children just before going to their jobs and then pick them up on the way home. A site close to businesses employing large numbers of women would be a likely place to consider for a school.

Nearness to an elementary school may be another consideration if the preschool also provides day care for children aged five to twelve. Parents find it convenient to be able to leave a child at a day care center from which the child can walk or be transported to his kindergarten or elementary class.

The general characteristics of the community should also be investigated before choosing a site. Some of the questions to be answered about the community concern the average size of families, the percentage of mothers who work, the number of one-parent families, the number of other schools and their enrollments, and the trend of enrollments in the local public schools — increasing or decreasing. Some of this information can be obtained from census records available in libraries. Some can be obtained by talking to people in the community — such as the elementary school principal, shopkeepers, and newspaper editors. Many directors of schools already established in a community are willing to give information to a prospective director. Realtors are a source of information concerning property values and buildings as indicators of income level of resident families and the potential for growth of the community.

NEW BUILDING, REMODELED BUILDING, OR RENTED SPACE?

Many attractive schools for young children are housed in renovated residences. In fact, many directors prefer the home-like atmosphere of this kind of building. If a large, older house can be obtained for a reasonable price and part of the renovation can be done by the owner, this is a good choice. Often, though, it is difficult to find this kind of building in the proper zone. In addition, the cost of meeting the many city, county, and state code requirements for licensing may increase the cost so that remodeling is not a viable solution.

A facility built specifically for use by young children has many advantages. Space can be allotted for the many components of the program. The building can be equipped with appropriate storage areas and include durable surfaces that will survive the wear and tear of young children.

Renting space is the third possible choice for the prospective operator of a school. Some landlords will renovate a building if extensive structural changes are not required. An attractive building originally built for commercial purposes can be made into a school by the use of sliding or movable partitions. Churches, private schools, and community centers may also rent space that can be used for a preschool.

Each of these decisions requires a great deal of information gathering and careful consideration. Costs for each must be weighed against the number of children the space can accommodate. The amount of income possible is, of course, directly related to the number of children enrolled in the program.

LICENSING REQUIREMENTS

Most schools for young children must have a license. The state department of welfare or its equivalent is the authority for licensing schools in most states. In other states, the state department of health has this responsibility. Therefore, the prospective owner of a school must contact the state agency and get full information concerning the licensing requirements. Most will have a packet of information available which lists the procedures, clearances, or permits that are necessary before the license can be issued.

Before awarding a license, most states require evidence that certain building requirements have been met. A visit from officials of the local department of building safety may be required to inspect the electrical wiring, plumbing, and provisions for utilities. The fire department makes sure that fire safety is planned for; extinguishers, alarms, fire walls or doors, safe storage of flammable materials, and plans for evacuation of the building will be checked. The health or sanitation department will cover food storage and preparation areas, toilet facilities, ventilation, lighting, heating, and provision for isolation of a sick child.

Three major types of day care facilities are required to obtain licenses in the United States. First is the *Family Day Care Home* which services a limited number of children and has the fewest requirements. Second is the *Group Day Care Home* which is an extension of the above; a larger number of children can be taken care of when an additional adult is employed. In some states the requirements

	Family Day Care Homes	Group Day Care Homes	Day Care Centers		Family Day Care Homes	Group Day Care Homes	Day Care Centers
	STATE LICENSES				STATE LICENSES		
ALABAMA	W	W	W	MONTANA	W		W
ALASKA	W	W	W	NEBRASKA	W		W
ARIZONA			H	NEVADA			W
ARKANSAS	W	W	W	NEW HAMPSHIRE	W		W
CALIFORNIA	W		W	NEW JERSEY			E
COLORADO	W		W	NEW MEXICO	H		H
CONNECTICUT	W		H	NEW YORK	W		W
DELAWARE	W	W	W	NORTH CAROLINA		W	W
FLORIDA	W		W	NORTH DAKOTA	W	W	W
GEORGIA	W		W	OHIO			W
HAWAII	W		W	OKLAHOMA	W		W
IDAHO	W			OREGON			W
ILLINOIS	W		W	PENNSYLVANIA	W		W
INDIANA	W		W	RHODE ISLAND	W		W
IOWA	W		W	SOUTH CAROLINA	W	W	W
KANSAS	H		H	SOUTH DAKOTA	W		W
KENTUCKY	W		W	TENNESSEE	W		W
LOUISIANA			W	TEXAS	W		W
MAINE	W	W	W	UTAH	W		W
MARYLAND	W		H	VERMONT	O	O	O
MASSACHUSETTS			H	VIRGINIA	W		W
MICHIGAN	W		W	WASHINGTON			W
MINNESOTA	W		W	WEST VIRGINIA			W
MISSISSIPPI				WISCONSIN			W
MISSOURI	W	W	W	WYOMING	W		W

H=Health
E=Education

W=Welfare
O=Office of Economic Opportunity

Fig. 3-1 Departments of State Government Responsible for Licensing Day Care Facilities

(State and Local Day Care Licensing Requirements, U.S. Dept. Health, Education, and Welfare. (OCD) 73-1006, p. B-1)

for this kind of facility are similar to the Family Day Care Home, but in others they more closely resemble day care center requirements. The third category, the *Day Care Center* allows for a larger number of children to be enrolled. Requirements are much more stringent and cover many aspects of the operation from the physical space to staff qualifications, to food service, fire safety, equipment, and program.

Some kinds of programs are excluded from having to meet licensing requirements. The general philosophy of state day care licensing agencies is to exclude from licensure:

1. Care provided to a child by a relative

2. Facilities which are operated by another state or federal agency

3. Facilities which provide day care on a short term or drop-in basis (Care provided for children whose parents are nearby.)

FINANCES

A preliminary budget is the next step for the prospective operator. Licensing requirements determine the number of children the school can enroll. A reasonable tuition must be set to cover the expected expenses. A survey of other schools in the area will help to find out what the "going rate" is. Whether a school offers a half-day program or provides all day care is also important in determining the amount of tuition that can be charged. Other sources of income such as supplementary programs, transportation charges, and registration fees should also be added to expected income.

Budget categories and the expected percentage of the total expenditures for each

---

TYPICAL INVESTMENT REQUIREMENTS
Capacity: 40 children
Building: 2,500 sq. ft.

	Ranges	
Renovation/Construction (exclusive of land costs)	$ 7,500	$ 60,000
Fixtures and equipment	11,000	30,000
Three-month operating expenses (Required by some licensing agencies)	12,075	12,075
Total Ranges	$30,575	$102,075

TYPICAL MONTHLY BUDGET
ESTIMATED GROSS INCOME

(40 children × $120 monthly fee)		$ 4,800
Less allowance for vacancy and collection losses (10%)		– 480
Actual Gross Income		$ 4,320

EXPENSES

Salaries		$ 2,700
Rent or mortgage		450
Supplies and equipment		150
Utilities		100
Food		400
Repairs and maintenance		105
Taxes, licenses, and insurance		35
Administrative service (accountant, etc.)		35
Advertising		50
TOTAL		$ 4,025
NET INCOME		405

Fig. 3-2 Financial Planning and Budgeting for Child Care

are discussed more fully in unit 13. These categories are identified: salaries and fringe benefits, consultant services, equipment, supplies and materials, food, space costs, utilities, and other costs (insurance, licenses, fees).

Expenses for the first year of operation of a school are usually greater than they will be once the school is established. Costs for initial equipment and supplies, for building renovations, and for planning time for staff must be included in the preliminary budget. This budget must also allow for the possibility that the school will not have full enrollment immediately. Many licensing agencies cover these costs by requiring that money be set aside for a specified number of months (three to six, for example) of operational costs before the license can be issued.

INSURANCE

In some states licensing includes requirements for insurance coverage. However, any school caring for children should be covered by adequate insurance whether it is required or not. Most schools have the following kinds of insurance:

- Liability and property damage — to provide legal protection for the owner/operator of the school

- Fire damage — to cover buildings and contents

- Fire, extended coverage — to protect against vandalism and malicious mischief

- Automobile — for vehicles used in transporting children as well as for non-owned vehicles that might be used for this purpose

- Accident — for children and staff

- Workmen's compensation (required by law if ten or more persons are employed) — to cover on-the-job injuries

It might be desirable to consider also the following kinds of insurance:

- Burglary and robbery — on the contents of the building

- Business interruption — payment for lost income while damaged property is being repaired

- Fidelity bond — to protect against theft by employees

LEGAL ADVICE

When the operation of a private child care facility involves more than one person, it is important to obtain legal advice. In a partnership, where two or more persons act as co-operators, this relationship may or may not be incorporated. When organized as a simple partnership, either partner is liable for all partnership debts. Each partner can enter into agreements or make contracts; the private assets of either one may be levied for payment of indebtedness. When the school is set up as a corporation, the individual is protected from personal liability. The details of these kinds of relationships should be worked out with the aid of a lawyer in order to ensure the rights of all those involved.

ADVERTISING AND RECRUITMENT

Advertising the school in order to attract enrollees is the next step for the director/operator. Small ads placed in local newspapers or neighborhood periodicals is a good way to begin. A notice on a bulletin board in places frequented by families is another possibility. Community centers, parks, a children's clothing or toy store, and a pediatrician's office are all places where the notice will be seen by families. Telephone book advertising is best in a long-range way. However, this may not suit the needs of the new school, because the opening of the school may not coincide with revisions in the telephone directory.

If possible, it is best to plan the opening of the school for the fall because this is the usual time when parents are thinking about school for their children. This is less true for day care programs, although in this case, too, parents often wait until after their summer vacation. The beginning of the calendar year is another possible time to consider for the opening of a school. Many schools find that there is a new surge of enrollments after the Christmas holidays.

A new school should be ready to be seen at best advantage before recruitment begins. A parent should not be expected to visualize the school in its finished state when shown an unrenovated building or a building in the early stages of completion. If recruitment must be done before the physical facility is completed, care must be taken to present the school and its objectives in other ways. Copies of plans or drawings will help parents picture the building. A brochure or other written materials covering the educational objectives and program will also help. A clear presentation by the director of the essential aspects of the program and of the ways that it will be different from other schools will be effective.

BOARD OF DIRECTORS

Certain kinds of nursery schools are governed by a board of one type or another. A church-sponsored school may be governed by the church board of directors or by an education committee that is responsible to the church board. A cooperative school that is incorporated is also governed by a board. A corporate school and a franchised school may have this kind of structure. Most private nonprofit or philanthropic schools are set up in this way. This means that the directors of many kinds of schools need to be knowledgeable in setting up guidelines for this kind of relationship.

It is helpful to understand the functions of the governing board as separate from the administrative role. A board of directors performs the following functions in a school:

- Formulates major school policies for overall goals
- With the director, formulates policies for the operation of the school — admission policies and hiring procedures, for example
- Participates actively in community relations
- Adopts and supports annual budget
- Approves all personnel hired
- Authorizes purchases and expenditures that exceed a specified limit, within the limits of the budget
- Explores sources of income other than tuition
- With the director, discusses enrollment requirements as needed
- With the director, considers problems that arise that cannot be resolved by staff
- Develops criteria for evaluating the center

Because a board of directors is a governing body that changes periodically as the term of office of each member expires, it is important to have a written manual of policies, or bylaws. Figure 3-3 shows a sample of a basic set of bylaws. These bylaws can be used during the term of office of each member as a guide to functions and procedures.

STAFF SELECTION

The entire process of staff selection is fully discussed in unit 9. Some guidelines for staffing the new school will be helpful here, however. The director should

- Choose the first teachers for the school with care. During the first year of

ARTICLE I.   Board of Directors:

Section 1.   The Board of Directors shall consist of not less than _____ nor more than _____ persons.

Section 2.   Members of the Board of Directors shall be elected at the membership meeting in _____ (month) and such directors shall be elected for terms as hereinafter provided.

Section 3.   The terms of office shall be for _____ years, beginning _____ .

Section 4.   The Board of Directors shall meet at least _____ times each year. A special meeting may be called at any time by _____ .

Section 5.   A quorum shall be constituted by _____ of the membership.

Section 6.   Any vacancy in the Board of Directors may be filled by the Board, pending next meeting of the membership.

ARTICLE II.   Officers:

Section 1.   The officers shall consist of _____ .

Section 2.   All officers shall be elected for a term of _____ .

Section 3.   Officers shall be elected at the membership meeting in _____ (month).

Section 4.   The Chairman shall have the following duties:

_____ .

Section 5.   The Vice-Chairman shall have the following duties:

_____ .

Section 6.   The Treasurer shall have the following duties:

_____ .

Section 7.   The following officers may be elected if desired:

_____ .

Section 8.   The Director of the school will serve as an ex-officio member.

ARTICLE III.   Standing Committees:

Section 1.   There shall be the following standing committees appointed by

_____ .

Section 2.   The function of the (Policy Advisory Committee, Finance Committee, Personnel Committee) shall be _____ .

ARTICLE IV.   Membership Meetings:

Section 1.   The regular annual meeting of the membership may be held during the month of

_____ .

Section 2.   Special meetings of the membership may be called by _____ .

ARTICLE V.   Amendments:

Section 1.   The bylaws shall be subject to amendment by _____ vote of the membership.

Fig. 3-3 Sample Bylaws

operation, the reputation of the school is being formed. The teachers are an important part of this process.

- Communicate the goals of the school program to the teachers. Help the teachers implement them.

- Hire teachers to begin work one or two weeks before the opening of school so that they can participate in pre-opening activities and plans.

- Get to know each teacher as quickly as possible and provide opportunities for teachers to meet each other.

WORKING CHECKLIST

Each of the tasks necessary for opening a new school may entail many weeks of work. Delays may be met when attempts are made to get all the licensing requirements fulfilled. Weather may interfere with building or renovation plans. Therefore, an adequate and realistic amount of time must be allowed. A checklist of tasks with a time line for completion of each will help the new operator/director.

SUMMARY

The location of a school may be determined by local zoning laws, but a prospective operator/director may want to find a site close to residential areas, to businesses employing many women, or to an elementary school. A community in which there are many families with children and where there are many working mothers will also increase the likelihood of the success of a school.

A school for young children may be housed in a renovated residence or in a facility designed and built for that purpose. Commercial buildings can also sometimes be remodeled to accommodate a school. Churches, community centers, and private elementary schools may rent space for a preschool.

Most schools are required to have a license issued by a state agency. In most states, the state department of welfare is the licensing agency, but in others this is done by the department of health. In a few, other state agencies have this responsibility.

First year expenses for the operation of a school are usually greater than will be

Task	Expected Completion Date	Date Completed
1. Choose community area		
2. Find suitable building or decide to build		
3. Contact state licensing agency		
4. Obtain insurance		
5. Set tuition — budget for first year		
6. Advertise		
7. Manual of policies or bylaws		
8. Hire teachers		

Fig. 3-4 Checklist of Tasks Needed to Open a New School

experienced once the school is established. Some states require that money for three to six months of costs be set aside before a license can be issued.

Some states include requirements for insurance coverage in licensing procedures. Liability, fire, automobile, accident, and Workmen's Compensation are the most important. It might be desirable to consider burglary, business interruption, and fidelity bond coverage.

When the operation of a private child care facility involves more than one person, it is important to obtain legal advice.

A new school must advertise in order to attract enrollees. Newspaper ads, bulletin board notices, and telephone book advertising are all effective.

Certain kinds of schools are governed by a board of one type or another. With this kind of administrative structure, it is important for the director to understand the functions of the board as differentiated from the administrative role. A set of bylaws will also serve as a guide to the board members.

The selection of the first teachers for a new school is important since during this time the reputation of the school will be formed.

STUDENT ACTIVITIES

- Visit the local zoning department to find out about zoning requirements for a school in your area.
- Visit the licensing agency for your state. Obtain and read the information regarding requirements for a license.
- Plan a preliminary budget for the first year of operation of a school.

REVIEW

1. List three things to consider in choosing a site for a school.
2. A building designed and built for a school is one kind of housing. Name two other possible types of building that can be used for a school.
3. Which state agency is responsible for licensing in most states?
4. Name three major types of day care facilities that require licenses.
5. Name three kinds of child care programs that are usually excluded from licensing requirements.
6. Are expenses during the first year of operation of a school less or greater than in following years of operation?
7. List five kinds of insurance that a school should carry.
8. When is legal advice recommended for setting up the organizational structure of a school?
9. List three ways a new school can advertise for enrollees without great expense.
10. When is the best time for opening a new school?
11. List five functions of a board of directors.
12. Discuss four suggestions for hiring teachers that would be helpful to the director of a new school.

Unit 4 Beginning the School Year

OBJECTIVES

After completing this unit, the student should be able to

- Identify tasks that are necessary for the beginning of a school year
- Plan procedures and routines for doing the "beginning of the year" tasks

In a school that is not in session all year round, preparation for beginning the new school year can be pretty hectic and exhausting for the director. Awareness of all the tasks to be done and careful planning for doing them can make this time somewhat easier. Year-to-year procedures that work can be developed and repeated so that they become routine. This helps the staff be sure that the many details are taken care of.

ENROLLMENT

During the several weeks immediately preceding opening day, enrollment of children should be taking place. Only a few schools complete their enrollment in the spring for the following fall; even in those that do, there may be unexpected vacancies when families move. The parents' first contact with the school is usually by means of a telephone call. Therefore, it is important to maintain a record of each call, with a procedure for follow-up. Printed cards on which the needed information is filled in or 3 x 5 cards on which to record the information will help to keep track of inquiries. Each call should be followed with some information by mail. If the parent

is really interested in the school, an application packet can be sent. The packet should include the application form, a brochure, and medical forms. If the parent does not ask for application materials, a brochure can be sent

---

INQUIRY REPORT FORM

NAME _____ DATE _____

ADDRESS _____ PHONE _____

_____

Child's Birthdate _____
                  (month-day-year)

How did you hear about our school? _____
_____ Application packet sent _____
                              Date

_____ Brochure sent _____
                          Date

Additional Comments:

Fig. 4-1 Sample Inquiry Report Form

so that information about the school is disseminated. Even parents who do not send their children to your school may pass the information on to someone else. Or, after seeing the brochure, they may decide that your school is the one they want their child to attend. Figure 4-1 shows a sample form that can be used to record inquiries about the school.

The parent, child, and director should meet before the application and acceptance are finalized. Some parents wish to come to the school, see the facility, and talk with the director before making application. Others already know about the school and schedule the visit after the application has been sent in. Whichever order is chosen for the visit, it is important that the family and the director have a chance to leisurely decide whether the school and child are suited to each other before enrollment. These visits usually take at least half an hour and often longer. For this reason, they should not be scheduled too closely.

Enrollment decisions may include deciding whether to accept a handicapped child into the school. Many schools are currently considering this idea, called *mainstreaming*. It

---

APPLICATION FORM

For school year _____

Name of child _____ Date of birth _____

Mother (or guardian) _____

Father (or guardian) _____

Brothers and sisters of child:

Name _____ Age _____

Name _____ Age _____

Name _____ Age _____

Name _____ Age _____

Number of days per week requested: 2 _____   3 _____   5 _____

Hours requested Half-day _____   Full-day _____

Is mother employed? _____

A registration fee of $ _____ must accompany this application. Paid $ _____ .

Signed _____
(parent's signature)

Date _____

Fig. 4-2 Sample Application Form

STATE OF CALIFORNIA — HEALTH AND WELFARE AGENCY   DEPARTMENT OF HEALTH

IDENTIFICATION AND EMERGENCY INFORMATION
To Be Completed by Parent or Guardian

CHILD'S NAME		TELEPHONE
ADDRESS		BIRTH DATE
FATHER'S NAME		BUSINESS TELEPHONE
HOME ADDRESS		HOME TELEPHONE
MOTHER'S NAME		BUSINESS TELEPHONE
HOME ADDRESS		HOME TELEPHONE
PERSON RESPONSIBLE FOR CHILD	HOME TELEPHONE	BUSINESS TELEPHONE

ADDITIONAL PERSONS WHO MAY BE CALLED IN EMERGENCY

NAME	ADDRESS	TELEPHONE	RELATIONSHIP

PHYSICIAN TO BE CALLED IN EMERGENCY

NAME	TELEPHONE
ADDRESS	

IF PHYSICIAN CANNOT BE REACHED, WHAT ACTION SHOULD BE TAKEN?

☐ CALL EMERGENCY HOSPITAL   ☐ OTHER

NAMES OF PERSONS AUTHORIZED TO TAKE CHILD FROM THE FACILITY
(CHILD WILL NOT BE ALLOWED TO LEAVE WITH ANY OTHER PERSON WITHOUT WRITTEN AUTHORIZATION FROM PARENT OR GUARDIAN)

NAME	RELATIONSHIP

TIME CHILD WILL BE CALLED FOR

SIGNATURE OF PARENT OR GUARDIAN	DATE

TO BE COMPLETED BY FACILITY DIRECTOR

DATE OF ADMISSION	DATE LEFT

LIC 700 (7/73)

Fig. 4-3 Sample Emergency Information Form

is based on the concept that educational placement of exceptional children should provide the least restrictive environment possible for the child. Both the parent and the director must decide if the school can meet the special needs of the child for curriculum activities to increase motor skills, perception, language, cognition, and self-help skills. Assessment of the child's needs can be made by using some of the instruments available. Discussions with staff must also take place before integration of a young handicapped child with non-handicapped children can be accomplished successfully.

Just prior to the opening of school, the director will be making decisions about scheduling children. Some mothers want their child to go to school less than five days a week. Some schools find this is a way to provide a needed service. It can also increase the total revenue of the school, since tuition for two part-time places can be more than tuition for one full-time place. On the other hand, some directors feel that anything less than five days a week will result in an incomplete experience for the child. The days in between attendance are too long a gap for the young child.

Other enrollment decisions concern the way in which children are grouped in their classes. Most schools use *peer-grouping,* meaning that all the children in one class are within six to nine months of each other in age. Other schools use *family-grouping,* meaning that children of widely differing age levels are together in a classroom. When these decisions have been made, group lists must be prepared. Then, parents are notified so that each knows what class the child will be in and who the teacher will be.

Enrollment time is also a period in which the files on each child are prepared. Each file should contain an application form, a medical evaluation, medical history, emergency information, and signed permission forms. Some

---

PERMISSION FORM

I hereby give permission for _____
                                         (Child's name)
to participate in the following activities at _____
_____School.

_____   Field trip with the class. I understand that I will be notified prior to a scheduled field trip, and will be given information regarding transportation, destination, lunch or other food, arrival and departure time.

_____   Pictures taken of my child to be used for educational purposes, teacher training or school use. I understand that my child's name will not be used at any time.

_____   Distribution of my address and/or telephone number to other parents of a child enrolled in this school. (Addresses will not be given out for any commercial purposes.)

Signature of parent _____

Date _____

Fig. 4-4 Sample Permission Form

schools add to this a financial agreement. In some states medical forms are available through the licensing agency. Other forms must be prepared by the school for its own use. Figures 4-2 through 4-5 show examples of some of these forms.

Some follow-up must be done to see that each file is complete. Directors can develop their own systems for accomplishing this. Several ways that directors have found helpful are discussed here. At a specified time, each file can be inventoried and then a contact made with the parent to complete needed forms. A running checklist can be used so what is missing can be seen at a glance, figure 4-6. Another system would involve putting completed files in one place and leaving uncompleted ones in another until they are complete. Whatever the system, it is important to see that the task of getting all needed forms on file is accomplished as quickly as possible at the beginning of the school year.

FINANCIAL AGREEMENT

I agree to pay $ _____ per month, payable in advance for tuition for my child. I understand there is no tuition allowance for absences.

I also agree to notify the school two weeks in advance of withdrawal, should that be necessary. I understand that without notification, I am obligated for two weeks' tuition or until the place is filled.

I have read the Parents' Handbook to the effect that there can be no refunds of tuition after May 1 of each year. Any child enrolled after May 1 will be charged tuition through the June closing date.

Signed _____
                Mother or guardian

Signed _____
                Father or guardian

Date _____

Fig. 4-5 Sample Financial Agreement Form

PARENTS

Parents with a child newly enrolled in a school need help at the beginning of the school year so that they and their child can adjust as quickly as possible to the new experience. For this purpose, the director can develop a handbook that contains much of the information that is helpful to parents.

- Health rules — when to keep a child out of school
- Safety — what the school does when a child is hurt or ill
- Arrival and departure — times and procedures for leaving and picking up the child
- Treats — kinds of foods to be used for special occasions
- Home toys — what the child can bring to school
- Visits of parents to classroom — how to be a good visitor
- Birthdays — how the parent can make a birthday a good time for the child and his class
- Clothing — what is appropriate for school

DIRECTOR'S CHECKLIST FOR FILE COMPLETION – CHILD

NAME	Application Form	Health Evaluation	Health History	Emergency Information	Permission Form	Financial Agreement	Registration Fee

Fig. 4-6 Sample Checklist for File Completion Used by Some Directors

- Lunch — suggestions for child's bag lunch

- Conferences — when scheduled

In addition to a parent handbook, an orientation meeting at the beginning of the school year is helpful. This is a time when parents and staff can get to know each other and begin to establish common goals for the child. The orientation is more fully discussed in unit 21.

The beginning of the school year is also a time when the director will want to be available to parents as much as possible. Parents need support during this first period of separation from their children. They may have questions and concerns that could be resolved before they become major problems. They may just want assurance that the children will be all right at school without them. Some time invested at the beginning of the year will often prevent time-consuming problems later on.

Fig. 4-7 A Happy Birthday

STAFF

It is important that all staff members work one or two weeks before the opening of school. Discussions between the director and staff can result in setting schedules for completing many of the details of operating a school. This is also a time when staff members are eager to get back to work with children and look forward to a new opportunity to do the best possible job. The director can use this time to set the tone for her relationship with the staff. Some of the tasks that the director and staff can accomplish at this time are listed:

- Give teachers a list of the children in their classes

    If files on children are complete, teachers will also have some information about the child and family available to them.

- Discuss group schedules

    It is sometimes necessary to rotate schedules of classes so that one group can use the play yard at a time.

- Set up a schedule for cleaning and maintenance to be done by teachers and the cleaning crew

    Teachers should have input into the cleaning tasks that are important to be done in their own classrooms.

- Review equipment and supplies in each classroom

- Order last minute items if needed

- Schedule home visits to the families if this is part of the school procedure

- Review attendance record procedures to be used by teachers

- Review emergency procedures for the safety of children in the event of a disaster

- Check to see that all personnel files are complete, especially the medical information.

- Complete W-2 forms for new employees
- Plan procedures for the first day of school

    There should be enough chairs for parents in each classroom and group lists or direction signs prepared for the halls.

- Review first day schedule with teachers

SUPPLIES

Some schools do an inventory before the end of the year and know during vacation time what items need to be ordered. If this has not been done, then it must be done at least a month or more before the opening of school. Some supplies can be obtained immediately, but others may take several weeks for delivery. Therefore, the director must plan to order so that the school is assured of an adequate supply of essential items when school opens.

Some schools have found it helpful to allow the teachers a specified amount of money to spend at the beginning of a year to purchase things needed in the classroom. This can relieve the director of some of the purchasing responsibility and also give teachers the opportunity to learn more about ordering. Other schools allow teachers a monthly sum from petty cash to use to purchase some of the small items that are needed as the year goes on.

FINANCES

Only a few schools can afford the luxury of a bookkeeper. Therefore, the director must collect registration fees and tuitions and keep a record of money taken in. This might be a time when the director reviews her procedures for these tasks and tries to determine if there are more efficient ways of completing them.

- Tuition payments are received.
- Checks can be accumulated for a short period of time before they are alphabetized and then posted on individual ledger sheets for each child, figure 4-8.

Name _____   No. of days per week _____

Address _____   Tuition Amt. _____

Telephone _____

Date	Item	Amt. Due	Amt. Paid	Credit	Balance

Fig. 4-8 Sample Individual Ledger Sheet Form

CASH RECEIPTS RECORD

Date	Item	Cash	Check/Number	Amount

Fig. 4-9 Sample Cash Receipts Record Form

- When cash is received, a duplicate receipt is made — one for the parent and one for the school records.

- All checks and cash are recorded in the cash receipts record.

- Deposits are made to the school account.

- At a specified time, usually ten days, individual ledgers are checked to see that all tuitions have been paid. Notices are sent out to parents who have not paid tuitions.

As expenditures are made during the month, they are recorded and a monthly summary is made. As the school year passes, this summary of expenditures is important as a record of expenditures to date. It is an excellent way of controlling expenses so that the budget limitations are maintained. Figures 4-9 through 4-11 show a record for cash receipts, expenditures, and summary.

FACILITY

The final task that the director must complete before the opening of school is to see that the physical environment is clean, repaired, and made attractive. Both indoor and outdoor areas need to be surveyed for safety, for cleanliness, and for appearance. A

EXPENDITURES RECORD

Date	Item	Check Number	Amount	From Account

Fig. 4-10 Sample Expenditures Record Form

MONTHLY BUDGET SUMMARY

Date	Item	Budget Amt.	This Month (last day)	Year to Date	Balance

Fig. 4-11 Sample Monthly Budget Summary Form

bright coat of paint on the tables or outdoor boxes will prevent splintering and also brighten the appearance of the room and yard. New sand in the sandbox will encourage children to use it — as will some brightly painted cans or buckets.

SUMMARY

The beginning of the school year requires the completion of many tasks by the director and staff. Routines and procedures need to be developed so that the many details get taken care of.

Enrollment must be completed and files established for each child. A child's file should include an application, a health evaluation, a health history, emergency information, permissions for field trips, and a financial agreement in schools where this is used.

New parents to a school need help at the beginning of a school year so that they and their children can adjust quickly to the new experience. For this purpose, the director can prepare a handbook with information that is pertinent to parents. In addition an orientation meeting will give parents and teachers a chance to get to know each other. The director will want to be available to talk to parents

in the first days of school, because this is a time when parents may have concerns or questions.

Staff members should begin work one or two weeks before the opening of school. The director and staff can use this time to discuss procedures for scheduling children, for cleaning and maintenance, and for reviewing procedures for the first days of school.

If supplies have not been ordered before the end of school, the director must do so at least a month, or possibly two months, before the opening day so that needed supplies are available. Some schools involve teachers in purchasing supplies by allowing each a specified sum of money to spend at the beginning of a year or by allowing a monthly sum throughout the year to be spent for small items needed in the classroom.

Only a few schools can afford to pay a bookkeeper, so the director must collect money and keep records of income and expenses. A monthly budget summary helps to show how much of the budget has been spent at any point throughout the year.

Before the opening of school, both indoor and outdoor areas should be cleaned, repaired, and made attractive as needed.

STUDENT ACTIVITIES

- Discuss enrollment procedures in your school. How might they be improved?

- Find out what forms are available through your state's licensing agency. Which of these are for children's files?

- Write a parent handbook for your school.

REVIEW

1. Describe the procedures for handling telephone inquiries as discussed in this unit.

2. What is the purpose of a visit to the school by the parent and child before enrollment is completed?

3. List items that should be in each child's file.

4. The text suggests three ways to be sure that children's files are completed. What are they?

5. What are five items of information that might be contained in a handbook for parents?

6. Teachers should start work before the opening of school. What was the time period suggested in this unit?

7. List tasks the director must accomplish with teachers before the beginning of school.

8. How much time should the director allow for the delivery of supplies needed for the opening of school?

9. Why is a monthly budget summary important?

10. What three final tasks must the director complete before the opening of school?

Section 2
PLANNING
THE PROGRAM

Unit 5 Formulating Goals and Objectives

OBJECTIVES

After studying this unit, the student should be able to

- Explain what is meant by a statement of goals
- State some general categories of goals
- Describe the process for formulating goals

Education of five-year olds in the United States began during the 1800s as an outgrowth of the European kindergartens. It was not until early 1900 that the education of children below kindergarten age was attempted. The first nursery schools used ideas and methods of the kindergarten, emphasizing learning through play. The focus was academic, but the curriculum was not designed specifically for preschool age children.

During the 1930s and 1940s, the needs of society were more urgent than the needs of children. Nursery schools were established for reasons other than the education of young children. The federal Works Progress Administration (WPA) schools provided jobs for unemployed teachers during the depression of the 1930s. When World War II began in the 1940s, nursery schools again were federally funded under the Lanham Act to provide child care so women would be free to work in essential war industries. At the end of the war most of these schools were abruptly closed. A few were taken over by community groups and, in some states, were funded on a year-to-year basis.

The 1964 Economic Opportunity Act once again brought federal support to schools for young children. When Head Start programs began in the summer of 1965, the nation's attention was focused on the importance of educating young children. Research in child development has shown that children can learn at a younger age than was previously

Fig. 5-1 This child wants to learn.

thought possible. In addition, it was recognized that early experiences were necessary preparation for later learning. Schools for prekindergarten children have now become an accepted part of our educational system.

Because education of the very young is being stressed, directors and teachers want to know what is considered to be important in the education of young children. They know that it is no longer enough just to provide good care for the child away from home. It is no longer enough just to provide a setting in which children can play, explore, and have fun. Teachers, and the directors who guide them, want to know what children are able to learn and what they should be learning.

PREPARING GOALS AND OBJECTIVES

The content and focus of learning experiences will vary from one group of children to another, from one school to another and from one community to another. For any particular school, this information will be contained in a *statement of goals* for the school. This statement of goals is then used by teachers as a basis for planning the day-to-day and month-to-month curriculum. Each goal can generate many curriculum or *behavioral objectives*. Both a goal and an objective can be defined as changes in behavior of a learner expected at the end of a specified period of time. However, the statement of goals is a long-range plan and the behavioral objective is short range in scope. Conversely, the sum of all the behavioral objectives then becomes the statement of goals for the school.

Who decides what the school should try to accomplish for each child? What are the desired behavioral changes? In the past, the decision was made by one person or only a select few who knew what was best for children, what they should learn and how they should learn. Today the trend in education is toward a decision-making process in which many persons participate. All those involved in the education and care of the child have an opportunity to take part in preparing and developing the objectives.

A group of parents, teachers, and community representatives may work together as a committee to formulate goals, or the director and her staff may perform this function using information gathered from others. Regardless of the method followed, the director of a school for young children must assume the role of educational leader. It becomes her responsibility to consolidate information and give direction to those who formulate the goals for the program.

The director is expected to help make decisions; to decide which goals are the most important for the school and for each group of children. The staff may want to emphasize the development of the child's social skills. The parents may be concerned that the children preserve aspects of their cultural background. The elementary school board may want the children to learn specific skills before entering kindergarten or first grade. Are all of these concerns compatible? Can they all be achieved, or must some be used and others eliminated?

Collecting Data

The first step in formulating a set of objectives for a particular school should be to gather information about what the children already know and what they are expected to learn. Staff, parents, and community can be involved in this initial phase. If the school is run by a board of trustees, they, too, should be included. If the school is part of a larger educational system, supervisors or other administrative personnel could take part in the process.

Information about what the children already know is sometimes apparent by looking at the neighborhood from which the children come. If the director and her committee could take a walk around the community, it would help them to understand its impact upon the children. A neighborhood of apartments with no outdoor play area is different from an area of single houses with large back yards. In the first, the children may have acquired social skills through play with other children, but may lack in physical skills because of the limitation on outdoor play. In a neighborhood of single houses, the children may have developed physical and cognitive skills but may lack in social skills.

The committee should also be familiar with the dominant culture of the neighborhood; this will give them an idea of what the children have already learned as part of their culture. This is particularly important when a language other than English is encouraged as part of the child's learning about that culture. It is necessary for the school to provide experiences so that the children will learn to communicate in English as well as in their native language.

A look at specific children adds further information. Applications filled out by the parents of the children are one source of information. Answers to questions about the children's abilities, skills, and interests are valuable. Assessment tests administered to the children at the beginning of the school year also yield information. General ability tests, language development tests, and perceptual and cognitive skills tests are all available for use in judging children's development. Observation of individual children and groups of children will provide further information about their level of functioning.

Information about what the children are expected to learn must also be gathered. A visit to the local elementary school, particularly to the kindergarten, is important. The kindergarten teacher can explain what is expected of

Fig. 5-2 The Neighborhood of a School

children at the time they enter. Elementary schools usually have some general expectations such as that children should be able to take care of their own physical needs or that they have acquired positive attitudes toward school. Elementary schools also may expect that children have acquired some specific skills — the ability to tie a knot, tell left from right, name colors, count objects, and recognize their own name when they see it printed.

Interviews with parents also indicate parents' expectations for their children. What do they want their children to know? What are their hopes for their children? How do they see their children's needs?

This kind of investigation should yield a great deal of information. It will provide a guide for assessment of the children's physical, social, emotional, and intellectual development. The director and her committee will also know what others expect or hope the children will be able to achieve as a result of the school experience. The difference between the two — the developmental level and expectations — represents the needs to which the school must direct its efforts.

General needs, those that are common to most of the children in the school, will be translated into goals. Needs common to certain groups only or unique to individual children are not usually included in the statement of goals. These will be reflected in the behavioral objectives that teachers use in planning curriculum.

Knowledge of Child Development

Before a statement of goals can be written, other information must be considered. Goals should be formulated with a knowledge of child development in mind. They should be realistic; most children at a particular age should be able to achieve the expected behavior. This is called the *norm* or normal range of ability.

In addition to knowing the normal developmental achievements of most children, those who formulate objectives must also recognize individual differences. Children from varied backgrounds learn different things and in different ways. Some children learn and develop at slower or faster rates than others. Therefore, the objectives become statements of expectations for most children of a particular age level from a specific environment.

Information concerning child development can come from many sources. The director will probably have gained extensive knowledge of child development through education and experience. This knowledge can be shared. Experienced teachers have had courses in child development. Teachers and parents know how children function because of their close association with them. Observations of children can supplement this information.

Reading materials on child development or research can be summarized by the director or a member of the group. Developmental information obtained from entrance forms or interviews with parents may also add to the knowledge of the child's development.

As the educational leader of the group or committee, the director can help the others to summarize available information on child development. She can assist in reaching agreement concerning the expected normal ability for the age level of each child in their care.

Values

The director must help the members of the group explore their own values. These are the beliefs concerning the most important needs of children to be met by the school. This process of exploring values also requires the group to make choices. Do they believe that it is more important for the school to help children develop social skills? Do they feel that the role of the school is to prepare the child for his future work as a productive member of society? If so, those involved in the program would probably want to stress the acquisition of intellectual skills. These may seem to be too future-oriented for the very young child and not related to the business of the childhood center. However, it is a basic question that concerns all levels of education: Is the purpose of education to help people to get along with each other or to prepare them for a job?

Many professionals who are concerned with young children believe that the child who develops a good image of himself and can get along with others will also be able to learn what he needs to know. Others believe that the development of learning ability, the acquisition of skills and knowledge, cannot be left to chance. They feel that the school must actively prepare the child for his future role in society. His feelings of self-worth will come with his ability to achieve.

Although it is unlikely that any group of teachers, parents, and community representatives will completely agree on values, it is important to reach a common ground. Many schools are ineffective because this issue has not been clearly thought out by all those involved with the children. The school administration and faculty may design a curriculum that helps children learn to get along with others, express their feelings, and develop creative outlets. The program will be unsuccessful if the parents and the elementary school authorities are more concerned that the children learn to read, to count, or develop verbal ability.

Beliefs

The final step before the committee decides upon a set of goals for the school is an exploration of their beliefs concerning how children learn. They may be aware that different children learn in different ways and even that the same children may need to utilize a variety of methods to learn. The committee members, though, will probably have ideas and opinions concerning the best method for helping children learn.

Members of the committee will probably explore their differences in seeing the child as (a) one who passively receives knowledge or (b) one who actively seeks knowledge. They may not have thought of learning in exactly these terms, but these are the two extremes in the many possible ways that children learn.

In the first instance, the child is thought of as a passive recipient of information. The teacher is viewed as the giver of the information. It is she who knows what children need to know, and it is she who teaches it. The meaning of the word "teach" is to impart knowledge. This view of the learner (child) assumes that he has limited capacity to determine for himself what he should learn; it also puts the primary responsibility and focus on the teacher.

This perception of how children learn results in a learning environment in which there is high input by the teacher. It is the traditional classroom in which the teacher provides the information and the motivation for learning. In this kind of classroom, the teacher must also provide opportunities for repetition and reinforcement of learning. The teacher is the activator, and the child is and remains the receiver.

In the second instance, seeing the child as one who seeks knowledge, there are also implications for both child and teacher. In this kind of environment, the child is expected to be actively involved and is encouraged to assume responsibility for his own learning. He may choose to learn some things and reject others. He may decide to learn some things by one method and others in a different way. The teacher becomes a *facilitator,* a resource person and a guide. She supplies information when asked or indicates where it can be found. The teacher also encourages

Fig. 5-3 **A child learns by exploring.**

the child's natural curiosity and helps him to broaden his search for knowledge. This view of the learning process assumes the child's ability to determine for himself what he wants and needs to know. It also views the learning process as focusing equally upon the child and the teacher.

This perception of how children learn best results in an environment that is arranged so that children have many possibilities to choose from. Each child is free to make choices, to move from one experience to another. This is the kind of classroom now being described in educational literature as "open" or sometimes as "the learning center approach." It would be characterized by high input from both children and teacher.

Most parents, teachers, and others who have thought about how children learn best probably fall somewhere between these two extremes. They accept the idea that some things must be taught to children and no choice can be allowed; other things may be left for the child to seek out or not. For instance, they may believe that the child must be taught to recognize letters and then to read. Still, they allow the child the freedom to explore the potential for learning with art materials.

Some committee members will have strong feelings and opinions concerning the effectiveness of one kind of learning environment over another. Many problems that could arise at a later time may be avoided if this question is thoroughly explored. What is best for the particular children in their school should be the determining factor in reaching agreement.

Questions concerning how children learn should be asked while objectives are being formulated and implemented. Beliefs determine to a large extent whether objectives are broad, allowing for what the children themselves want to learn, or narrow, reflecting only what adults believe they should learn.

SELECTING GOALS

Goals prepared and developed as a result of the process described must represent a balance of the needs of the children, parents, staff, and community if a childhood center or school is to be successful. Children must get the kind of educational experiences they need. Parents must trust the school to educate their children with consideration of their desires and expectations. Staff must believe that they are doing what is best for the children. The community must know that when the children leave the school, they are better prepared for their next challenge.

Not every person involved in setting goals will agree with every one. Agreement should be reached on as many as possible, with final decisions left to the director.

Also, it must be kept in mind that the process of selecting objectives cannot be accomplished overnight. It may take many months of gathering, discussing, and sorting information. It may take many hours of talking about values and beliefs before even a few objectives can be decided upon.

A director should also be aware that goals designed for a particular school may be appropriate at one time but not at another. Goals should not be seen as absolutes, but as guides that should be reviewed frequently, changed when necessary, and used to develop a good curriculum for children.

THE STATEMENT OF GOALS

The *statement of goals* is a list of expected changes in the behavior of children as a result of the educational experiences provided by the school. Since changes in behavior are extremely slow, a short list may be less frustrating than a long one. It will be easier to see changes in a few areas of behavior than in many. It will also be easier if behaviors can be put into groups. One or two objectives can be stated for each group.

GOAL	DEVELOPMENTAL LEVEL	VALUES	BELIEFS
The child will be able to initiate, carry through, and take pride in a variety of learning experiences available in the school setting.	Three-to-five-year olds are alert to the world around them. The child is eager to channel his energies into constructive "work." The child is striving toward *autonomy* (control over himself). He has an increasing ability to concentrate.	It is important for children to learn to value work.	Children learn best by doing and by being actively involved in a learning experience. Greater motivation will be present when the activity is initiated by the child.

Fig. 5-4 Formulating a Goal

Ralph Tyler, in his book *Basic Principles of Curriculum and Instruction,*[1] categorizes behavior into ten areas:

1. acquisition of information

2. development of work habits and study skills

3. development of effective ways of thinking

4. development of social attitudes

5. development of interests

6. development of appreciations

7. development of sensitivities

8. development of personal social adjustment

9. maintenance of physical health

10. development of philosophy of life

These categories are not the only ways that behavior can be classified. Other educators have made different lists. This list can serve as a beginning for the development of one's own list.

[1] Ralph Tyler, *Basic Principles of Curriculum and Instruction* (Chicago and London: The University of Chicago Press, 1970), p. 58.

Three major points concerning objectives should be kept in mind. First, the statement is made in terms of changes that should take place in the child. The objective should state that the child will be able to do a specific thing as a result of the learning experience. Teacher behavior should not be included in the statement; this can be interpreted by each teacher according to her style. Further discussion of this point will be found in unit 6, Implementing Goals and Objectives.

The second point concerning objectives is that the objective must be clearly stated to provide a base for evaluation of the behavior. The objective is clear if the behavior can be illustrated or described. The behavior should be recognizable when seen.

The third point to remember is that a list of ten goals may be broad statements: they will be considered long-range objectives. When planning for day-to-day implementation of goals, these broad statements will have to be broken down into more specific statements. These will be short-range or behavioral objectives. Many steps may be necessary to achieve a single goal. Each step will be stated in a behavioral objective. The reader is again directed to unit 6 for further discussion of this point.

SAMPLE GOALS

The achievement of one goal may take some children as long as a year in a preschool program. The many steps along the way to reaching this end will have been reflected in the day-to-day and week-to-week behavioral objectives that are part of the long-range process.

In order to help readers state their own long-range goals, some samples are given for several of the categories listed earlier from Tyler. Tyler's category *the development of work habits and study skills* may at first not seem applicable to young children. Yet it is during this early period that the ability to pay attention develops. It is also at this age that the child learns to begin a project himself and carry it through to completion. It is also a time when he learns to be pleased with his own achievements. All of these are necessary preparation for his later involvement in the learning experiences of the elementary school.

Therefore, based on this category, an appropriate goal might be chosen:

The child should be able to initiate, carry through, and take pride in a variety of learning experiences available in the school setting.

This goal is stated in terms of the changes in the behavior of the child. One could observe the child begin a project without the help of the teacher. He could be seen to finish the project without urging. He could be heard to express pleasure in what he had done.

In some schools, Tyler's category *the development of social attitudes* might be stated as the goal:

The child should begin to understand and accept differences in people based on ethnic or cultural background.

Again, this is stated in terms of changes in the behavior of the child. An observable

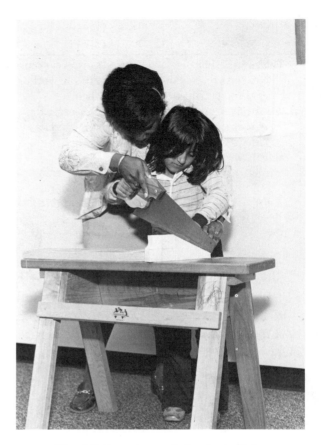

Fig. 5-5 **Learning with Teacher's Help**

example of understanding ethnic differences would be the child's recognition that a friend has brown skin because he is a Negro. He could be seen to accept this child as a friend, not reject him because the friend looks different from himself.

As a last example, Tyler's category *the maintenance of physical health* might be stated in this way:

The child should develop habits and attitudes that promote and maintain his physical health and well-being.

The goal states what the child will be able to do. Observable behavior might be putting on a jacket when it is cold without having to be told by the teacher. The child who can play in water without fear that he will catch a cold is one who has developed the attitudes desired. The child who eats a variety of food because it tastes good and is good for him is also achieving this objective.

The readers are encouraged to formulate their own objectives from Tyler's categories. Each goal should be considered in terms of child development; stated with values and beliefs in mind; and given in terms of changes that can be recognized.

SUMMARY

The director of a preschool program provides guidance to the staff in setting the goals of the school. The process begins with gathering information about the community from which the school draws its enrollment and continues with gathering information about the children in each class.

Before stating goals, the staff members must consider their ideas in terms of child development and what they believe is appropriate for children at each age level. Their values about important needs of the children which can be met by the school and their beliefs about the education of children are topics which must be thoroughly discussed.

A statement of goals should be short and should be in terms of changes that take place in the child. Teacher behavior can be interpreted by each according to her own style. An objective is clear if teachers can describe or illustrate the behavior the child is expected

Fig. 5-6 Friends

to acquire and can recognize the behavior when they see it.

The statement of goals is a list of expected changes in behavior as a result of the educational experiences provided by the school. Goals can be categorized in the following ways: the acquisition of information, the development of work habits and study skills, the development of effective ways of thinking, the development of social attitudes, the development of interests, the development of appreciations, the development of sensitivities, the development of personal social adjustment, the maintenance of physical health, and the development of a philosophy of life.

STUDENT ACTIVITIES

- Write one long-range goal for your school.

- Test your goal against your knowledge of child development, your values, and your beliefs concerning how children learn.

- Discuss the part that parents should play in determining the goals for your school.

- Contact a local Head Start program. Find out if they have a list of goals. Inquire about how the goals were formulated.

REVIEW

1. Explain what is meant by a goal or an objective.

2. Name five of Tyler's general categories for goal preparation and development.

3. List the four factors to be considered when first preparing goals.

4. Whose needs should be represented in the process of formulating goals?

5. How do objectives contribute to the evaluation process?

6. Name three major points to consider in writing goals.

Unit 6 Implementing Goals and Objectives

OBJECTIVES

After studying this unit, the student should be able to

- State general principles for implementing objectives
- Explain what is meant by integration, continuity, and sequence when applied to curriculum
- Describe how short-range objectives evolve from long-range goals

The staff of many schools for young children are often overwhelmed by attempts to put goals and objectives into practice. They do not know how to separate each goal into individual objectives or to organize learning experiences into a curriculum for the year. There is also confusion about which experiences should be chosen for each objective and which should be left out or postponed. Some guidelines for implementing goals are given to help the director in her role as educational leader to the staff.

The statement of goals for the school must be thought of as end results; these are the changes in the child's behavior that will occur by the end of varied periods of time. Sometimes these time periods may cover a full school year. Therefore, it can be seen that the goals are the basis for long-range curriculum planning.

The steps necessary to achieve the end result must be outlined for each goal. What series of behaviors learned over a long period of time will help the child to achieve the expected end result? These behaviors will be included in the objectives for short-range curriculum planning. They will be the basis for the daily, weekly, and monthly activities.

In short, the transition from long-range to short-range curriculum planning involves separation of the expected end behavior into the steps leading to that behavior. The curriculum planners start by describing the terminal behavior; they can then outline each of the steps leading to that end result.

An example from the objectives discussed in unit 5 may be helpful to the reader. The following objective is used to illustrate the point:

The child will be able to initiate, carry through, and take pride in a variety of learning experiences in the school setting.

What observable behavior would lead a teacher to decide that a particular child had indeed achieved this objective? There are many situations that could be used, but the child's use of blocks is a good example. The teacher might observe the following incident.

John goes to the block shelf and begins taking down a pile of long blocks.

He lays these out in a square, goes back to the shelf, and chooses four more blocks the same size. He continues in this manner until he has a structure that is three blocks high. He looks around to find suitable materials for a roof. He decides against using blocks and chooses a square piece of plywood. It fits.

John now tries to park some small cars on the roof of the building. To get the cars up on the roof, he builds a long ramp with several inclines and square blocks to lift the inclines to the proper height. It is a difficult problem to solve, but he does it. As he drives the first cars up the ramp and parks them on the roof, he sits back with a look of pleasure on his face. At snack time, he asks the teacher if his building can be saved to show his mother when she comes to pick him up.

This child has chosen his own activity, solved the problems that arose as he carried his project to completion, and was pleased with his accomplishment. He has achieved the objective in this situation.

What steps were necessary to reach this end result? There would have been numerous ones over a period of time; however, only a few will serve as examples.

Initiate:

- When the teacher suggests an activity, John willingly takes part.
- When three activities are suggested, John is able to choose one of them.
- When told that it is free choice time, John is able to choose an activity by himself.

Carry Through:

- John is able to complete an eighteen-piece puzzle with some help from the teacher.

- John is able to put together a twelve-piece puzzle by himself.

Take Pride:

- John gets frustrated when he is unable to build the structures he wants and stops building.
- Upon completing a task, John expresses with words his pride in his achievement.
- Upon completing a picture, John carefully puts it in his locker to save for his mother.

BEHAVIORAL OBJECTIVES

Each of these steps has been stated as a behavioral objective used for daily, weekly, or monthly curriculum planning. The behavioral objective is written in a prescribed manner so that it is easily understood and used:

- The objective is stated in terms of the child's behavior.
- The conditions for learning are included in specific terms.
- The behavior must be observable.
- The amount or extent of expected behavior is stated.

Certain words are helpful in clarifying objectives. They are used

To describe conditions for learning:

- When asked
- When shown
- Having completed
- Having used

To describe observable behavior:

- The child will select
- The child will place
- The child will express pride with words
- The child will return
- The child will identify
- The child will match

Some of the behavioral objectives that would be necessary to achieve the particular goal that is being discussed can be outlined:

Goal:

- The child will initiate, carry through, and take pride in a variety of learning experiences in the school setting.

Behavioral Objectives:

- When three activities are suggested, the child will be able to choose one of them.

- When told it is free time, the child will be able to initiate his own activity from the materials available.

- When asked to complete an eighteen-piece puzzle, the child requires help in finding fewer than three pieces.

- When shown a puzzle with twelve pieces, the child is able to put it together without help.

- When the child completes a task, he expresses with words his pride in his achievement.

- Upon completing a task, the child will show he values his achievement by wanting to show it to others.

Each step reflects the weekly and monthly objectives which had been formulated earlier. The teacher carefully plans the kinds of activities and experiences that the child needs from the beginning of the school year to the end. Daily, weekly, and monthly activities are not haphazardly put together. They are planned in an organized and meaningful way.

IMPLEMENTING OBJECTIVES

After the long-range goals and behavioral objectives have been formulated, steps are taken to implement them, that is, to put them in operation. This can be done by following some general principles.

Implementing Objectives Begins with Setting up the Environment. The teacher organizes the environment and structures the learning experiences in ways that stimulate the kind of reaction desired in the child. For instance, one of the general objectives might be to develop the child's ability to make choices. The classroom must be set up so that the child really has opportunities to make choices. By placing materials and equipment on shelves that the children can reach easily, the teacher makes it possible for each child to select what he wants.

The Child Must Have Many Opportunities to Practice the Kind of Behavior Implied by the Objective. It was stated in the previous unit that changes in behavior are achieved slowly. Therefore, for any objective, the child must be able to participate in a variety of learning experiences designed to meet the objective. He must also repeat the same learning experiences many times. A child will build up a tower of blocks and knock it down many times. Some children spend hours each day for a week learning to ride a tricycle. Others will paint ten pictures, each time experimenting with brush strokes or mixing colors. All these experiences provide the child with opportunities to practice a skill.

The Child Must Gain a Feeling of Satisfaction from Carrying on the Behavior Expected to Result from the Experience. Each selected learning experience should give the child satisfaction from having participated in it. It is the nature of human beings that attempts will be made to avoid repetition of unsatisfying or painful experiences. If the experience is not a satisfying one, the child will not learn the behavior for which it was designed. In fact, he may even learn the opposite of the desired behavior.

An example of this principle will help to emphasize its meaning. A stated objective may be

To begin developing attitudes that promote and maintain the child's physical health and well-being.

All experiences involving food must be set up with this objective in mind. The child should find that eating at school is fun and free from pressures. He should feel satisfaction in assuming some of the responsibility for what he eats or does not want to eat. He should be able to enjoy the preparation of food.

The Child Must Be Able to Achieve the Behavior Expected to Result from the Learning Experience. It is important for the teacher to know about the development of children in general. It is even more important for her to know the needs and abilities of the particular children in her class. Only in this way is she able to judge whether an expected behavior is within the ability of the children.

When a learning experience is designed to produce behavior that is far beyond the children's level of functioning, they become discouraged. If the learning experience is far *below* this level, children will not be challenged to move on to other levels of behavior.

Good examples of this principle can often be observed in the art activities of a school. Most three-year-olds have not developed the ability to cut with scissors; an art activity that requires cutting will soon be terminated by these children. On the other hand, clay and water may often encourage four-year-olds to go back to an earlier, messy stage when they are really capable of using clay more productively.

The Child Should Have a Choice of Experiences That Can Result in the Desired Behavior. The children in any one class have a wide range of interests and abilities. Interests and even abilities in the same child may also vary from one day to another. Choices will allow each child to find the experience from which he can achieve the expected behavior.

For instance, the development of sensitivities can be achieved through a variety of experiences. Art, music, and movement activities are the most often used by curriculum planners. Preparing and eating food, playing in water, or digging in mud can also develop the child's senses.

The Child Should be able to Repeat Familiar Activities in Order to Achieve the Desired Behavior. Every learning experience has many possible outcomes in terms of the changes in the child's behavior. At one time, an activity may bring about one change. At another time, the changes in behavior may be on quite a different level.

At age three, a child may use clay to explore how it feels and how it changes under different conditions. He will cut it, roll it, pound it, and squeeze it. At age four, clay may provide the opportunity for the child to develop skills in controlling himself and his

Fig. 6-1 Water play is one way to develop the senses.

Fig. 6-2 All ages can enjoy clay and dough.

environment. He can pound the clay and find release for his feelings, thus gaining better control of them. His feeling of success at controlling an inanimate object (the clay) leads him to believe he can control other parts of his environment. At age five, he may use clay to express an idea. He will make a figure, a snake, or a bird, for example.

Many teachers get bored with the same activities or materials. With freedom and encouragement to explore, children seldom do. At each age level there are new possibilities in the use of the materials.

Learning experiences must be put together in an organized way in order to achieve maximum effectiveness. No single experience can achieve an objective. It may take many experiences over a long period of time. Each experience must lead to the next. Each must have a sequence that is logical in terms of the way children learn. Experiences offered over a period of time must be integrated with each other. The total of the learning experiences must constitute a meaningful and cohesive whole.

Integration means combining into a related, unified whole. In curriculum planning, this means that each part must be brought together with other parts. Behaviors developed in one situation should be encouraged in others in order to bring about a unified program.

If the ability to make choices is to be encouraged, making a choice should be expected in as many situations as possible. The child cannot learn if he is allowed to make decisions about the kind of activities he engages in, but is forced to stay at the table until he cleans his plate. He will be confused about whether he is able to make choices or not.

Continuity means uninterrupted connection — persistence without essential change. When applied to learning it means the provision for continuing with related experiences to meet each objective. It provides the opportunity for each child to practice the desired behavior in an organized way, each step related to the next.

If an objective requires the development of speech as a tool for thinking and communicating, organized activities must be provided to meet that end. The child must have a chance to hear language used in the desired way. He must have the opportunity to hear language used in ways that are important to him, such as in storytelling and reading aloud. He must be encouraged to use speech himself in as many ways as possible. He must not be required to be silent on too many occasions.

Sequence is the following of one thing after another. Applied to the planning of curriculum, it means the logical succession of one experience after another. Thus, each experience will reinforce the previous one.

An example of sequencing is making an excursion to the pet store, after which the children can take part in many related activities. A book about pets can be read to the children at storytime. The children can be encouraged to tell a story or paint a picture about something they saw at the pet store. Listening to a record about animals may help the children relive the experience. Adding figures of animals to the block-building area can stimulate play about the field experience. Teachers can also reinforce the excursion experience in other ways.

DESIGNING A CURRICULUM

Putting into practice the principles and guidelines suggested may still be difficult for those who have not done so before. Planning and carrying out an organized curriculum has to begin somewhere. It might be helpful for the beginner to start with one short-range objective, and outline experiences planned for a week as indicated in figure 6-3.

GOAL: The child will develop habits and attitudes that promote and maintain his physical health and well-being.

Behavioral Objective: When presented with a new food, the child will taste it.

Activity	Monday	Tuesday	Wednesday	Thursday	Friday
Learning Centers	Vegetable Lotto Game	Taped reading of *Carrot Seed*	Video cassette on food and nutrition	Categorize foods — cut and paste pictures	Seed collage
Story	*Carrot Seed*		*Stone Soup*		
Play Activity	Prepare carrot and raisin salad for lunch		Cut up vegetables for lunch soup		
Lunch	Throughout the week, the children will set the table and serve their own portions from serving dishes.				
Outside	Throughout the week, the children will be getting soil ready and then planting a vegetable garden.				

Fig. 6-3 Sample Plan for One Week

It will also be helpful to keep a daily log of the learning activities offered each day and some brief notes concerning how the children reacted to the experience. The teacher may find that some things interested the children and others did not.

The daily notes may also include suggestions for setting up the activity in another way. With a different presentation, the objective might be achieved more easily. Over a period of months, the record of activities and reactions related to a particular objective will yield a great deal of information for the teacher, and help in planning for other objectives.

SUMMARY

Using objectives for planning curriculum often appears to be an overwhelming and confusing task. There are some general principles that might be helpful.

- Putting objectives into practice begins with setting up the environment in such a way that the desired reaction is stimulated.

- The child should have many opportunities to practice the kind of behavior implied by the objective.

- The child must gain a feeling of satisfaction from carrying on the behavior expected to result from the experience.

- The child must be able to achieve the expected behavior as a result of the experience.

- The child should have a choice of experiences that can result in the desired behavior.

- The child should have the opportunity to repeat familiar activities in order to achieve the desired result.

Learning experiences must be put together in an organized way in order to achieve maximum effectiveness. Continuity, sequence, and integration should be part of the organization.

STUDENT ACTIVITIES

- List three characteristics of three-year-olds. Observe some children who are three years old. Are the characteristics that you listed present in these children?

- List three characteristics of four-year-olds. Observe some children who are four years old. Are the characteristics that you listed present in these children?

- Based upon one objective, plan a weekly curriculum for a group of three-year-olds.

REVIEW

1. Do you feel that children must enjoy a learning experience? Explain.

2. Can an objective be satisfactorily achieved by providing the child with a single experience? Explain.

3. Give an example of how sequencing may be used.

4. Name the general principles that help in planning the curriculum.

5. Select the explanation which best explains the individual components of learning experiences given below.

A.	Continuity	a.	Logical succession where each experience reinforces the previous one.
B.	Integration	b.	Combining related experiences into a unified program.
C.	Sequence	c.	Combining parts to bring about a unified whole.

Unit 7 Evaluating the Outcomes

OBJECTIVES

After studying this unit, the student should be able to

- Explain what is meant by evaluation
- Describe steps in the evaluation process
- List methods of evaluation that can be used in a school for young children

In order to determine if the learning experiences offered by the school are effective, the director and teachers must carry out a continuing evaluation of the curriculum. *Evaluation* is the process of determining the degree to which expected changes in behavior have actually taken place. Have the children been able to achieve the expected changes in behavior? Have they achieved the objectives of the school? Have some children been able to meet the objectives, but others have not?

In addition to information about the children's development, the process of evaluation may produce side benefits for the school staff. The staff may discover that objectives need to be redefined in order to evaluate what they are doing. If the objectives have not been clearly stated or are not appropriate for this group of children, the expected behavior will not occur. In this case, the objectives must be studied and replaced.

The evaluation process may force the staff to reexamine the ways in which objectives are being implemented. If few of the children have achieved the expected behavior, the fault may be in the way that the daily or weekly activities are presented rather than with the objectives themselves. The staff may want to reconsider their beliefs concerning the ways that children learn best.

EVALUATION PROCESS

Evaluation requires the expected behavior to be observable just as writing and implementing objectives require it to be observable. The evaluator must know exactly what behavior or behaviors indicate that the objective has been achieved. If the objective has been stated correctly, it will contain a description of the behavior. Some examples of descriptions of behavior are shown:

... the child **completes a puzzle** . . . . . .
... the child **shares a toy**. . . . .
... the child **unbuttons his sweater**. . . .
... the child **returns the books to the shelf**

Standards for judging behavior must also be set up. The evaluator should determine the acceptable level of performance. Should the child be expected to achieve the behavior only part of the time or must he be able to do it all of the time? Must the child be able to complete all of a series of tasks or only part of them? Some illustrations of this kind of statement are given:

... shown four kinds of classroom equipment, the child will be able to **return at least three of them** to their storage places.

... shown the colors yellow, red, and blue, the child will correctly **name each of them**.

... shown five name cards, the child will correctly pick out his own name **75% of the time**.

The evaluation process must also include a determination of where to look for evidence that the objective has been met. This is especially true of the affective areas of the child's development. Affective areas include social and emotional aspects of the personality and are demonstrated by feelings, emotions, interests, attitudes, and values. For each objective, the director and teachers should list the situations in which there is an opportunity for the expression or performance of the desired behavior.

If the evaluators wish to determine the extent of the child's personal social adjustment, they must observe situations in which the child is interacting with other children or adults. They would not look for this behavior when the child is playing alone. The dramatic play corner, the block-building area, and the sandbox are places where interaction might take place. Children and adults also interact during lunch time, when the children arrive and leave, during play times, and during transitions from one activity to another.

METHODS OF EVALUATION

Methods of evaluation are the ways in which the achievement of objectives is tested or judged. The evaluators must choose a method appropriate to the objective. A variety of methods may be used. Valid evidence

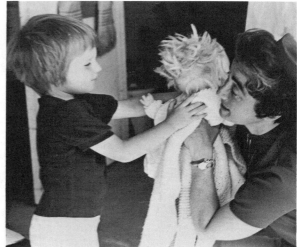

Fig. 7-1 An Interaction between a Teacher and a Child

of the child's achievement is obtained by an evaluation before the learning begins and again at the end of the time period.

Tests

Testing may be as complex as using a commercially prepared ability test. It may also be as simple as asking a child to perform a single task. Some currently used assessment tests for preschool age children are the Denver Development Test, the Peabody Picture Vocabulary Test, and the Minnesota Preschool Scale.

Observations

Observe the child in the situations where there is opportunity for expression or performance of the behavior. Anecdotal records, film, videotape, or taped records are used. A checklist might also be appropriate for recording observations of the child. When judgment of behavior is held in doubt, more than one observer might be used to evaluate achievement. At times a single observer must make several observations in order to make an accurate determination.

Collection of End Products

Collecting and examining things made by the child will reveal a great deal about his progress. For example, pictures taken of block buildings made over a period of time may show an increase in complexity and manual agility. A collection of paintings may show increased awareness of color and form.

Samplings

Time interval sampling of the presence or absence of behavior is helpful. The observer can record what the child is doing during periodic five-minute intervals. The number of

---

CHECKLIST OF LARGE MOTOR SKILLS

Child's name _____ Date _____

Directions: Place a plus sign (+) if the child can do it. Place a minus sign (–) if he cannot do it.

1. Locomotor Movements

   ____ Runs forward.   ____ Slides.
   ____ Runs backward.   ____ Rides tricycle.
   ____ Hops on one foot.   ____ Walks on stairs with alternating feet.
   ____ Hops (jumps) on both feet.   ____ Climbs up and down (jungle gym).
   ____ Skips with one foot.   ____ Gallops.
   ____ Skips with both feet.

2. Nonlocomotor Movements

   ____ Bends down.   ____ Pushes and pulls.
   ____ Stretches upward.   ____ Twists and turns body.

3. Manipulative Skills

   ____ Throws ball.   ____ Catches ball.
   ____ Rolls ball.   ____ Bounces ball.

Fig. 7-2 Checklist of Motor Skills

Elinor T. Massoglia, *Early Childhood Education in the Home* (Albany, NY: Delmar Publishers, 1977), p. 258.

| Child Observed _____ Date _____ |
| Age of child _____ Time _____ |

Activity	Behavior	Description

Fig. 7-3 Observation of an Individual Child

| Child Observed _____ Date _____ |
| Behavior being observed _____ |
| _____ |

Time	Activity	No. times behavior occurred
9:00–9:15		
9:15–9:30		
9:30–9:45		
9:45–10:00		

Fig. 7-4 Time Sample Record

times the behavior was present can then be counted. Examples of the kinds of behavior that can be readily assessed by the time-sampling method are incidence of aggression, language development, and interest span.

Questionnaires

Answers written on a questionnaire provide a record of a parent's evaluation of the child's progress. Questions regarding the development of language or the acquisition of information could be answered. Parents might be asked to comment about changes in the child's ability to get along with his family and friends. If a written questionnaire seems unsuitable for a particular group of parents, the same kinds of information can be gathered in interviews with them.

Interviews

The parent interview can provide information about the child's abilities before and after learning experiences take place. An interview with the child might also be considered. The teacher can talk with the child to determine his level of achievement for some of the objectives. Talking about people or friends will reveal his ability to accept others. Conversations can also reveal information that the child has acquired from participation in the program.

When information has been gathered, it must be put into an organized form so that the director and teachers can use it to further the child's development. This is usually called a *profile* and is seen as a picture of the child's development at a particular time.

A profile should be made with the categories for objectives in mind. Each profile should be dated, should include the child's name, and contain a summary of the information obtained from each of the methods used for evaluation. Profiles are done at different periods and then compared; they give the teacher a valuable tool for her work with the child.

Acquisition of information   John G. Smith   June 2, 1975

John has learned to count from one to ten. Usually recognizes the numbers when he sees them, although sometimes confuses six and nine. Has been observed to count out blocks for his friends. Mother reports that he uses numbers a great deal at home. He counts out cookies for his sister, recognizes numbers in magazines.

Development of work habits and study skills

John comes in each morning and goes immediately to the block-building corner. He starts a building and stays with it for most of the time indoors. Pictures taken of his buildings, over the last month, show that they have become increasingly complex. He is now also using cars and people in his buildings. His mother reports he is very interested in how buildings are really put up and asks to be taken to construction sites.

Development of effective ways of thinking

John asks many questions at school. When he doesn't understand and wants more information, he is very demanding of the teacher until he gets an answer. He is also beginning to go to books for pictures that will help him to find out what he wants to know. His mother says that at home he follows his father around as father works in the yard or on the car. John watches and asks questions.

Fig. 7-5 Sample Profile

SUMMARY

An evaluation process is used to determine the degree to which expected changes in behavior have actually taken place. Serious consideration must be given to the source where evaluators may look for evidence that the objective has been met. Those involved in evaluation must also determine how to find valid evidence of the child's level of achievement. They might use one or more of the following methods: tests, observation, a collection of the child's products, samplings of behavior, questionnaires for parents, and interviews with the parents and/or the child.

By using various methods, those who work with children can evaluate their achievements and guide the young ones toward development of their full potential.

When information regarding a child's achievement has been gathered, it must be put together in organized form. This is called a profile and should be done with the categories of objectives in mind.

STUDENT ACTIVITIES

- Submit a written report about your feelings on evaluation and the effectiveness of evaluation tools.

- Based on outside readings, give a talk on evaluation or submit a report, citing reading references to support your statements.

- Select one goal and develop two or three behavioral objectives based on it. Make up an evaluation tool to measure the educational outcomes desired. In conference with your head teacher, determine if the evaluation tool may be tested in the school.

REVIEW

1. What is meant by evaluation?

2. Name six methods used to evaluate children in schools for young children.

3. What steps are involved in the evaluation process?

4. Explain what is meant by a profile, including what it should contain.

5. Give three general headings contained in a profile.

Unit 8 Supervising the Children's Program

OBJECTIVES

After studying this unit, the student should be able to

- Identify ways in which a director can help teachers implement curriculum objectives
- Describe procedures for simplifying the record keeping required of teachers

The leadership abilities of a director are most often used to ensure that the curriculum objectives of the school are being fully and appropriately implemented. Teachers and the director work together to set the objectives; however, teachers carry out these objectives in the daily activities of the classroom. The goals of the school are achieved only to the extent that teachers do their jobs well. It is the responsibility of the director to provide the support, encouragement, and means needed for teachers to function at an optimum level.

ROOM ENVIRONMENT

It has been said elsewhere in this text that the physical environment is the basis of the curriculum of a school. The director must encourage individuality in the way that teachers arrange their rooms. She must also make certain that each arrangement reflects the objectives of the program. The room arrangement should provide for the comfort of both children and adults. It should allow for the teacher's creativity and taste in decoration. The furniture should be designed so that it is flexible; the teacher should be able to change the arrangement as adult, child, or school needs change.

The director will want to provide materials that bring color and beauty to the rooms. Many teachers find that a variety of plants add a special feature to their rooms. Colorful posters, pictures, bits of fabric, or pieces of sculpture all help to brighten a room.

Bulletin boards used as added interest centers enhance children's learning. Bulletin boards should be at the eye level of the child, not the adult. They should display things that the child is interested in and that he can touch, feel, or smell. The display should be colorful, and the arrangement should be pleasing to the viewer. The theme of the display should fit in with other areas of the curriculum. Lastly, the bulletin boards should be changed periodically as the children's interests change or as the curriculum changes.

The director should encourage a feeling of sharing among the teachers so that materials can be used by as many children in the school as possible. If the director, herself, acts as a resource for materials and ideas and encourages teachers to learn from each other, this feeling of sharing will develop.

FIELD TRIPS

If insurance coverage allows it, the director should encourage teachers to plan and arrange field trips so that the children's experiences will be broadened. Field trips can be short walking trips to the park, to the mailbox, or to the store. They can be trips that need transportation — such as trips to a bakery, the harbor, or the zoo.

So that the field trip will be pleasurable to both children and adults, the director should remind teachers of several steps to be taken before the trip begins:

- Visit the site ahead of time. See what is available. Arrange what the children will do or see.

- Notify all parents of children participating. Be certain that every child has a signed trip consent.

- Know the person who will be the contact at the site. Give information about the ages of the children and their interests. Follow visit with a thank-you letter or telephone call.

- Provide enough adults for adequate supervision and safety.

- Plan some travel activities or games to keep the children amused on the bus or in the car.

- Schedule the visit for an appropriate amount of time. Allow enough time so that children do not have to be rushed, but not so much that they get bored.

- Take along a snack or lunches. Lunch bags are easier to manage than lunch boxes which tend to get lost. The school should provide a beverage.

- Prepare the children for the trip. Tell them where they are going, how they will get there, what they will see, what the rules are, and when they will return to school.

- Do a follow-up. Plan an activity appropriate to the age level of the children that will allow them to review what they have learned.

- Record information about the trip for future use. (Figure 8-1 shows an example of the kind of information that would be helpful.)

CURRICULUM RESOURCES

The director can be extremely helpful to teachers in providing information concerning sources of materials to enhance the curriculum. There are many catalogs put out by equipment companies that show materials and make suggestions for their use. These should be kept in the staff lounge so that they are readily available. There are also many books that give suggestions for learning activities or show how scrap materials can be used for exciting activities for young children.

It is helpful to keep a current list of materials available throughout the school so that teachers can trade materials around from one class to another. Some schools find it effective to keep learning materials in some central place from which they can be checked out like library books. A set of materials can be boxed and labeled; everything needed for an activity or learning center is kept together.

Another way of adding to the supply of small equipment and materials is to schedule workshops as part of staff training. Most teachers would like to increase their picture file, add to their games, or learning center materials, but find it difficult to make these at home after working all day. A workshop

FIELD TRIP RECORD

Place _____   Telephone Number _____

Address _____   Contact Person _____

_____

Time in Transit _____

Things to See _____

_____

_____

Follow-up Activities _____

_____

_____

_____

Fig. 8-1 Field Trip Record Form

SOURCE OF FREE MATERIALS

Place _____

Address _____   Phone _____

_____

Kinds of Materials _____

_____

When Available _____

_____

Pick-up at _____

_____

Fig. 8-2 Free Materials Source Form

PARENT SIGN-IN/SIGN-OUT				
Date _____		Group or Class _____		
Child's Name	Time of Arrival	Signed	Time of Departure	Signed

Fig. 8-3 Sample Sign-in/Sign-out Sheet

provides a social time for teachers as well as the opportunity to make some needed materials.

A director can also compile a list of places in the community that provide free materials. As a source is discovered, it can be recorded on cards that are kept in a file box. Information should include the place, kinds of materials, and when they are available. Some places such as furniture manufacturers may have scrap wood that they put out once a week; newspapers may put out ends of rolls of paper at certain times of the day.

TEACHER RECORD KEEPING

In every school there are certain records that teachers are required to keep. The number and kind vary with the type of program. Record keeping should never be allowed to interfere with the teacher's responsibility for the children, however. By planning the most efficient way of keeping records, the director can save teacher time that could be spent with the children.

Sign-in/Sign-out Sheet

In day care schools where children arrive and depart at different times and where staff shifts are staggered, a parent sign-in and sign-out sheet is necessary. A glance at this sheet will show which children are present at any time. The sheet should be kept at a convenient place so that each parent upon arrival or departure is reminded to sign it. Some schools keep one record at the front entrance. Other schools have found that it is important to have this record in each classroom. If one record is used, it should be divided into classes or groups of children so that a count of children in each group can be quickly determined. Figure 8-3 shows an example of this kind of record.

Daily Log

Teachers should be encouraged to keep a daily log on important happenings to each child, figure 8-4. This is a record that is to be

```
┌─────────────────────────────────────────────────────────────────┐
│              DAILY LOG OF CHILDREN'S BEHAVIOR                     │
│  ─────────────────────────────────────────────────────────────   │
│                                                                   │
│  Date _____  Group or Class _____ │
│                                                                   │
│  John C.    Didn't sleep at all at rest time.  Seemed to be very  │
│             restless and couldn't get comfortable.  When asked    │
│             what was the matter he could not give any reason.     │
│             Saw no signs of illness coming on.                    │
│                                                                   │
│  Mary F.    Had a slight bump on the back of her head when she    │
│             tumbled over backward out of the sandbox.  It wasn't  │
│             a long fall, so bump was slight.  Mother should       │
│             be told about it, though.                             │
└─────────────────────────────────────────────────────────────────┘
```

Fig. 8-4 Sample Daily Log

used by teachers and is not open to parents. This should be set up like a diary, with a page for each day. The morning teacher should record significant events so that the afternoon teacher is able to understand a child's behavior. Ideally, teachers should have a chance to talk together about these things. In reality, there often is not time during a busy day. Examples of the kind of record useful in this diary are incidents when a child has hurt himself or when he has had a difficult time with another child. Descriptions of unusual behavior might be recorded so that an attempt can be made to understand it as the day goes on. If a child seems listless or tired, this should be entered in the log so that the afternoon teacher can watch the child for similar behavior after a nap. If necessary, unusual behavior should be reported to the parent.

Attendance Records

Attendance records must be filled in each day. These should be done at the same time each day so that they will not be forgotten. Many teachers do this the first thing in the morning. However, some children may arrive after that time. To avoid having to check the record twice, attendance can be taken at snack time or lunch time so that late arrivers are included. Obviously, a school in which some children leave at noon while others remain will have to use an earlier time than the school in which all children stay throughout the day.

Periodic Evaluation Records

Some program types require that teachers do periodic evaluations of each child's progress. These may be tests of motor skills in which the child is asked to perform a series of tasks and the results are recorded. The evaluation may consist of a series of cognitive tasks that the child is asked to complete. Either of these tasks can be done more efficiently if the teacher is free of other duties during the evaluation time. Two teachers may combine groups for a time so that one is free. The director may help out in the classroom, or an extra aide could be used. The director can also help by seeing that there is a place free of interruptions where the tests can be done. This is especially important for any test involving cognitive tasks. If extra time is needed to record evaluation information, it should be allowed for within the teacher's working hours.

HOME VISITS

Many schools schedule visits to each child's home at the beginning of the school year; others make a visit to each family at the time the child is first enrolled in the school. A teacher's visit to a child's home provides an opportunity to develop a different kind of relationship both with the child and with his family. The visit should be scheduled with the mother by telephone for a time that is convenient. Both the child and any members of the family at home should be present. The teacher might suggest to the parent that she would like to have a chance to visit briefly with the child and then have a short visit with the other members of the family. The mother might serve refreshments during this time, involving the child in her activities.

A home visit is not to be seen as a time in which problems are discussed; it is not a conference. The teacher gains some information about the home, and the family learns more about the teacher. The primary purpose of this visit is to foster a closer relationship, thus bringing the home and the school closer together. Many children are pleased to have their teacher visit their home and often show even greater eagerness to attend school afterwards. Children who have found it hard to part from their mothers at school may find it easier after this visit.

It must be remembered that some parents may not want to have a teacher visit the home. This feeling should be respected until the parent is ready for a visit. The school must be willing to find other ways to bring the school and the home together.

Some schools foster a close relationship between the school and home by making a field trip to each child's home during the year. When the setting allows it, the whole class can go to the child's house for snack time. A family living in an apartment or without a yard, might find this a hardship.

Even where there is adequate space for a visit, it must be planned carefully so that the visit does not create havoc for the mother. The children should have time to play in the yard, with activities planned by the teacher if necessary. It may be that some materials will have to be brought from school so that the children remain occupied during the visit. If the host child wishes, the children may have time to see his room. Snack should be served; then, the children return to school. The entire visit probably should not be for more than forty-five minutes — depending upon what there is available at the home for the children to do. Most children look forward to having their friends visit; a few will not want this kind of invasion. These children may be allowed to postpone the visit until they have seen how it goes at their friends' homes — or they may not want a visit at all.

SEPARATION

Most children look forward to the first school experience with pleasure and excitement. They see it as a sign of growing up. Their parents probably have told them they will meet new friends and have lots of fun. Problems arise for a few children when they fully realize that going to school means leaving their mothers. The younger the child, the more difficult it may be. The two- or three-year-old will have more difficulty than a four-year-old.

Parents, too, sometimes have anxieties about leaving the child at school. They worry that school staff may not understand their child's needs or that they might not take proper care of him.

The fears of both the child and the parent can be minimized if proper procedures are used and if the director and staff are sensitive to their feelings. Several steps that the parent and child can go through help make the separation process simpler. These steps may take a day for each or may be accomplished in a shorter time.

- Parent and child visit school together before the opening day. Fifteen minutes to half an hour should be allowed for the child to explore the environment and meet the teacher.

- The first group session should be shorter than a usual day.

- When the child seems comfortable, the parent should leave the room for a short time, but should remain at the school.

- The parent should leave school and go home for a short time.

- The parent should stay only a few minutes after bringing the child to school. She should return to pick him up at the end of the session.

- The parent should bring the child to school and return at the end of the session.

- Each time the parent leaves, whether she has been there for a few minutes or longer, the parent must never be allowed to sneak out of the room without saying goodbye to the child, telling him how long she will be gone. She should then go even if the child cries. The length of her absence might be shortened if the child is really in distress.

- In a day care school where the mother may not be able to be absent from work several days to help with the child's separation, it will be easier for the child if she does stay with him throughout one complete day. It is especially important for her to be there at meal times and at nap time.

- The director can help parents understand that the child's anxiety is normal and that their own worries are normal. A supportive attitude and reassurances that the child will be all right usually suffice.

It sometimes helps the child if he brings a favorite toy or blanket from home to comfort him.

- The director can introduce parents and make opportunities for them to be together. As they get to know one another, they can lend support to each other.

SUMMARY

The leadership abilities of a director are used to ensure that the curriculum objectives of the school are being fully and properly carried out. The teachers carry out the objectives which means that the goals of the school are achieved only to the extent that teachers do their jobs well.

The basis of the curriculum is in the physical environment. The director must encourage individuality in the way that teachers arrange their rooms. She must be sure that each arrangement reflects the objectives of the school.

- The rooms should be comfortable for both children and adults.

- The director should provide materials to bring color and beauty to the rooms.

- Bulletin boards are used as an interest center for the children.

- The director encourages teachers to share materials and resources.

Field trips must be carefully planned so that the children's experiences will be broadened — and also be fun for the children. Teachers should be reminded of ways to make field trips more effective:

- Visit site ahead of time
- Notify parents
- Know contact person
- Provide enough adults
- Plan travel games or activities
- Take a snack or lunch

- Prepare children for trip
- Do a follow-up
- Record information for future use

The director can help teachers by providing information about sources of materials to enhance the curriculum:

- Equipment catalogs
- Books
- Current list of materials in school
- Workshops for making materials
- List of free materials

The director can devise efficient methods for doing the records that teachers must keep.

- A parent sign-in/sign-out sheet
- Attendance taken once a day
- A daily log of significant behavior in children
- Evaluations of children's progress

Many schools schedule teacher visits to each child's home at the beginning of a school year. Other schools have the children's groups take field trips to each child's house. Home visits and field trips are scheduled for the purpose of bringing the home and the school closer together.

Although most children anticipate going to school with pleasure, a few have difficulty parting from the parent. The school can help both the parent and child by taking the separation in slow steps. The director and staff must be sensitive to the feelings of parent and child. Parents need to know that anxiety in the child is a normal reaction.

STUDENT ACTIVITIES

- Look at the arrangement of a classroom in a school for young children. Is it attractive? Does it reflect the objectives of the school? Are the bulletin boards at the child's eye level?
- Find out about one field trip site. Fill out an information record for this site.
- Compile an inventory of learning resource materials in your school.

REVIEW

1. Why is it so important for the director to use her leadership abilities when planning for implementation of objectives?
2. A classroom environment should provide for the comfort of both children and adults. In what other ways can the environment be enhanced?
3. List things to remember when planning a field trip.
4. In what ways can the director provide additional curriculum materials for the staff?
5. List the kinds of records that teachers may have to keep.
6. What is the purpose of a home visit?
7. How does the director help the parent and child through the period when separation is a problem?

Section 3
STAFFING THE PROGRAM

Unit 9 Staff Selection

OBJECTIVES

After studying this unit, the student should be able to

- State factors to consider when determining staff qualifications
- Name some sources for recruitment of staff
- Plan and carry out a recruiting process
- Describe the process of selecting a staff member from qualified applicants

The staff members carry out the functions of the school; they create the atmosphere in which children grow and develop. They determine whether a school remains static or meets the challenges of early childhood education.

QUALIFICATIONS

It is essential that the director of a school develop procedures for finding qualified staff. The first step is to determine the requirements for the position. What kind of person is needed? What skills or knowledge must that person have? These questions must be answered for each position in the school: the food service personnel, the maintenance staff, the secretary, and the teachers.

Educational Requirements

Determining the qualifications for a job may begin with an investigation of the regulations governing the position. In some states there are regulations concerning the academic background of teachers of young children. In California and New York, for instance, the qualifications for teachers in privately owned schools are subject to regulations attached to licensing laws. All teachers must have at least twelve semester units of college level courses. If these units have not been completed before she is hired, the teacher must be working toward their completion during her period of employment. Publicly funded schools have other regulations.

Personal Characteristics

The personal characteristics needed for the job should be listed. It is generally accepted that teachers should like to be around children, but what about other employees? Will the secretary come in contact with the children? Is flexibility a requirement for teachers or for all employees? Does the director want employees who can make their own decisions? What kind of person will fit in best with other staff members? There are many questions that might be explored based on the director's knowledge of each job and her awareness of her staff. Some of the personal characteristics that are recommended

| | DAY CARE CENTER | | FAMILY DAY CARE |
	DIRECTOR	TEACHER	HOME OPERATOR
ALABAMA	+	HS	NS
ALASKA	HS	NS	(NS)
ARIZONA*	NS	NS	NS
ARKANSAS	HS	NS	(NS)
CALIFORNIA	+	+	NS
COLORADO	+	HS	NS
CONNECTICUT	+	HS	NS
DELAWARE	+	+	(NS)
FLORIDA	NS	NS	NS
GEORGIA	HS	HS	NS
HAWAII	+	+	NS
IDAHO**	NS	NS	NS
ILLINOIS	+	+	NS
INDIANA	+	+	NS
IOWA	+	+	NS
KANSAS	+	NS	NS
KENTUCKY	NS	NS	NS
LOUISIANA*	NS	NS	NS
MAINE	+	HS	(NS)
MARYLAND	NS	NS	NS
MASSACHUSETTS*	+		NS
MICHIGAN	+	+	NS
MINNESOTA	NS	NS	NS
MISSISSIPPI**	+	+	NS
MISSOURI	+	NS	(NS)
MONTANA	NS	NS	NS
NEBRASKA	+	+	NS
NEVADA	+	NS	N/AP
NEW HAMPSHIRE	HS	HS	NS
NEW JERSEY*	+	+	N/AP
NEW MEXICO	NS	NS	NS
NEW YORK	NS	NS	NS
NORTH CAROLINA*	NS	NS	(NS)
NORTH DAKOTA	HS	NS	(NS)
OHIO*	+	HS	NS
OKLAHOMA	HS	HS	NS
OREGON*	NS	NS	N/AP
PENNSYLVANIA	+	+	NS
RHODE ISLAND	+	+	NS
SOUTH CAROLINA	NS	NS	(NS)
SOUTH DAKOTA	+	+	NS
TENNESSEE	+	+	NS
TEXAS	HS	NS	NS
UTAH	NS	NS	NS
VERMONT	NS	NS	
VIRGINIA	+	HS	NS
WASHINGTON	+	NS	NS
WEST VIRGINIA*	HS	NS	NS
WISCONSIN	+	+	N/AP
WYOMING	+	+	NS
DISTRICT OF COLUMBIA	NS	NS	NS

+   Some college or equivalent experience   *   No mandatory licensing requirement for family day care homes
HS   High school   ** No mandatory licensing requirement for day care centers
NS   Not specified   No licensing law for homes
N/AP Not applicable   ( ) Also a requirement for group day care homes

Fig. 9-1 Education and Training Requirements For Day Care Center and Family Day Care
(*State and Local Day Care Licensing Requirements*, U.S. Dept. Health, Education, and Welfare. (OCD) 73-1006, p. G-1)

for people who work with young children include a sense of humor, a cheerful disposition, enthusiasm, good health and the ability to communicate well.

Required Skills

A statement regarding skills needed for the position should be the third step. A word currently being used in early childhood education is competencies. It simply means that persons are able to demonstrate by their behavior that they can perform the skills required for a particular job. It is applicable to all positions. Does the secretary need to take shorthand as well as type? Must the teacher be able to plan experiences so the children will learn to read? Must the cook be able to plan meals as well as prepare them?

The skills required of a teacher include the following:

- Ability to plan and implement learning experiences

- Ability to create a learning atmosphere through the arrangement of the room environment

- Ability to assess and measure achievement of goals

- Ability to use a variety of media and resources for learning

Knowledge of the Field of Interest

The person in this position must have certain knowledge of the specialized area. Should the teacher have a knowledge of child development? Does the cook need to have a basic understanding of nutrition? Does the secretary have to have knowledge of public relations techniques? Again, the director must have an understanding of the functions and needs of each job in order to make these determinations.

Some examples of the knowledge required of a teacher are listed:

- Understanding of child development including knowledge of expected behavior at each stage

- Knowledge of the learning process

- Knowledge of the curriculum areas appropriate to the preschool

RECRUITING SOURCES

The director can begin the recruiting process as soon as she has determined the qualifications. A concise, written statement for distribution or a discussion by telephone will help at this point. The items the statement should include are listed:

- The name of the school

- Address of the school

- Job title and brief description

- Contract period (September to June or the calendar year)

- Salary range

- Brief statement of qualifications

- Name and phone number of person to contact

- Application process

- Starting date of position

This information should be widely distributed; the more people who see it, the better are the chances of finding the right person. However, if there is an expectation of large numbers of applicants, the director may want to eliminate the telephone number from distributed information. Written applications should be requested first. Fifty phone calls in a day can be extremely time-consuming. Fifty written applications can be screened at leisure with follow-up phone calls to qualified candidates.

The Village Early Childhood Center at 8126 West 8th Street is seeking a Head Teacher for a group of 18 four-year olds. Responsibilities include planning and conducting the program of the group, working with parents and participating in staff planning and decision-making.

The applicant selected will be awarded a one-year contract with a salary ranging from $7,200 to $9,500. The school is in session all year, with each staff member entitled to 15 days paid leave each year. Starting date for this position is August 1.

Applicants should have a B.A. degree in child development or related fields and have had at least two years experience in a preschool program.

An application, resume and three letters of reference are required. The application form may be requested by calling

Mrs. Anton
924-8659

Fig. 9-2 Sample Recruiting Notice

Notification of Staff Vacancies

What are the sources the director can use in order to find qualified staff? First, existing staff should be notified of openings. In some situations, the opening may offer opportunity for advancement. Staff members may also know of persons who would be interested in the job.

Second, professional organizations and placement services should be notified. These organizations often have journals or newsletters that could carry information regarding the position. Placement services allow wide distribution of information.

The placement offices of colleges which offer programs in early childhood education or related fields may be another source. A local community college may have vocational programs for food service workers, secretaries, and teachers. Universities which offer majors in teacher education should also be included. Some states have universities that offer credential programs in early childhood education. They may have trained teachers looking for jobs.

Other schools in the area may be another source for application. Many directors either know of or keep a file listing the names of persons who have applied for jobs in their school. If they have not been able to use the applicant, they may refer the person to another school.

Related agencies which provide services for children and their families should also receive recruiting information. Licensing agencies and social service agencies may have contacts with persons seeking positions in schools for young children. Medical and recreational agencies are another source. Community youth organizations may know of young people who wish to begin a career working with young children.

If necessary, an advertisement can be placed in the local newspaper. A written response should be requested in this case, since advertising often brings a large number of replies.

APPLICATION INFORMATION

Application forms should be developed and used each time a position is to be filled. There may be a basic form to be used for all positions with additional information as needed for each position. Whatever proce-

EMPLOYMENT APPLICATION

Name _____ Date of Application _____
      Last   First   Middle

Address _____ Phone _____
                                        Social Security
_____ Number _____

Position Applied For _____

Previous Employment (List most recent experience first)

Employer	Address	Position	Dates

Educational Background

School	Major Subject	Courses Related to Preschool	Degree	Date Completed

Number of High School years completed: 1   2   3   4

Certificates or Credentials: _____

_____

Fig. 9-3 Sample Employment Application (Page 1)

Special abilities _____
(Music, art, etc)

_____

Significant experiences with children _____
(Sunday school, camps, volunteer, etc)

_____

Significant experiences with adults _____
(PTA, Adult Education, etc)

_____

Professional Affiliations _____

_____

Publications _____

_____

_____

Personal References:
    Name   Address

_____

_____

_____

Fig. 9-3 Sample Employment Application (Page 2)

dure is used, the forms should be simple and short. Questions on the form should be clear and related to the job. The application should include

- Date the application is made
- Name of applicant
- Address of applicant
- Telephone number of applicant
- Job or volunteer experience (should include dates and type of volunteer work)
- Age
- Position applied for
- Social Security number
- Educational background
- Credentials and/or academic degrees
- Hobbies or special interests
- References (include name, address, telephone)

In addition, the application for the position of teacher may include:

- Professional affiliations
- Published works

Some applicants may need help in filling out an application form. Language handicaps, inexperience with forms, or limited education should not prevent a potentially qualified person from applying. Either the director, secretary, or another staff member should be available to help with the application.

SELECTION PROCESS

When enough applications have been received, the selection process can begin. It is recommended that more than one person be involved in the selection process. The final decision to hire a specific applicant must be made by the director or board of trustees but other staff members can be involved in the recommendation of candidates. Many direc-

tors fear the loss of their authority if others are involved in staff selection. Involving others in decision-making processes allows for staff development as well as fosters a feeling of staff solidarity.

Screening

Experience, age, credentials or licenses, references, and academic background are examined before actual selection of individuals is undertaken. It has been found that the use of three categories is helpful; the application forms of applicants who meet all, some, and none of the job requirements are separated into three piles. Those applicants in the first group, who meet all the requirements, are contacted first. Depending upon the number of applications, either the first group or the first two groups may be called for interviews. Five to ten applicants in each of the first two groups will likely yield at least one person to fill the position and possibly more.

The references listed by the applicants should be checked, preferably before the scheduled interview. If a written reference is required or a form returned, it should be immediately placed with the file. If references have been asked for but have not been received, it should be the responsibility of the applicant to follow-up on the references. The

Fig. 9-4 The director helps an applicant.

director may telephone one or more of the references for further information. This step may also be reserved only for final candidates for the position.

The Interview

Personal interviews with each applicant are essential. Interviews should be scheduled, allowing thirty to forty-five minutes for each. Ten to fifteen minutes between each interview should be allowed for jotting down notes about it.

More than one person should be involved in interviewing prospective candidates. The director, a board member, a parent, a supervisor, or a teacher may be included depending upon the organization of the school. Some programs require that staff selection be done by an interview committee. If several people are to be involved, more than one interview might be scheduled. Most applicants are able to deal with two interviewers at a time, but more than two may be overwhelming and unproductive.

The actual interview may be preceded by a tour of the school. Although this adds time to the process, it will allow the applicant to gain information about the school. It may also offer the opportunity for the director to observe the reactions of the applicant to the physical plant and to the children. Comments or questions during this tour may provide important insights regarding the applicant.

Where the interview takes place is an important consideration. The room should be comfortable and free from interference. The room should be arranged so that all persons present can be included in the discussion. The applicant should not sit facing a row of interviewers; the interviewer should not be barricaded behind a desk.

For purposes of later evaluation, the interview should have some structure to it. If more than one staff interviewer is involved,

Fig. 9-5 The director and applicant tour the school.

one should be designated to lead. It is helpful to ask all applicants the same questions. Time should be allowed for the interviewers to get additional information or to clarify information. Time should be allowed for the applicant to ask questions.

Some suggestions are given which will help to find out how an applicant functions:

- In order to determine the applicant's ability to plan or organize, a hypothetical situation could be outlined. "What would you do if.....?" The kind of situation described would be determined by the type of job opening.

- The applicant's knowledge of the job might be determined by asking her to plan for a specified period. A teacher could plan a typical day; a cook could plan a week's menu.

- In order to determine the applicant's ability to get along with others, she can be asked to describe how she would handle typical situations. A teacher could be asked how she would handle a child who bites. The applicant for the position of maintenance man could be asked what he would do if the children put sand in the drinking fountain.

- To determine how the applicant views herself, she might be asked to describe what she thinks are her best abilities in relation to this job.

- If it is important to determine the applicant's feelings about and understanding of children, she might be asked what is most likable about children. She might also be asked what is most bothersome about children.

- Commitment to the job and desire for professional growth may also be areas which should be discussed.

If separate interviews are scheduled, the areas to be explored by each interviewer should be determined beforehand. The interviewers may divide the questions to be asked, based on their own abilities to evaluate the answers. They may decide to ask the same kinds of questions in different ways and then compare the answers.

Interview information should be recorded immediately following the interview. (No notes should be taken while talking to an applicant.) Answers as well as reactions might be included in the interviewer's notes. A short notation of the applicant's general appearance might also be included. Finally, the interview record should include a tentative recommendation for hiring or not hiring.

The Evaluation

Evaluation of the applicants is the final step of the selection process and the most difficult. It is well to remember that the evaluation will be based on several sources of information: the applicant's background and experience, the applicant's responses to questions, and the image projected by the applicant.

The applicant's background and experience is probably the easiest to evaluate. If a specific requirement such as a degree or license is needed, it can be easily determined whether or not the applicant meets that requirement. Experience can also be easily determined by information included on the application or through the interview. In some cases, additional information may be obtained from resumes or from the confidential files of a college placement service.

Answers to questions in an interview will give a great deal of information regarding the applicant's thoughts and knowledge. Again, it is important to remember that two people interviewing an applicant may hear the same answers but interpret them differently. It is also true that some teachers talk well about teaching, but may not perform well. Whenever possible, it is helpful to observe an applicant in a working situation, let the applicant demonstrate her teaching abilities.

An applicant's appearance and manner are the most difficult to evaluate. A well-qualified applicant may be judged unqualified because the interviewer could not see beyond his or her appearance. Some applicants may be well qualified but are unable to communicate this to others. More than one interview will help to counterbalance the negative or subjective reactions to an applicant.

In the end, selection of a particular applicant is based on speculation. However, experience with hiring staff will add to the director's ability to make good choices.

NOTIFICATION OF EMPLOYMENT OR NONSELECTION

When an applicant is chosen for a position, notification should be made in writing. A letter is sent to the applicant who has been appointed to the position; it should give the starting date of employment. If a contract is used for employees, the contract should be enclosed with a date for signing and returning. A copy of this letter or the contract is placed in the personnel file of the employee.

VILLAGE NURSERY SCHOOL

(Date)

Dear _____,

   After interviewing several candidates for the position of teacher at Village Nursery School, it is the unanimous decision of the selection committee that you fulfill our qualifications for the position. We would like you to become a member of our staff for the school year beginning on ____(date)____.

   I am including a copy of our employment contract and our personnel policies. If the terms of the contract are to your satisfaction and if after reading the personnel policies, you agree to abide by the statements they contain, please sign the contract and return it as soon as possible.

   We are looking forward to working with you in the coming school year.

                                                                Sincerely,

                                                                Marion Smith, Director

---

Fig. 9-6 Notification of Employment

   In addition to notifying the applicant who is hired, the applicants who were interviewed and not selected must also be notified. They should be thanked for their interest in the school and possibly told that their application will be kept on file for future openings. They should not be left wondering about the outcome of the interview and selection process. Depending upon the number of applications, others who applied might also be notified of the appointment.

SUMMARY

   The people in a school are its most important resource. It is essential that a director develop procedures for finding qualified staff who will stay for a reasonable period of time.

   Before beginning the recruiting process, the director must determine the qualifications for the position. She should list the personal characteristics needed for the position and determine what competencies are needed.

VILLAGE NURSERY SCHOOL

(Date)

Dear _____,

   Thank you for your interest in Village Nursery School and your desire to become a member of our staff. We wish to inform you that we have made a selection from the applicants for the recent opening.

   Your application will be kept on file and should an additional opening become available, you will be notified. If you are still interested in working with us, we would hope that you would reapply.

                                                                Sincerely,

                                                                Marion Smith, Director

---

Fig. 9-7 Notification of Nonselection

Regulations governing the job should be explored.

Once these determinations have been made, recruiting can begin. A concise statement written for distribution would be helpful. Information to be included should be the following: name of the school, address of the school, job title and brief description, contract period, salary range, qualifications, name and phone number of person to contact, application process, and starting date of job.

Information regarding the opening should be distributed as widely as possible. Application forms are used for all positions and should be clear and related to the job. The initial screening of applications is based on qualifications as stated in the application.

An interview with qualified applicants is the next step. More than one person should interview applicants. The applicant should be given the opportunity to ask questions about the position.

Evaluation of the applicants is the final step of the selection process. Background and experience, responses during the interview, and the applicant's appearance and manner are all taken into consideration in evaluating the qualifications for the job. The applicant should not be left waiting for a response for longer than two weeks.

STUDENT ACTIVITIES

- Write a statement for recruiting applicants for your job.
- Obtain application forms from three different schools. Compare and analyze the kinds of information that each requests.
- Role play an interview with a prospective teacher. Evaluate an interview demonstrated by fellow students. Discuss the applicant's answers and behavior.

REVIEW

A. Answer and discuss the following questions.

1. What factors are to be considered in determining qualifications for a staff position?
2. Name five sources for recruiting possible applicants.
3. What would you include in notes taken after interviewing an applicant?
4. How would you go about selecting an applicant who answered an ad and appears to be very well qualified?

B. Briefly answer the following questions. Give the reason for your answer.

1. Should the existing staff be notified about job openings?
2. Who should be involved in choosing staff members?
3. How much time should be allowed for each interview?
4. Should the interview be structured?
5. Once the selection has been made, who is to be notified?

Unit 10 Personnel Practices

OBJECTIVES

After studying this unit, the student should be able to

- Identify and discuss items that should be contained in a contract agreement
- Outline a statement of personnel policies
- List contents of a personnel file

Qualified staff members must have a sincere desire to work in the school setting and plan to stay long enough to contribute to their own growth and to that of the school. One way to attract and keep qualified staff is to establish personnel policies that provide job security and adequate benefits. Personnel policies include all matters relating to staff employment, fulfillment of job responsibility, and job benefits.

CONTRACT

A *contract* is a binding written agreement between two or more parties to do some specific thing. A contract between the school and the employee is the first step in assuring that a school will attract and retain qualified staff. The contract indicates a commitment between the parties for a specified period of time. During that time, each party has certain responsibilities to the other.

Working in a school for young children involves interaction with other people. In order to teach, effective relationships with children must be developed. Rapport must be established with other adults in order to work toward common goals. This takes time. A contract allows an employee to be assured of employment for a specified period of time. The staff member can think about doing the job rather than about job security.

Teachers, especially, should have a contract in order to allow for time they need. It is possibly less important for other staff members who are not as closely involved with the children. Nevertheless, the director might consider a contract for all employees. This could be a way of stabilizing all adult relationships.

The type of school determines who actually awards a contract to an employee. In a private school, franchise school, educational corporation, and hospital or apartment-owned school, the contract is between the owner(s) and the staff member. In a nonprofit school, a laboratory school, or a college or university school, the contract is awarded by a board of trustees. In children's centers, the contract is awarded by the school district.

The contract should be a statement covering the conditions of employment. The following points should be included:

This agreement is made the _____ day of _____, 19 _____, by and between (name of school, board of trustees, etc.) and _____(employee).

It is mutually understood that he/she is employed as _____(position) for a period of one year, beginning _____, 19 _____and ending _____, 19 _____. During that time, he/she will perform each and every duty pertaining to such position prescribed by (name of school, board of trustees, etc.) or by any state laws or ordinances governing said position.

He/she shall serve for twelve (12) calendar months and shall be entitled to twenty-two (22) vacation days. One (1) day sick leave will be allowed for each month of service to a maximum of twelve (12) days. The employee shall be entitled to any and all other employee benefits provided by (name of the school, board of trustees, etc.). It shall be understood that should this agreement be terminated, the employee shall be entitled to compensation for such accumulated vacation time as shall be accrued at the time of termination but shall have been unused as of the date of termination.

The employee will serve one (1) month probationary period after which the full contract will be in effect. This agreement may be terminated at any time if it is determined that said employee has not fulfilled the responsibilities of the position as prescribed. Termination by either party to this agreement must be preceded by a notification period of thirty (30) days.

The (name of school, board of trustees, etc.) agrees to pay the employee as compensation for his/her services, the sum of _____. Said sum shall be payable at the rate of _____ per calendar month, beginning _____, 19 _____.

In witness whereof, the (name of school, board of trustees, etc.) has caused this instrument to be executed by its duly authorized (director, secretary to board, etc.) and _____ has subscribed his/her signature the day and year first above written.   (Name of employee)

_____

Signature (director, secretary to board, etc.)

_____

Signature of employee

Fig. 10-1 Sample Contract

Time period of the contract — the date when the contract goes into effect and the termination date

Probationary period — the time before the full contract goes into effect, usually from one to three months

Salary — the pay for the period covered by the contract

Fringe benefits — the number of days of vacation and sick leave (Any other benefits such as medical plan or retirement could be included.)

Termination — conditions for termination of the contract (This would include causes for termination by the employer. It would include requirements for termination by the employee.)

STATEMENT OF PERSONNEL POLICIES

A *statement of personnel policies* is a written document covering employer-employee relations. It is an important framework for the development of good staff morale. When it is given to a new employee, information regarding the job is conveyed efficiently. The director can then spend time getting to know each new employee rather than in discussing the details of employment. Many of the items contained in such a statement are things each employee should know. The director can expect staff members and new employees to assume the responsibility for getting the information by reading the personnel policies.

A written statement does not guarantee that employment problems will be avoided. Not every staff member will read the statement. Not every staff member will understand what is written. Still, the written statement is important and each employee should be urged to read it.

The written statement of personnel policies can prevent later misunderstandings and possible conflicts between the director and staff members. If work hours, vacations, illness leave, and similar items are clearly stated, there should be less difficulty when problems arise. Job descriptions for all staff members indicate what the job responsibilities are. A chart showing the organization of the school helps employees see themselves as part of the larger unit.

The statement of personnel policies should be as short as possible. Each item should be covered in a few sentences. The pages can be typed and photocopied. If available, the mimeograph machine can be used to duplicate the pages.

Many directors will say that they do not have a written personnel policy statement because items change each year. Some things do change each year, but many stay the same. It is fairly easy to retype a few pages in the statement to meet changing conditions in the school. In the long run, time and effort are saved by having a written statement of the personnel policies — always current and always available.

Each director must decide what to put into a statement of personnel policies and how long the statement should be. A director can choose what is appropriate for a particular school. An overview of sections that might be included are discussed in the following paragraphs.

Details of Employment

A section should be devoted to the details of employment; that is, the number of working hours per day, holidays, and vacations. A calendar showing holidays and starting dates of the school year is helpful. The length of the probationary period and what is to take place during this period could be outlined. As an example, it might be stated that during the

---

The teacher will be responsible for planning and conducting a program for a group of children and all activities related to that program.

The teacher will

1. Plan and conduct daily experiences for the children based upon the objectives of the school.

2. Prepare all materials required to carry out the program.

3. Supervise personnel assigned to assist with group activities.

4. Plan and maintain a physical environment that is conducive to meeting the objectives of the school.

5. Attend and participate in staff meetings.

6. Plan and participate in activities designed to include parents in the education of their children.

7. Observe and record significant individual and group behavior of children.

8. Participate in community activities that can bring about increased professional competence.

Fig. 10-2 Sample Job Description

probationary period of one month's duration, the director will observe the teacher at least once a week. At least one conference between director and teacher will be scheduled to evaluate the teacher's performance. If performance has been satisfactory, the full contract goes into effect.

Physical Environment

Issues concerning the physical environment might be another section of the personnel policies. How to obtain the keys to the classroom and where to park could be included. There might also be a statement regarding the teacher's responsibility for maintaining her room and equipment. Directions for obtaining new supplies are also included.

Health and Safety Matters

The employee should be told if health examinations are required and how often they are needed. Does the employee pay for the examinations? Does the school contribute toward the cost or provide free examinations? How many days sick leave does each employee have? Can the days be carried over from one year to another? Procedures for reporting employee accidents should be stated. Procedures dealing with disasters such as fire, bomb scares, earthquakes, or tornadoes should be clearly explained.

Fringe benefits provided to the employee should be included in the statement of personnel policies. If employment includes participation in a health plan or hospital plan, the details of enrollment are given. A retirement plan might be outlined. Other kinds of benefits such as group life insurance, unemployment insurance, and workmen's compensation might be covered.

Termination of Employment

The personnel policy statement should include termination procedures. How much notice must either the director or staff member give before ending the employment? A period of two weeks to thirty days is customary. Also, when a staff member has a grievance, is there a procedure that can be followed? Such a procedure might prevent termination of employment, increase morale, and lower staff turnover.

The Job Description

Each employee should be provided with a job description. A job description is a statement of the duties and responsibilities of the person filling that particular position. It should include all the tasks each person must do in order to fulfill the responsibilities of the job. For example, a teacher's job description would include teaching activities, attendance

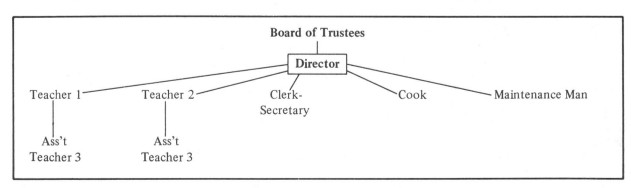

Fig. 10-3 Organization Chart (Numbers refer to level of position.)

at parent meetings and at staff meetings. It might also include keeping records on children.

An organization chart should also be included. All the jobs in a school and how they relate to each other are diagrammed. This diagram gives a clear view of the lines of authority. It tells the child care assistant that she is responsible to her teacher; it tells the cook that she should take problems to the director. An example of a table of organization is shown in figure 10-3. (The number after *teacher* refers to the level of the position.)

Promotional Opportunities

A statement of personnel policies should include position levels and salary schedules. Opportunity for advancement and basis for promotions must be clearly stated. It should be made clear that a move up the scale is achieved through specific acts or time. For example, if an increase in salary comes from completion of additional college courses, and/or from the number of years of service, this information must be clearly indicated.

The section on advancement procedures should also include ways the school encourages professional growth. It might show payment for workshops, courses, or conferences. The school might also offer payment of time taken from the job for participation in these activities.

PERSONNEL RECORDS

Positive staff relations are essential to the success of a school for young children. Staff relationships are built more easily on a foundation of good personnel policies and practices. Every director who wishes to attract and keep qualified staff must establish policies and procedures that meet the needs of both the school management and the individuals who make up the staff.

Personnel records are an important part of the framework that a school sets up to attract and hold qualified staff. A file for each employee implies a commitment to that employee during school *tenure* (a status granted after a trial period). Time that is saved by

		SALARY				
	Academic	Number of Years Experience				
Level	Background	1	2	3	4	5
1	MA Degree	$10,000	$10,100	$10,500	$11,000	$11,500
2	BA Degree	9,000	9,200	9,400	9,600	9,800
3	AA Degree or 60 units	7,700	7,900	8,100	8,300	8,500
4	HS Diploma and less than 60 units	6,700	6,900	7,100	7,300	7,500

Note: Teacher salaries shown are based on twelve yearly payments.
Employee can move across the scale at the completion of each year of experience.
Employee can move up a level upon completion of the academic requirements for the next level.

Fig. 10-4 Sample Salary Scale, Public Day Care Center

SAMPLE SALARY SCALE (HOURLY RATE)							
UNITS 0	4	8	12	16	24	42	60
STEPS							
1	3.10	3.15	3.20	3.25	3.30	3.40	3.60	3.80
2	3.15	3.20	3.25	3.30	3.35	3.50	3.70	3.90
3	3.20	3.30	3.35	3.40	3.45	3.60	3.80	4.00
4	3.25	3.40	3.45	3.50	3.55	3.70	3.90	4.20
5	3.35	3.50	3.55	3.60	3.65	3.80	4.00	4.40

Note: Each step is equivalent to one year of teaching experience. Units indicate the number of academic units completed. (One unit is defined as 20 hours of college or university level work.) As an example, teachers starting without experience, with 4 units of college work will begin on Step 1, Column 4.

Fig. 10-5 Sample Salary Scale (Hourly Rate) — Private Proprietary School

keeping accurate records is time that can be spent on developing staff relations. Problems and questions concerning vacation and illness time used will be lessened if written records are available.

Application Form

Personnel records begin with the application for employment. The application is placed in a folder which should be made up as soon as a person is hired. References that accompanied the application are also kept in the file. Written records of the application interview might also be included.

Health

Reports on the health status of the employee should be in the file. This should begin with the physical examination required for hiring and should include yearly examinations. This is an appropriate place to record the number of days the staff member was absent. Any injuries received while on the job and the treatment given should be recorded here.

Evaluation

If the school has a system of evaluation, the record of each evaluation should be in the personnel file. A series of evaluations over a period of time provide the director with a record of individual job performance. It may also point to areas where the staff member could be helped to further his or her ability.

Employment Record

Forms can be made up or purchased commercially to maintain an employment record. This form would show the starting date, any leaves that might have been granted, and the final date of employment. Also included would be a record of changes in status during the period of employment. These changes would be promotions within the school or transfers to another school within the organization. The form would also allow space for the salary for each position.

STATE OF CALIFORNIA—HEALTH AND WELFARE AGENCY   DEPARTMENT OF HEALTH

PREEMPLOYMENT EXAMINATION

Persons that work in Community Care Facilities, whether as licensee or employed staff, must demonstrate that their health condition allows them to perform the type of work required. This report is to be completed by a physician who has knowledge of the person's health condition.

Person's Name _____ Age_____

Position Title_____ Work Days Per Week_____Work Hours Per Day_____

Duty Statement _____

_____

_____

Persons Served. (Check appropriate items)

☐ Children   ☐ Adults   ☐ Physically Handicapped   ☐ Developmentally Disabled
☐ Mentally Disordered   ☐ Aged Adult   ☐ Drug/Alcoholic Addiction
☐ Other (specify)

AUTHORIZATION FOR RELEASE OF MEDICAL INFORMATION

I hereby authorize the release of medical information contained in the report of the examination   ☐ Yes   ☐ No

I agree to pay any expenses incurred.   ☐ Yes   ☐ No

Signature of Prospective Employee	Date	Address

Note to Physician

Staff in Community Care Facilities shall be in good general health, free from communicable disease, free of disabilities which would adversely affect persons to be served and be adequately able to perform work expected of them. Please complete the following information on the above named person.

Evaluation of General Health_____

_____

Evaluation of Ability to Perform Work In Duty Statement _____

_____

Significant Health History (Note any illnesses, injuries, etc., that would affect work)

_____

_____

_____

_____

Date of Last Examination _____ Length of Time Applicant Known to You _____

SIGNATURE OF PHYSICIAN _____ Date _____

Upon Completion Return to: _____

Facility Name _____

Facility Address_____

LIC 503 (12/74)

```
┌─────────────────────────────────────────────────────────────────────┐
│                         FOR EMPLOYER'S USE                          │
│                                                                     │
│  CHEST X-RAY OR INTRADERMAL TB TEST INFORMATION                     │
│                                                                     │
│  Referred to_____   Date_____  │
│                                                                     │
│  Report Received_____   Results_____ │
│                        Date                                         │
│                                                                     │
│  ANNUAL X-RAY OR INTRADERMAL TB TEST                                │
│                                                                     │
│  Date_____   Results_____  │
│                                                                     │
│  Date_____   Results_____  │
│                                                                     │
│  Date_____   Results_____  │
└─────────────────────────────────────────────────────────────────────┘
```

Fig. 10-6 Sample Employment Health Examination Form

There should be allowance for staff-requested inclusions in the personnel file. Such things as special awards or achievements might be in this category. Letters of commendation might be another.

Conferences

The purpose, discussion, and outcome of conferences are included. Conferences that are concerned with performance of the staff member should be brief and to the point; a few sentences covering the content of the conference are all that is necessary.

Termination of Employment

The reason for termination of employment should be a part of each file. A note stating the reason should be enough. It should be objective and factual.

Recommendations

Requests for references after an employee has left the school may also be added. When a letter of recommendation is written for any employee, a copy should go into the file. Future requests, unless asking for specific information, can be filled by copying the first letter of recommendation. A notation can accompany the file copy showing the dates and to whom copies have been sent.

SUMMARY

One may attract and keep qualified staff in a school by establishing personnel policies that meet their needs as well as the needs of the school. Personnel policies include all matters relating to employment, fulfillment of job responsibility, and job benefits.

A contract between the school and the employee is the first step in assuring that a school may attract and keep qualified staff. It indicates a commitment between the parties to allow the time necessary to develop working relationships.

A written statement of personnel policies provides a framework for the development of good staff relations. It contains information regarding (1) details of employment, (2) details of probationary period, (3) issues concerning the physical environment, (4) health and safety matters, (5) fringe benefits, (6) termination

Name				Social Security No.

Street Address				Telephone No.

City   State   Zip Code

POSITION _____ Starting Date _____ Salary _____ Leave of Absence From _____ To _____

_____

_____

_____

_____

_____

_____

Termination Date _____

Reason for Leaving _____

_____

_____

_____

Fig. 10-7 Sample Employment Record Form

procedures, (7) a job description, (8) a table of organization, and (9) opportunities for advancement.

Good personnel records for each employee include (1) the application for employment, (2) reports on health status, (3) evaluations, (4) employment record and termination date, (5) staff-requested information, (6) conferences with director, (7) reason for termination of employment, and (8) requests for references. Good staff relationships are important to the success of a school for young children and are built on a foundation of sound personnel policies and practices.

STUDENT ACTIVITIES

- Find out if a school with which you are familiar has a statement of personnel policies. Compare it with items discussed in this unit.
- Draw an organizational chart for the school with which you are associated.
- Write a job description for the position of child care assistant.
- Invite several teachers to discuss salaries and fringe benefits with your class.

REVIEW

1. What is the purpose of an organizational chart?

2. What details of employment are contained in a statement of personnel policies?

3. What two parties are involved in an employment contract of a private school?

4. What is the customary period of time given for termination notice by the employee or the employer?

5. How would you define a contract?

6. What does a job description contain?

7. What items should be contained in a contract between employer and employee?

8. What reason do some directors give for not having a written personnel policy?

9. Name the items which should be part of the employee's personnel file.

10. Give some examples of fringe benefits.

Unit 11 Supervision and Evaluation of the Staff

OBJECTIVES

After studying this unit, the student should be able to

- Define supervision and evaluation
- Identify tasks that a director performs as supervisor
- Describe the process for evaluating staff performance

Administration refers to the performance of executive duties. Included in these executive duties are the tasks of supervision and evaluation. Although these terms are used in many kinds of work situations, it is necessary to understand their meaning within an educational setting.

Supervision means the process of overseeing workers during the execution or performance of a job. In an early childhood program, it refers mainly to observing and monitoring teachers during their acts of teaching and related activities. It also means overseeing other staff members whose activities affect the teaching and learning process.

Most often in schools for young children the director is also the supervisor of her staff. In schools that are part of a school district, there is likely to be another person who is responsible for supervision. Educational corporations or laboratory schools may also have a person other than the director serve as a supervisor.

In educational settings, *evaluation* means the process of determining the effectiveness of teaching activities. It can also mean judging the job performance of other staff mem-

bers in activities that affect the teaching functions of the school. This is done through assessments of the three components of the school: staff, children, and curriculum. Curriculum evaluation as part of the development and implementation of goals is discussed in unit 7. Evaluation of the child's progress is more appropriately covered in a text on teaching than one on administration. Therefore, only staff evaluation is discussed here.

Evaluation is a procedure carried out jointly by the person to be evaluated and the evaluator. The director has the responsibility for the evaluation process, but if it is to be effective, it must be a cooperative effort. Both the staff member and director must be involved in designing and carrying out the procedure.

SUPERVISION OF STAFF

Good supervision of staff performance begins with the development of an effective relationship between the director and individual staff members. The director must feel that the employee has the ability and desire to do a good job. The staff member must accept and respect the knowledge and help offered by the director. Each must recognize that they have to work together to achieve their goals.

The development of this kind of relationship takes time. The director's availability and responsiveness provide the climate in which it can grow. The director must make herself available at the key times during the day.

The early morning arrival time for the staff is an important time of the day. If the director plans her time so that she is free for a short chat with each member or a greeting to each, she will go a long way toward developing rapport with her staff. This is the time when teachers can discuss the day's activities or schedules. It is the time to get ready for the day ahead.

During the school day, the director can get to know her staff by visiting each classroom. This will let them know that she is interested in what is happening in the classrooms. It also gives her an opportunity to share the pleasure of seeing children actively involved in learning.

At times, the director may help teachers by teaching for short periods. In a small school, relief time may be scheduled to allow a break for the teacher. It is essential that the director be available when an emergency arises. The director may have to stay in the classroom while the teacher cares for an injured child. At times, she will need to be available to help with a child who is having other difficulties.

The end of the school day is also an important time for the director to be available to her staff. This may be a time when teachers are tired or discouraged. It may be the best time to discuss a problem the teacher is having in the classroom. A chance to talk with the director may help to relieve some of the negative feelings or resolve the problem.

When the director is available and offers support to staff members, she goes a long way

Fig. 11-1 The director and teacher talk at arrival time.

towards establishing a relationship that brings about effective supervision. The task of supervision is complex and difficult. How the director goes about this task determines the effectiveness of her efforts towards achievement of the stated purposes. Her skills as a communicator are important. Her style and ability as a manager and organizer also influence successful supervision.

Supervision of staff involves seeing that directions are carried out. The director is responsible for the operations of the school. At times she must give directions to her staff regarding schedules or materials. She must be able to communicate these directions clearly. A follow-up must be made to see that her directions are being carried out.

Supervision also involves trying to change attitudes and behavior. Some attitudes are destructive to the effectiveness of the educational program.   If negative attitudes are observed in a staff member, it is the responsibility of the director to try to change them.

Attitudes are difficult to recognize. They are even more difficult to change. If a good relationship has been established between the teacher and director, the task may be a little easier. Changes in attitude can sometimes be brought about through listening. A director who is available to listen without criticism may gradually help the teacher to recognize attitudes that interfere with effective teaching. A supportive relationship can then help the teacher to develop new ways of thinking.

Supervision of staff also involves helping each staff member to develop the skills needed for the job. The teachers, the cook, and the secretary all want to do a good job. An effective director supervises in such a way that each staff member can develop the skills necessary for the particular job.

Through observation, the director may be able to see the cause of a problem. For instance, a teacher may be having difficulty keeping the children occupied. By observing the teacher and the children in the classroom, the director may be able to see the cause. She may be able to tell the teacher that some of the children are not occupied because there are not enough choices of activities available to them. She may also see that the children do not remain long at an activity when the teacher is too busy to sit down with them.

The director can help the staff to develop their skills by offering alternate ways of performing. She should be familiar with each job. She may then be able to make suggestions that will make each job easier. For example, if she is familiar with the cook's job, she will know the difficulty involved in getting all the food ready at the same time. She might suggest to the cook that time can be saved by cooking bacon in a shallow pan in the oven instead of frying it on the stove, for example.

Fig. 11-2 **The director supervises all staff members.**

Suggesting sources of information is another way that the director helps her staff to develop their job skills. She may be able to tell a teacher where to find information about a particular subject. She may refer teachers to books on curriculum for new ideas. She may suggest that the cook look at a reference on nutrition in order to do a better job of menu planning.

Supervision involves helping teachers to develop the personal characteristics essential to teaching. The director in her role as supervisor can help teachers to understand themselves, to recognize their own strengths, and to find ways to alleviate their weaknesses. This is a most difficult task for the director and takes a great deal of skill.

In a school for young children, the teacher is an extremely important person. The kind of person she is, how she reacts, and how she is able to respond has immediate effect

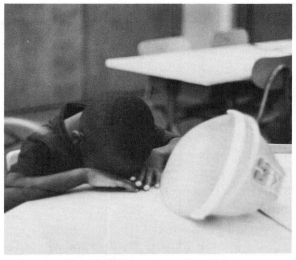

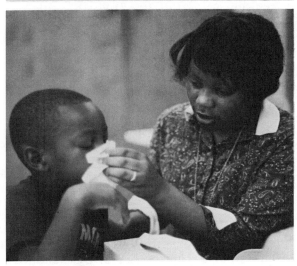

Fig. 11-3 The teacher responds to a child's feelings.

upon the children. The teacher must be a reasonably stable person without extreme changes of mood so that the children can learn to anticipate her reactions. She must be able to develop warm, personal relationships with the children and be sensitive to the ways in which they relate to her and to other children. Her behavior and responses serve as a model to the children.

The teacher must be able to remember what it is like to be a child so that she can be more tolerant of children in their process of growing up. Remembering will also help her to appreciate the kinds of play activities and learning experiences that children enjoy. She must be able to appreciate childlike experiences while remaining a mature adult herself.

It takes time for teachers to develop these characteristics and reach this level of maturity. Each teacher is at a different stage of development — some at the very beginning level and others further along. Most teachers and directors agree that this process continues throughout the career of working with children.

In order to help teachers to understand themselves, the director must get to know the characteristics of each. She listens and she observes. She learns how they react to people and experiences. She tries to understand how they feel about themselves. She recognizes that some teachers are ready to look at themselves and that others are not.

Once the director has developed her own understanding of each teacher, she will be better able to make decisions about how to help. For example, the director can do several things to help a teacher to understand that her behavior makes others angry. She can decide to tell the teacher, she may decide that the behavior is important to the teacher at this time and not say anything about it, or she may get the teacher to talk about incidents in which the behavior occurred. This may help the teacher see that others reacted with anger and why they did so.

However the director proceeds in her task of helping teachers develop an understanding of themselves, and then develop the characteristics needed for teaching, it must be done slowly and with care. The director must use all her own skills in relating and communicating with others.

EVALUATION OF STAFF PERFORMANCE

While supervision is a daily process carried out by the director, evaluation is done at specified intervals. Many educational programs require that an evaluation of teachers be completed at least once a year and sometimes more frequently. Most teachers want to know for their own satisfaction if they are achieving what they have set out to do; a periodic evaluation procedure will give them the answer.

Although most teachers and directors see evaluation as a means of growth and the basis for increasing job performance, the whole concept of evaluation has some built-in problems. First, the idea creates anxiety both in the person to be evaluated and the one who will do the evaluating. As a general rule, few teachers are completely comfortable about having someone judge their performance. Also, many directors are uneasy about judging the performance of staff members.

The second problem is that there are two different levels of performance to be evaluated if it is to be an effective evaluation. On one level are the things that are obvious. The performance can be seen. The secretary types ten letters a day or does only eight. The teacher keeps her room in order or leaves it in an absolute mess. On the other level are the factors that cannot be seen or touched or heard. How does a director evaluate the ability of the teacher to encourage decision-making in the children? How does the direc-

tor evaluate the secretary's ability to create a welcoming atmosphere for visitors? If only one of these performance levels is used to evaluate job performance, the director may get an incomplete picture of the staff member's ability.

Third, it must be decided who is to be responsible for the evaluation of each staff member. Final responsibility lies with the director. The actual evaluation may be done by any one of several persons in a school. Also, more than one person may be involved, each having a specific part of the procedure.

In a small school, the director will probably be the one to evaluate all employees. She may work with her staff to develop the procedure, but she will be the one to carry it out.

In a larger school there may be a more complex organization for accomplishing evaluation. Staff members at different levels may be responsible for those under their authority. The head teacher evaluates the assistant teacher, and the head cook evaluates the assistant cook, for example.

In a large system or organization there may be a person designated to evaluate all employees. This evaluator works with the director and possibly other staff members to design and carry out the evaluation process. It is possible that in some situations, persons on a particular job level might evaluate others on the same level. As an example, a teacher might evaluate another teacher. This is called evaluation by one's peers.

Some systems for evaluation may include self-evaluation by the employee. This would not be done in place of other evaluations, but in addition to other evaluations.

The director must decide if all employees should be evaluated or only those in certain job categories. Should only teachers and aides be evaluated or should the performance of all employees in the school be examined? If a school is to create an atmosphere in which children can grow and change, no staff member can remain static. Each employee must be aware of his or her own strengths and weaknesses and be helped to find ways to change. If the atmosphere is truly to be one in which learning is encouraged, it must apply to every staff member.

THE EVALUATION PROCESS

Obviously, evaluation cannot focus in minute detail on all areas. An overall evaluation in some areas may be enough with emphasis in specific areas at certain times. Whatever the focus, the decision should be a joint one between the evaluator and the person to be evaluated. No employee should be evaluated on something without knowing about it in advance.

Objectives

The evaluation process should begin with an agreement between the director and the staff member concerning what is to be accomplished during a given period of time. These expectations may be taken from the statement of goals for the school or from the job description for the position. They may also be personal characteristics that are important to the teacher's performance. As an example, one of the goals of the school and an important one for a particular teacher might be the development of decision-making skills in the children. Director and teacher then list as many ways as possible by which this can be done. Evaluation of the teacher will then focus on the ways in which she successfully met the goal. Obviously, a supplementary evaluation of the effectiveness of her methods would come with an evaluation of the children's progress, but that is a separate procedure.

Standards

There should also be agreement on the standards to be used in judging achievement or nonachievement. The staff member should know what will be considered satisfactory. In the case of the example just given, the teacher should know whether she has to use all of the ways to implement the goals that were listed or if a certain percentage will be considered adequate.

The evaluator and the staff member should know when the evaluation is to be done. Each should understand clearly that the evaluation will be done at a certain time and will cover a specified period of time. For instance, the evaluation will be done in March and will cover the period from September to March.

The evaluator and the staff member should also understand the methods of evaluation. Each should know that a checklist will be used or that two observations followed by a conference will be the method. If a checklist is used, the staff member should know what items are included on the list. If observation is the method, the focus of the observation should be made clear.

METHODS OF EVALUATION

In an earlier unit, methods of evaluating curriculum were discussed. Similar methods can be used for evaluating staff members in a school.

Tests

Commercially prepared tests or tests devised by the staff may be used to judge the acquisition of specific knowledge. Colleges and universities which offer teacher-training programs are a possible source for finding out if there are available tests that may be used. Educational testing services provide another source for prepared tests. Knowledge of child development, curriculum, nutrition, and first aid may be tested in this way. Some services are also developing teacher competency tests.

Fig. 11-4 A camera may be used to record teacher behavior.

The staff can also make up their own tests to determine whether they are accomplishing what they set out to do. Performance to be achieved should be stated as objectives. The test is then designed to find out if each objective has been reached. For example, if one of the teacher's objectives was to teach every child to count to ten, the test would simply consist of asking each child to count to ten. The teacher would have achieved her objective when every child could count to ten.

Observations

With specific objectives in mind, the evaluator observes the staff member. The observation should be made in situations in which the expected behavior is likely to occur. Recordings or notes that are related to the objective should be made. Videotapes or filmed records would also be helpful.

More than one observation should be used to determine achievement or nonachievement of the objectives. Some evaluators schedule a series of observations done at different times of the day. Others use ongoing observations scheduled at regular intervals such as twice a month, once a month, or every other month.

Fig. 11-5 The teacher should be able to encourage a variety of responses.

Sampling of Achievements

The evaluator may take samples of teacher performance by recording specific kinds of behavior. For example, a teacher might decide that one of her objectives for the year would be to increase her ability to encourage language in the children. A way to measure success in meeting this objective would be to count the number of words said by the teacher and by the children during a specific time period. Analysis of the results would show whether the children were allowed and encouraged to talk. Comparison of observations over a period of time would indicate changes in the children's verbal ability.

Performance might also be evaluated by collecting products made by the children. Increase in the number or changes in the quality would determine whether an objective has been achieved. As an example, if a teacher's objective was to develop more extensive use of the art materials, a comparison of the number and quality of paintings at the beginning and at the end of a semester would give some information.

Questionnaire or Checklist

Questionnaires or checklists may be completed by the evaluator. Questions can be designed to be answered *yes* or *no*; they can also be designed to require longer answers or so that a rated response can be given. An example might be, "Does the teacher encourage the children to take care of their own physical needs?" This question could be answered by *yes* or *no*; it could also be answered by a rating such as *often, sometimes, never.*

Conferences

Another way to assess achievement is by a conference between the evaluator and the staff member. This method is helpful when the objective to be reached concerns a personal characteristic. The attainment of this kind of objective may be based upon subjective information rather than observable behavior. A discussion between the evaluator and staff member allows for an exchange of information between them. Evidence can be presented by both individuals to determine if the objectives have been reached.

USE OF EVALUATIONS

Whatever the method or combination of methods of evaluation, a record should be kept of the results. The personnel file of each staff member should contain the periodic evaluation. In this way, the staff member can see his own progress and the evaluator has a record of past performance.

Evaluation results should also be given to the staff member. This can be in the form of a written copy of a rating or it can be done through a conference. Each should know exactly what the rating or evaluation is and what the areas are in which improvement is recommended.

When a staff member receives an unsatisfactory or borderline rating, effort should be made to bring about improvement. Both the evaluator and the staff member should discuss specific steps to be taken to bring about the needed improvement. There is nothing as discouraging to an employee as being told that work performance is unsatisfactory without being told how to bring about improvement.

Evaluation is an effective and powerful tool — to be used with great care and sensitivity. It can be an instrument for change toward self-growth. It can bring about discouragement if it is not done well. The following suggestions may be helpful to the evaluator:

- **Be objective**
  Describe specific incidents to illustrate the behaviors being discussed

- **Be gentle**
  Discuss the positive things that have been observed before proceeding to the others

- **Establish a climate for discussion**
  Let staff members know what you are criticizing, but allow time to listen to their points of view
  Try to look at the behavior from the teachers' points of view

- **Be constructive**
  Help teachers or other staff members to find alternative methods
  Provide resources for further information when applicable
  Offer help and continued support

- **Be professional**
  Evaluations are not discussed with other staff members unless they share the responsibility for evaluation

PERSONAL QUALITIES	Often	Sometimes	Never
Name _____			
Date _____			
By Whom _____			
1. Expresses a desire to learn			
2. Is able to evaluate self			
3. Is enthusiastic about teaching			
ASSUMING RESPONSIBILITIES			
12. Is independent in assuming responsibility			
13. Achieves an efficient and orderly room arrangement			
14. Discusses pertinent problems with director			
WORKING WITH CHILDREN			
20. Is aware of differing moods of children and adjusts standards accordingly			
21. Encourages children to make appropriate decisions for themselves			
22. Creates a stimulating environment for learning			

SPECIFIC STRENGTHS OF TEACHER

AREAS FOR IMPROVEMENT

OTHER COMMENTS

I have read this evaluation.

Signed   _____
                Employee name and title

Date   _____

_____
                Supervisor

Fig. 11-6 Sample Form Used in Staff Evaluation

SUMMARY

The words *supervision* and *evaluation* are part of the educational scene today. To supervise means to oversee workers during the execution or performance of their jobs. To evaluate means to determine the effectiveness of teaching activities.

Good supervision of staff performance begins with the development of a relationship of trust and respect. A director can help to foster this kind of relationship by being available at key times of the day.

The task of supervision is difficult and complex. Part of the task involves seeing that directions are carried out. Another part involves trying to change attitudes and the behavior that results from attitudes. The director also tries to help each staff member develop personal characteristics essential to the job and acquire the skills that are needed.

Many educational programs require an evaluation procedure to determine their effectiveness. The director must consider the problems of evaluating two levels of performance. She must also consider who is to be responsible for the evaluation of each staff member.

The evaluation procedure begins with an agreement concerning what the person to be

Fig. 11-7   The director and a teacher discuss an evaluation record.

evaluated is expected to accomplish and what standards will be used.

Methods of evaluation may be a combination of tests, observations, samplings of behaviors, questionnaires, checklists, and conferences.

Evaluation is an effective but powerful tool. It must be used with great care and sensitivity.

STUDENT ACTIVITIES

- Discuss your feelings about evaluating someone else with your class.
- Discuss your feelings with your class about being evaluated by a supervisor.
- Describe how you would carry out an evaluation process for the school with which you are associated.

REVIEW

1. How does administration differ from supervision? Discuss the meanings.
2. Who is usually responsible for supervision in a school for young children?

3. In order to develop a relationship conducive to good supervision, what times of day should the director be available to her staff?

4. List the four tasks of supervision.

5. What is meant by evaluation?

6. Name four methods of evaluation.

7. Name the two levels of performance which must be evaluated.

8. What action should be taken when a staff member receives an unsatisfactory or borderline rating?

Unit 12 Developing Staff Skills

OBJECTIVES

After studying this unit, the student should be able to

- Name a variety of training methods
- Explain problem solving and decision-making techniques
- Plan an effective staff meeting

Young children model their own behavior after the significant adults in their lives. Therefore, it is important that all adults in the early childhood education setting practice the behaviors that are desired in children. While it is generally accepted that children grow and change rapidly, the changes that constantly take place in adults are less readily recognized. Adult changes are the focus of a good staff training program, however. These changes can be guided, enhanced, and reinforced so that the adults will acquire the characteristics and skills that they want for children.

Another purpose of staff training is to help each member learn the skills necessary to enrich the job being done. An assistant teacher must understand the principles used to plan a curriculum, as well as be able to set out the materials that are planned by the head teacher. The food service worker may want to understand the importance of her relationship with children in developing good health attitudes. The teacher may wish to add to her knowledge of human behavior so that she can be more effective with parents.

A third purpose of staff training is to help those who are interested to move to new job categories. The assistant teacher may eventually assume full responsibility for the management of a classroom. The food service worker may be able to take over the tasks of an assistant teacher. The teacher may find that she is capable of assuming some administrative tasks.

PLANNING STAFF DEVELOPMENT

The questions most often asked by directors or others responsible for developing staff skills are "Where do I start?" and "How do I choose the right method?". "Where to start" is probably the easier of the two questions to answer. The starting point must be with the knowledge that employees already have concerning each of the tasks listed in their job descriptions. The staff should be asked to evaluate themselves on each of these tasks to determine what they already know and then what they need to learn in order to fulfill their responsibilities adequately or to enrich their job. This self-evaluation plus the director's evaluation will be used as a basis for setting the objectives for training. When the employees are actively involved in an assessment of needs and the setting of goals, the training process is simplified.

The choice of the best method is more difficult because it is affected by many variables. Some of the factors affecting a choice of training methods are discussed.

Composition of the Group

Is the group diversified or homogeneous? A diversified group has many levels of knowledge and skills. Therefore, training methods must provide for individualized learning. A homogeneous group starts with a common base of knowledge. Members can learn together to achieve a new level of knowledge.

Size of the Group

Is the group large (over ten members) or small? A large group is sometimes unwieldy for discussions, but functions well with individual participation kinds of activities such as workshops. A small group lends itself to discussions. However, a small group may need outside stimulation at times — such as films, lectures, or field trips.

Time

Is training to be scheduled during working hours or after? If training is done during working hours, participants must be free from their usual job duties during that time. The session should be well organized; it should begin on time and end on time. If training is done after working hours, the possible fatigue of the participants must be taken into account. Active involvement, such as a discussion or workshop, helps to stimulate interest and lessen fatigue.

Place

Is the setting appropriate for the training method? If the session is a workshop, there should be adequate space for each member to work. A good discussion needs a room large enough so that each member can be included in the group. Comfortable chairs also help.

Special Abilities of Staff Members

Are there staff members who have special skills that can be used to train others? Some teachers are very capable of helping other adults to learn. These teachers can be assigned as assistants for on-the-job training. Other teachers may have special talents such as music or storytelling and can help others to learn these skills in a workshop setting.

Attendance

Is attendance at training sessions required or encouraged? If attendance is required, training methods and content must be planned so that the participants will be motivated to learn. Workshops, discussions, a film with discussion — all require some active participation. Therefore, these methods may be suitable for required meetings. When training sessions are voluntary, the interest in the topic is important. One way to achieve active participation is to involve the staff members in planning training activities. If they have a chance to say what they want and have opportunities to provide feedback concerning the effectiveness of the training, they are more likely to feel it is worthwhile to participate.

Application of Skills

Does the school provide an opportunity to practice the skills that will be taught at the training session? Unless staff members have an opportunity to practice newly learned skills, they will not be motivated to participate in training. A workshop on curriculum planning or new ideas for science lessons is not effective unless the teachers have the materials available to use. A lecture from an expert on working with parents should be

Fig. 12-1 The director encourages staff participation.

followed by encouragement and with time to spend with parents.

Learning Styles

Has the staff been asked to state the ways that each learns best? Have the needs of the individuals then been met as adequately as possible? If staff members indicate they learn best by active participation, methods that allow this, such as workshops or discussions, should be chosen. If some staff members learn best by oral or visual means, they may want to watch films or read.

POPULAR TRAINING METHODS

A variety of methods can be used for staff training activities. Some of the most frequently used ones are briefly discussed in the following paragraphs.

Staff Meetings

The staff meeting is the most frequently used method for conveying pertinent informa-

tion, for discussing problems, and for reaching decisions. Other purposes of this kind of training may be to increase understanding of individual children, to formulate plans for future operation of the school, and to foster a spirit of cooperation and harmony among staff members.

Workshop

The workshop provides an opportunity for individuals to broaden their practical skills by giving them first hand experiences with a wide range of materials and techniques. This method is most frequently used for teachers since it is an ideal way to try out new techniques for working with children. A workshop could just as easily be planned for other job categories in a school. Usually this is not done, however, because there may be only one food service worker or one secretary in a school. If there are several schools in a district or corporation, a workshop may be planned as a cooperative effort.

Group Discussion

Group discussions are usually planned for the purpose of discussing a specific subject. This method allows for an easy exchange of information, questions, and feelings. Discussions are effective in helping teachers to understand children's behavior, to increase their curriculum planning skills, and to enhance their knowledge of working with adults. For others in a school setting, a group discussion can be a primary means for exploring and resolving problems that arise in the daily activities of the school.

Lecture

An expert in a particular field speaks, presenting information. An opportunity for questions or discussion may also be provided during the session. The lecture is a means by which staff members can acquire a common body of knowledge on which to base their working together. It is also an opportunity to be exposed to new ideas and new stimuli from a source outside of the school setting.

Role-playing

A few participants role-play, or act out, a problem or situation. The audience then discusses the action and the solution. This method lends itself to solving problems that entail interactions between adults or between adults and children. Role-playing can only be successful, however, when the participants are familiar with each other and have a common bond of support for each other.

Demonstration and Practice

One person demonstrates a method, technique, or procedure. The participants then have an opportunity to practice the activity that was demonstrated. This method can be used effectively for demonstrating curriculum methods such as preparation and presentation of learning activities, techniques of group music or storytelling activities, and procedures for introducing a reading lesson. This method is also effective when used for training any of the other job categories — more effective kitchen procedures can be demonstrated, for example.

On-the-job Training

Pairing a less-experienced worker with an experienced one is another training method. The experienced teacher has an opportunity to demonstrate proper techniques, to plan learning experiences with her coworker, and to evaluate the progress of the assistant. The amount of time involved in this kind of training plus the opportunity for continuity of experience makes on-the-job training extremely effective.

Films, Slides, Tapes

Commercial or school-produced audiovisual materials are used to convey information. There are many good films having to do with early childhood teaching. Slides, 8-mm films, or tapes can also be made fairly inexpensively for use by a school. When videotape becomes more widespread and less costly, this medium, both commercial and school-produced, will be valuable.

Field Trips

Field trips are a method by which a school can broaden the learning experiences of its staff. Visits to other schools, to special programs (schools for handicapped children), and to instructional-materials centers give staff members new areas for learning. This method can help teachers to broaden their understanding of children, increase their knowledge of curriculum, and get new ideas for arrangement of the learning environment.

Conferences

Many directors or trainers schedule regular meetings with each person involved in a training program. Through individual discussion, each has an opportunity to assess the progress that is being made toward the goals that have been set with the employee. A conference provides time to discuss problems and to reassess the direction of the training process.

Reading

Some employees may find that their own learning is enhanced by reading. Each may have particular interests that can be pursued through this method. The director or trainer should have knowledge of the resources available for finding the right books or journals. If the school can afford it, these materials should be readily available; if not, booklists and knowledge of nearby library resources will be helpful.

FORMAT FOR TRAINING SESSIONS

There are some general principles of good planning for effective training sessions that hold true for any method used. With only slight variation they are important to follow whether a staff meeting, a workshop, or an individual conference is being planned.

- Arrange the setting for the purpose of the session
- Inform the participants of the purpose of the session
- Prepare the setting ahead of time
  a. Put out materials, arrange chairs, provide coffee
  b. Check audiovisual equipment
- Carry out the procedure as planned
  a. Begin and end on the time schedule that was planned
  b. Remember the purpose and stay as closely as possible to that purpose
  c. Have an agenda

- Evaluate immediately whenever possible
  a. Written evaluations are more helpful than verbal ones.
  b. Evaluators can take more time to do written evaluations and they can be done anonymously.
- Follow through
  a. Allow participants to practice newly acquired skills
  b. Provide new materials or new opportunities to practice
  c. Get feedback as to the effectiveness of the skills when put into practice

OTHER TRAINING METHODS

An innovative director might want to consider some other possibilities. **Exchange observations between teachers could be effective.** By mutual agreement, two teachers observe each other in the classroom. They then share their observations and learn from each other.

Encouraging the staff to write is another way to bring about growth. Ideas about teaching, curriculum, and child development can be written down. This may be kept as a body of knowledge for the staff or be prepared for publication.

Staff could be encouraged to give talks to community groups — such as women's clubs, professional organizations, or service agencies. Often the director herself takes on these tasks. If the director views this function as part of staff development, she will encourage teachers to accept some of these assignments. In this way, they can gain from the experience of telling others about early childhood education.

A staff development program should also include encouragement and possibly **financial support for participation in professional activities.** Conferences, professional meetings, and workshops are opportunities for teachers to get a broader perspective. They can talk to other teachers from other schools, possibly with different ideas about teaching. They have an opportunity to see how what they are doing in their own school fits into the whole field of teaching.

Staff development should also offer **incentives to teachers to continue with their academic education.** Tuition support or salary increments encourage teachers to continue to take courses.

Most staff training programs provide a variety of activities. Several kinds of activities may be scheduled during the year. However, it should be remembered that more learning will take place if there is continuity to the program. For instance, a series of workshops on curriculum can be scheduled, or training activities which concentrate on interaction skills can cover a one-year period. The next year, focus can be placed on another area of teacher performance.

STAFF RELATIONSHIPS

A discussion of staff development would not be complete without considering how the people in a school get along with each other. They must be able to work together toward common goals. Each must feel secure. Each must know that he has a place in the group.

Again, as has constantly been emphasized in this text, the director is the key person. She must create an atmosphere in which each person is valued.

She must also be sensitive to the kinds of skills that are necessary for group efforts. These are usually called human-relationship skills, but could also be called interaction skills. They include the ability to communicate and to express feelings; problem-solving and decision-making are also important.

Communication

The development of communication skills begins with the example provided by the director. Obstacles to good communication and ways to overcome them were discussed in the first unit.

In addition, the director can use every opportunity possible to help others develop the ability to communicate. At staff meetings, each person should be encouraged to listen to what is said. The listener can be asked to repeat what is heard. The speaker confirms or denies that the message has been heard properly. Also, training sessions can be set up to practice the art of listening.

Practice should be provided in the interpretation of nonverbal cues. Films, still pictures, and slides can be used for this purpose. Several people looking at the same nonverbal cue may interpret it quite differently. By sorting out what each person was responding to, teachers develop awareness of these cues.

Practice in saying exactly what one means is important. Everyone should speak as directly and clearly as possible when conveying thoughts or ideas. Any staff discussions can be used to provide practice in this skill. When the meaning is unclear or indirect, the director should encourage the speaker to try again.

After staff members have developed the ability to communicate with each other, they will be ready to try to express feelings. When teachers understand their own feelings and can express them, they can help children understand and express their feelings.

In order to express feelings, persons must recognize what feelings are. Each must be able to say "I know I am angry — or resentful — or happy." This sounds simple, but most people have been taught to hide their true feelings.

Soon comes the recognition that others probably have similar feelings. Sometimes this fact comes as a surprise — that others get angry at certain kinds of behavior. At times it is a relief to know that one is not alone with unpleasant or painful feelings.

Each staff member must be helped to find satisfying ways to express feelings. It is not always necessary to use words; but, it is necessary that the expression be clear to the other person. A sensitive director will recognize that each person must find his own way.

In a supportive atmosphere, staff members can come to a mutual respect and understanding. They are able to develop the feeling of group solidarity which is the basis for solving problems.

Problem Solving

Problem-solving skills are needed when a group of people work together; these are the skills that find solutions to everyday difficulties, both concrete and interpersonal. The types of problems teachers face may range from how to make a piece of equipment to how a room may be shared by two teachers.

When she is presented with a problem situation, the director can demonstrate her problem-solving skill by the way she helps her staff solve the problem. Eventually they will be able to do it themselves.

The first step in problem solving is to state what the problem is. For example, the problem may be how to make a balance scale so that the children can learn about weights. A concrete problem is easy to state but interpersonal problems are not so easy. For example, an apparent problem may be that one of the teachers who share a room is sloppy and always leaves it in a mess. With investigation, the real problem is found — the teacher does not feel that she has a place in the school. She feels the room is not hers because she does not belong there. Therefore, it does not matter if it is kept clean or not.

The next step is to find out what resources for solution are available. In the first example, the library would certainly yield some information about balances. Other teachers may have found ways that were successful. Experi-

Fig. 12-2 The director creates a supportive atmosphere.

mentation with materials might also result in a solution to the problem.

In the second example, the director would have to explore all possible ways to help the teacher who leaves the room in a mess. Available alternatives would have to be considered: Are there possible changes in room arrangements or assignments that would give the teacher a feeling that she had her own space? Can the director, herself, do more to help the two teachers? Are there ways that other staff members can help?

The third step in problem solving is to find out what obstacles get in the way of a solution. The obstacles to building a balance scale might be a lack of proper tools or materials. In the example of the teacher, an obstacle might be the teacher's difficulty in communicating her feelings to others.

The last step is the solution. For building a balance, one can get the tools and materials. For establishing a feeling of belonging, the solutions are less precise: The director would have to find ways to help the teacher let others know how she feels. She may help the teacher to feel she has a place in the school by asking her to share her expertise in music with the other members of the staff. The director may decide to develop her own relationship with the teacher.

Decision Making

Decision-making skills are necessary when a group works together in a democratic setting. The staff may be asked to decide between two very expensive pieces of equipment. Which one should be purchased since they cannot afford both?

With leadership from the director, the staff will gather information as the first step. They will find out as much as they can about the two pieces of equipment: They will want to know what the two pieces look like and how long each is expected to last. Furthermore, the ways that children can use the equipment should be explored. Also, where could it be placed so maximum use can be obtained?

Next, the staff must set priorities based on their objectives. One piece of equipment may lend itself to more imaginative play. The other may be primarily used for the development of physical abilities in children. Based on the objectives of the school, the staff should be able to rate one as having a higher priority.

How to implement the decision is the next step: Is the equipment to be purchased immediately? Will it be installed during school hours so the children can watch or on a weekend so the children can be surprised?

For future reference, the staff should evaluate the decision to find out if the choice was a good one: Do the children use the equipment as predicted? Are there other ways it is used that were not predicted? Should a different choice have been made?

This procedure for decision making has been described in terms of a concrete object, the piece of equipment. It can be adapted to other kinds of decisions. These same steps can lead to making choices concerning schedules or activities and also to decisions concerning people.

DIRECTOR RESPONSE TO STAFF DEVELOPMENT

For some directors, staff development may at first cause anxiety. A director may feel that if the staff is trained too well, the director will have nothing to do.

If the staff is involved in making decisions or solving problems, what does the director do? She assumes a different role. In a school where there is emphasis on staff participation, the role of the director can truly be that of a leader.

Some directors fear that if they train their staff too well, teachers will be dissatisfied with their jobs. They are afraid that well-trained teachers will want to leave and seek better jobs. Perhaps a few will. Most teachers, however, realize that there is a great deal to learn about teaching and about getting along with people. They are challenged by the opportunities that a good staff-training program can offer. The opportunities to continue to learn are appreciated. When the staff is growing and learning in a dynamic environment, the children, too, can learn.

SUMMARY

Young children model their own behavior after the significant adults in their lives. One purpose of a good staff-training program is to help the adults in a school setting acquire the characteristics and skills that they want for children.

Another purpose of staff training is to help members learn the skills necessary to enrich their jobs. A third purpose is to help those who are interested move to new job categories.

The starting point of staff training is the knowledge that the trainee already has concerning each of the tasks listed in the job description. A self-evaluation plus an evaluation by the director is used as a basis for setting the objectives for training.

The choice of the best training method is difficult because it is affected by many variables:

- Composition of the group
- Size of the group
- Time
- Place
- Special abilities of staff members
- Attendance
- Application of skills
- Learning styles

A variety of training methods should be used. There are the usual methods: staff meetings, workshops, group discussions, lectures, role-playing, demonstration and practice, on-the-job training, audiovisual materials, field trips, conferences, and reading. Some innovative methods are also available: exchange observations between teachers, writing, and giving talks to community groups. Staff members should also be encouraged to participate in professional activities and continue to take college courses.

The director must be sensitive to skills necessary for group efforts such as communication skills. Staff members should be encouraged to listen carefully, to interpret nonverbal cues, and to say exactly what they mean.

The second skill to be developed is the ability to express one's feelings. Staff can become increasingly aware of their own feelings and those of others. They can be helped to find satisfying ways to express feelings.

Problem-solving skills are also needed when a group of people work together. The steps in problem solving are stating what the problem is, finding the resources for solution, finding the obstacles to solution, and solving the problem.

The staff also needs to develop decision-making skills. They will learn to gather information, set priorities, implement the decision, and evaluate the decisions.

Some directors fear that if they train them too well, some of the staff members will no longer be satisfied with their jobs. However, teachers appreciate the opportunity to learn. They realize that there is a great deal to learn about working with people and about teaching.

STUDENT ACTIVITIES

- Obtain a large photograph of a person. Ask five people to tell you what the person in the photo might be feeling. Compare similarities and differences in their interpretations.
- Discuss a problem you might encounter as a teacher. Try to solve the problem effectively following the steps outlined in the text.
- Plan and conduct a training session suitable for your school. Ask the participants to evaluate its effectiveness in meeting their needs.

REVIEW

A. Select the phrase which best completes each of the following sentences.

1. A director who is planning staff development activities should consider
   a. the size of the group
   b. the composition of the group
   c. the place where the activities take place
   d. all of the above

2. The director may achieve active participation in staff training by
   a. requiring the staff to attend
   b. showing films
   c. having a good lecturer talk to them
   d. involving staff in the planning

3. Communication skills can best be developed by
   a. encouraging staff to talk a lot
   b. lectures about communication
   c. viewing films on communication
   d. practice in listening to others

4. A staff development program which emphasizes staff participation would find the director's role is that of
   a. a friend
   b. an authority figure
   c. a discussion leader
   d. a decision maker

B.   Briefly answer the following.

1. Name three innovative methods of staff training.

2. Name the four steps in problem solving.

3. What is involved in the decision-making process?

Section 4
OPERATING
THE PROGRAM

Unit 13 The Budgeting Process

OBJECTIVES

After studying this unit, the student should be able to

- Name the items to be included in a budget
- Prepare a budget for a new or ongoing school
- Identify records that should be kept for budget planning

Financial management of a school can determine the success or failure of its educational program or even of the school itself. The cost of providing a quality program is high. The income of a school for young children is often very limited. A budget that has been carefully planned and administered is essential to good financial management.

A *budget* is a list of every item connected with a school operation for which cash pay-

Fig. 13-1 Supplies are necessary for "playing house."

ment may be made. A budget might also be viewed as a statement of all the services and programs of the school expressed in money terms.

DEVELOPING BUDGET ITEMS

It may be necessary for a director who knows nothing at all about financial management to seek help with the first budget she prepares. An accountant may help her in preparing the budget and in setting up a book-keeping system. There are some suggestions that can be made before the director begins the mechanics of budgeting.

Services, Programs, and Goals

A budget begins with a list of the services to be provided, programs to be included, and goals to be reached. All staff members should have an opportunity to be involved in this phase of the planning. In a small school, staff meetings provide the director with an opportunity to gather ideas from the staff. In a larger organization, information from the separate departments may have to be gathered by the staff member in charge of the departments.

This information is then brought to the director at budget planning sessions.

When services, programs, and goals are clearly stated, costs for providing these can be figured. It is true that estimated income may not be enough to cover the projected costs. Nevertheless, the budget should begin with services, programs, and goals, not with expected income. Adjustment of budget to income is the second step of the process, not the first.

Justifications

Budget justifications should accompany the budget. Budget justifications are explanations of any items that might raise questions in the mind of someone reviewing the budget. Examples of the kinds of justifications to be included would be unusual items or unusual amounts. If the method of computing a particular item is not obvious, it should be explained. Explanation of the need for a certain item or service might also be included.

Clear and complete justification statements indicate a well-planned and well-prepared budget. Inadequate or generalized justification statements may indicate poor planning. Lack of planning can be the reason for poor financial management.

THE START-UP BUDGET

Financial planning for a new school is different from planning for an ongoing school. As was discussed in unit 3, a new school will have some costs even before it is ready to open. These are called *start-up costs*, and a separate budget should be prepared to cover them. A sample of this kind of budget is shown in figure 3-2 (refer back to unit 3).

Capital Costs

A sizable amount of money to be spent during the initial stages of planning a new school is for the cost of land and building. Whether land is purchased on which to build, an existing school is bought, or a structure is renovated, the cost will be high. Renting or leasing property may also be expensive since often rent for the first month and the last month — plus a security deposit — are required.

Capital costs in the start-up budget must also include the equipment and supplies needed to begin operation of the school. Kitchen equipment, playground equipment, classroom and office furniture, all entail a fairly large investment. Supplies such as art materials, food, and office materials must be on hand when the school opens. Figure 13-2 shows that one estimate of capital costs is between $714 and $1,899 for each child.

Working Capital

Working capital is needed to cover operating expenses during the first months. It is hard for many small proprietary schools to get through the first year before total enrollment is achieved. The director must plan for

---

Estimated Costs

Capital cost of land, building and equipment may range from $714 to $1,899 per child.

Working Capital needed may range from $13 to $625 per child.

Labor and miscellaneous start-up costs may range from $250 to $1,167 per child.

Total start-up costs may thus range from $1,000 to $3,750 per child.

Source: *The Costs of Child Care: Money and Other Resources,* Day Care and Child Development Council of America, Inc., Washington, D.C.

(These figures reflect costs for several different kinds of programs: day care homes, small proprietary schools and large centers that are part of a system.)

Fig. 13-2 Estimate of Start-up Costs

the possibility of less than maximum income during the first several months. In addition, some licensing agencies require that a new school have cash, other liquid reserves, guarantees by a responsible governing board, or predictable income to cover the estimated cost of operation for at least three months. Figure 13-2 shows these costs to range between $13 and $625 per child.

Labor and Miscellaneous Costs

The cost of the human effort needed to plan and implement the new program must also be added to start-up costs. At least a director and possibly a secretary are needed during the early planning stages. Teachers, aides, kitchen workers, and maintenance staff can be added later as the need arises. Additional personnel costs may include an accountant, lawyer, and architect.

Miscellaneous costs should be anticipated and will vary from one region to another and from one program to another. Included are license fees, permit fees, and inspection costs. A tax assessment for sewers or sidewalks, a fire alarm system, and fire extinguishers might also be included. A director who is careful in her planning will expect some additional overlooked costs and will provide for them in the start-up budget. Figure 13-2 shows that labor and miscellaneous costs range from $250 to $3,750 for each child.

THE OPERATING BUDGET

The budget for an existing school is called the *operating budget*. It will contain some fairly standard items. Publicly funded programs will probably have a standard format to follow.

Staff Salaries

Staff salaries make up a large proportion of the operating budget. All personnel must be listed in this category from the director to the person in charge of maintenance. Salaries usually account for 70 to 80 percent of the budget expenditure.

It is important that the director decide carefully the number of persons needed. More teachers and aides will be included than any other job category. The director must know how to determine the number of teachers needed to maintain the quality of program desired. The method for computing the number of teachers is shown in figure 13-3.

Fringe Benefits

All of the services that the school makes available to its personnel are referred to as *fringe benefits* and make up the second category of the budget. Social security, unemployment benefits, retirement, disability insurance, medical coverage, sick leave, and vacation pay are included. A standard estimate of costs is 10 to 20 percent of salaries.

Consultant Services

The third category of the budget lists consultant services. These consultants are people who contribute to the program but on an infrequent basis. They are not actually staff. It is easier to pay for their services on a *per diem* basis, that is, by the day. Consultant services that a school might use could range from medical examinations for the children to demonstrations by an artist. Other services might be provided by a social worker or an educational consultant. Fees for consultants usually range between $25 and $100 per day.

Equipment

There should be a category for equipment. Equipment includes all those items that are fairly permanent, that is, not regularly used up. Some definitions indicate it refers to all those items that last three years or more.

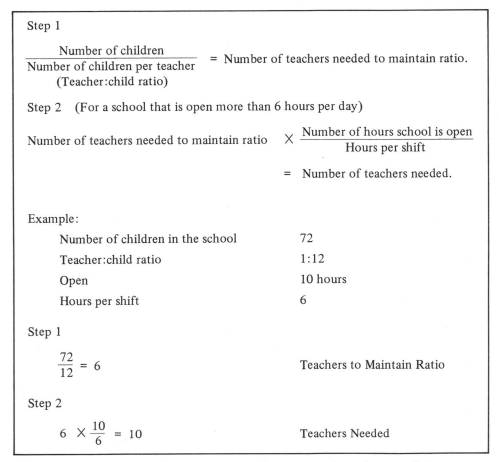

Fig. 13-3 How to Compute the Number of Teachers Needed

Various kinds of equipment are needed throughout the school. Typewriters, garbage pails, and educational toys are all considered equipment. It is easier to separate equipment into several sections such as educational or curriculum equipment, caretaking and housekeeping equipment, office equipment, and kitchen equipment.

Supplies and Materials

These items are used up in the process of carrying out the functions of the school. This category includes art materials for the classrooms, floor wax and cleaning agents, and office supplies. As with equipment, supplies should be broken down into smaller subcategories such as curriculum supplies, caretaking and housekeeping supplies, and office supplies. (Food is treated as a separate category.)

Transportation

Some schools may include money for transportation in their budget. Field trips and transportation to and from school might be provided for the children. The staff may be allowed travel money to other schools, conferences, or workshops.

Food

The category for food will include all the meals and snacks served at the school. The budget should indicate the number of meals and snacks, the cost per day, the number of days covered, and the number of children being served. Costs for two meals and two snacks each day range between 60¢ and $1.00 per day per child. During periods of inflation, the cost may be even higher.

Space Costs

Space costs refer to building and yard areas. The item should show the number of square feet of space needed and the total cost of that space. From this data, it can be judged if the space is adequate for the number of children involved. Cost for space will vary greatly from one area to another. Careful comparison of costs for additional space should be made when expansion of the school is planned.

Fig. 13-4 Delivering Food for Snack Time

PERCENTAGE EXPENDITURES

Typical ranges of percentages of total expenditures for a small (less than 50 children) proprietary school which is open a full day. A noon meal is served.

GROSS INCOME	100%	100%
EXPENSES:		
Salaries (directors, teachers, part-time secretary, plus payroll taxes)	55.0%	60.0%
Rent or mortgage	9.0%	12.5%
Supplies and equipment	1.5%	3.0%
Utilities (water, gas, electricity, telephone, trash, laundry)	1.5%	2.5%
Food	8.0%	10.0%
Insurance	1.0%	2.5%
Repairs and maintenance	2.0%	3.0%
Taxes and licenses	1.0%	2.0%
Administration and professional services (accountant, lawyer, etc)	1.0%	2.5%
Advertising	1.0%	1.5%
Bad Debts	1.5%	1.5%
TOTAL EXPENSES	82.0%	100.0%
NET PROFIT RANGE	18.0%	0.0%

Fig. 13-5 Sample Percentage Expenditures

Utilities

Utilities include such items as telephone service, heat, trash removal, water, and electricity. In some communities, a charge for sewage disposal may be included. When renting space, one or more of these items may be covered by the rental fee.

Other Costs

An item should be in the budget to cover anything that does not fit into the above categories. This will be called other costs and usually includes license fees, insurance, advertising, and accountant fees. Some schools prefer to have a separate item for insurance. Each director will change the budget format to suit the needs of the particular school. A more detailed discussion of insurance is found in unit 3.

Figure 13-5 shows some expected percentages of the total expenditures for each budget item. In order to illustrate the budget items, a sample budget for a publicly funded day care program is shown in figure 13-6 and an example for a private proprietary school, in figure 13-7.

Income

An operating budget shows the expected income for the period it covers. All sources of income and estimates of expected income should be included. In the case of a government grant, total expected income is usually computed on a cost-per-child allowable under the grant conditions. Income from fund-raising has to be an estimate based on a goal to be reached. Income from tuition, registration fees, transportation, and meal charges should allow for a vacancy in enrollment plus some fees that cannot be collected. A reasonable allowance for this kind of loss is 10 percent of the total income.

BUDGET ANALYSIS

The budget should be reviewed when it is completed. In a small private school, the director may do this. In other small schools, there may be a separate owner or board of trustees who will review the budget before it is adopted. In larger organizations, budget review may be done by a finance committee or chief administrative officer. The following considerations should be made when reviewing the budget.

- Is every service or component included that would meet the goals of the school? Services or components justifiable at one time may no longer be necessary in order to achieve goals. Additions may also be necessary as goals and priorities change.

- Have all costs been included? The inexperienced director may easily forget important items in the budget and should, therefore, review it carefully. It may be necessary for the director to rely upon the more extensive experience of the person or persons who review the budget.

- Is there a marked difference in the budget projection from that of previous years? The director of a new school may need to compare the budget with that of other schools in the area or with budget information available in the literature. Justifications for any radical changes in the budget should be clearly understood by all those involved in the budget process.

- Are there certain items that show marked increase over previous budget years? Marked increases may reflect changes in the way objectives are to be implemented. Changes may also indicate that cost control measures are necessary.

- How can the budget be adjusted to stay within the anticipated income? At this

INCOME		BUDGET			$176,890
EXPENSES:					
Category	%Time	No.	Salary	Total	%Expenses

I. Staff
   A. Administrative

	%Time	No.	Salary	Total	%Expenses
1. Director	100	1	$10-14,000	$ 12,000	

   B. Teaching

	%Time	No.	Salary	Total	
1. Head teacher	100	5	7-9,000	40,000	
2. Assistant teacher	100	5	5-7,000	30,000	
3. Aides	100	7	4,000	28,000	
C. Cook	100	1	6,000	6,000	
D. Maintenance	50	1	6,000	3,000	
E. Secretary	100	1	7,000	7,000	
				$126,000	71.3%

	Total	%Expenses
II. Fringe benefits at 10% of salary costs	12,600	7.0%
III. Consultant Services		
A. Health-related		
1. Physician at $100 per day for 12 days	1,200	
2. Dentist at $75 per day for 10 days	750	
3. Nutritionist at $25 per day for 12 days	300	
B. Training and curriculum related		
1. Educational consultant at $50 per day for 12 days	600	
	$ 2,850	1.6%
IV. Equipment		
A. Educational	$1,500	
B. Caretaking and housekeeping	700	
C. Kitchen	200	
D. Office	500	
	$ 2,900	1.6%
V. Supplies and Materials		
A. Educational	1,200	
B. Caretaking and housekeeping	600	
C. Office	500	
	$ 2,300	1.3%
VI. Food		
For two meals and two snacks: 75¢ × 60 children × 260 days	$ 11,700	6.6%
VII. Transportation		
A. Bus rental for field trips	1,000	
B. Local staff travel	200	
C. Long-distance staff travel	500	
	$ 1,700	1.0%
VIII. Space Costs		
4,500 square feet at $3.00 per square foot	$ 13,500	7.7%
IX. Utilities		
A. Telephone: 2 at $40 per month each	960	
B. Heat at $65 per month	780	
C. Electricity at $50 per month	600	
	$ 2,340	1.3%
X. Other Costs		
License fees, insurance, etc.	1,000	0.5%
GRAND TOTAL	$176,890	99.6%
(Cost per child)	2,948	

Note: Costs per child were used to show the high cost of quality care for children ten hours a day. See unit 3 for a lower cost budget.

Fig. 13-6 **Budget for a Publicly Funded Day Care Center, Open Ten Hours per Day. (Sixty children are enrolled. The teacher/child ratio is 1:6.)**

TYPICAL MONTHLY BUDGET		
ESTIMATED GROSS INCOME	AMOUNT	%
(50 children × $65 tuition)	$3,250	100%
EXPENSES		
Salaries:		
Director @ $800/mo.	800	
2 teachers @ $3.50/hr	616	
1 teacher @ $3.00/hr	264	
	$1,680	51%
Payroll Taxes	168	10%
Rent	450	13%
Utilities	100	3%
Supplies & equipment	100	3%
Food (35¢/day per child)	357	12%
Insurance	50	2%
Repairs and maintenance	100	3%
Taxes and licenses	35	1%
Administrative & professional services	40	1%
Advertising	35	1%
TOTAL	$3,115	100%
NET INCOME	$ 135*	
*Note that no allowance has been made for uncollected tuition or for less than full enrollment.		

Fig. 13-7 Budget for a Private Proprietary School, Open Three Hours a Day (Fifty children are enrolled.)

point, the budget reviewer may need to consider changing services or components in order to stay within the income. It may be necessary to make decisions about buying certain pieces of equipment or supplies. It is essential to the existence of the school as an educational institution that these decisions are made wisely.

Decisions about budget items should always be made with the goals of the school in mind. By reviewing the goals of the school and how these goals have been implemented, the reviewer and director can set priorities.

However, the final decision rests with the person or persons responsible for the budget.

IMPLEMENTING THE APPROVED BUDGET

Having an approved budget set down on paper does not assure that the budget will be followed. The director of a small school as well as the director of a large organization must use good management methods to insure adherence to the budget.

- One person should be responsible for the purchasing of all equipment and materials. If several staff members do the purchasing, it is difficult to maintain controls in order to achieve maximum use of funds. One person can more easily seek out and use the most economical vendors.

- One person should be responsible for the disbursement of all monies. As with purchasing, it is easier to maintain control if one person is involved in writing checks or spending cash. Often in a small school, the director assumes both the purchasing and disbursing functions. In a larger school one person may do both. In a very large organization, separate positions may be required for the two functions.

- Each person concerned with purchasing or disbursement should have a copy of the budget. No one can be expected to stay within a budget without clear understanding of that budget. It is also recommended that all staff members have information regarding the budget. It will give them a greater appreciation of the problems involved in providing for the needs of the school.

- Monthly statements should be prepared showing expenditures for each budget item. The statement should indicate the amount spent for the period covered and the cumulative expenditures for the year. At the end of the budget year, an annual report of income and expenditures should be made.

- The staff member responsible for purchasing and/or spending should make every effort to stay within the budgeted amount. Overspending or underspending should be investigated by the director. Overspending may indicate that staff members need to be encouraged to conserve supplies. Underspending may indicate that needed personnel have not been hired or necessary equipment purchased.

RECORDS FOR FUTURE PLANNING

Good records will make the task of preparing each year's budget progressively easier. Records that are required for budget development and administration should include the following:

- Current costs of items included in the budget

- Budget forms used by the school or by any funding agency

- Copies of current costs of taxes, insurance, licenses, and assessments

- Copies of approved budgets for at least three previous years

- Copies of any cost-control practices and procedures of the school

- Correspondence relating to the budget

- Minutes of budget review meetings

- Copies of the annual reports for at least three previous years

SUMMARY

A budget is a list of every item connected with a school operation for which cash payment is made. It begins with a list of the services to be provided, programs to be included, and objectives to be reached.

The following items should be included in the budget for a school:

- Staff salaries

- Fringe benefits

- Consultant services

- Equipment

- Supplies and materials

- Other costs

- Transportation

- Space costs

- Utilities

The review of the budget should determine if all of the objectives have been met.

Implementing the budget requires good management procedures. One person should be responsible for the purchasing and disbursement of all monies. Each person concerned with purchasing or disbursements is given a copy of the budget. Prepared monthly statements show how much was spent for each item. The staff member responsible for buying and/or spending must make every effort to stay within the budgeted amount.

Good records make the task of preparing each year's budget progressively easier.

STUDENT ACTIVITIES

- Plan a budget for a school with which you are familiar, or for a school you would like to have.

- Obtain several budgets prepared by others. Compare them with your budget.

- If you were asked to cut back your budget by 10 percent, what changes could be made? Justify your choice.

REVIEW

1. Name six points to consider when planning the start-up budget.

2. Explain what is meant by a budget.

3. Before beginning work on budget planning, what factors must be considered?

4. How often should a statement be prepared showing expenditures for each budget item?

5. Who is responsible for making the final budget decisions?

6. What item constitutes a large proportion of the operating budget?

7. What other costs must be considered under budget operation?

8. Once the budget is put together, who should review it before it is adopted?

9. Is a listing of items needed all that is necessary in preparing the budget for consideration? Explain.

10. What items should be included in records for future planning?

Unit 14 Food Services

OBJECTIVES

After studying this unit, the student should be able to

- Explain the value of good nutrition
- Discuss factors to consider in purchasing, preparing, and serving food to young children

Proper nutrition has a critical role in the development of young children. During a period of rapid growth from birth to five years, nutrition — adequate or poor — has immediate and sometimes lasting effects. Studies have shown that nutrition affects physical health and growth patterns. Mental development and intellectual ability are also affected by what the child eats.

The director of a nursery school may be responsible for supervising a nutritionist and cook or she may plan and sometimes even prepare meals herself. Some knowledge of the nutritional needs of children is necessary. The foods required for optimum growth and health can be divided into four basic groups:

(1) vegetables and fruits (2) milk and milk products (3) breads and/or cereals and (4) meat and/or alternate protein.

PLANNING MENUS

The length of the school day determines the proportion of daily nutrition that must be provided by the school. In general, during a school day of four hours or less, one-third of the daily food intake must be provided. One midmorning snack and lunch are adequate. A school day that extends beyond four hours may have to provide as much as two-thirds of the child's daily food intake. Breakfast, two snacks, and lunch must be planned.

FOOD GROUP	NUTRITIONAL NEEDS	FOOD
Vegetables and Fruits	Vitamin C, Vitamin A, Iron	Green and yellow vegetables; All fruits and melons; Dried fruits; Beans — green, wax, lima
Milk and Milk Products	Calcium, Riboflavin, Protein Calories	Milk, cheese, ice cream, cottage cheese, yogurt, butter
Breads and/or cereals	B Vitamins, Minerals, Protein Calories	Whole grain or enriched bread; Biscuits, muffins, crackers (whole wheat flour); Cookies made with whole grains; Enriched or whole grain cereal
Meat and/or alternate	Protein, Iron, B Vitamins	Meat, poultry, fish, cheese, eggs, peanut butter, beans, peas

Fig. 14-1 The Four Food Groups

GUIDELINES

In order to determine how much food to prepare and serve, it is necessary to know the serving portion that will provide the required amount of nutrition. The basic food groups can be translated into serving amounts. Recommendations from *Special Food Service Program for Children* by the United States Department of Agriculture are shown in figure 14-2.

Foods Children Like

Children are more aware of flavor, texture, and appearance of food than are adults. Meals should be planned with that fact in mind. Often, children reject food that has a strong flavor or smell. Children usually do not like foods that are mixed together, such as in a casserole. They also react negatively to unattractive color or an unfamiliar texture.

Facilities and Equipment

Meals should be planned according to the facilities and equipment available for preparation and serving. For example, two items requiring oven space cannot be on the same menu unless the oven space is adequate for cooking both at the same time. A finger food may be prepared for dessert if all the bowls are to be used for the meal.

Available Personnel

Food should be planned according to the number of personnel available for preparation and serving. A school large enough to employ a cook and an assistant is better able to serve

PATTERN	CHILDREN 1 to 3 yrs.	CHILDREN 3 to 6 yrs.
BREAKFAST		
Milk, fluid whole	1/2 cup	3/4 cup
Juice or fruit	1/4 cup	1/2 cup
Cereal and/or bread, enriched or whole grain		
Cereal	1/4 cup	1/3 cup
Bread	1/2 slice	1/2 slice
MIDMORNING OR MIDAFTERNOON SUPPLEMENT		
Milk, fluid whole, or juice or fruit or vegetable	1/2 cup	1/2 cup
Bread or cereal enriched or whole grain		
Bread	1/2 slice	1/2 slice
Cereal	1/4 cup	1/3 cup
LUNCH OR SUPPER		
Milk, fluid whole	1/2 cup	3/4 cup
Meat and/or alternate. One of the following or combinations to give equivalent quantities:		
Meat, poultry, fish	1 ounce	1 1/2 ounces
Cheese	1 ounce	1 1/2 ounces
Egg	1	1
Cooked dry beans and peas	1/8 cup	1/4 cup
Peanut butter	1 tablespoon	2 tablespoons
Vegetable and/or fruit	1/4 cup	1/2 cup
Bread, enriched or whole grain	1/2 slice	1/2 slice
Butter or fortified margarine	1/2 teaspoon	1/2 teaspoon

Fig. 14-2 Serving Portions

different kinds of meals than one in which there is only a part-time cook. In a very small school where the owner-director may have to do the cooking, meals must be simple and easily prepared.

Appetizing Meals

Meals should be planned to provide appetite appeal. There should be a variety of foods, but also a repetition of familiar favorites. Contrasts of color, shape, texture, and flavors should be considered. A combination of hot and cold foods provides a contrast of temperature.

Desserts should be planned as a part of the menu, not as a special treat. Only desserts that have nutritional value beyond calories should be included. Fruits, cakes made with whole wheat flour, cookies made with nuts and raisins, or milk puddings are all good desserts. Ice cream also contains valuable nutrients. All of these desserts are just as important as any other part of the menu.

The special meanings of food should be considered in planning menus. Significant foods for holidays or birthdays are in this category. Cultural or ethnic foods might also be included. Planning these foods as part of the child's school experience can bring home and school closer together.

MENU INFORMATION FOR PARENTS

Parents frequently ask what their child has eaten at school. This information is helpful when meals are planned for the family. It may avoid giving the child the same thing for dinner at home. The director of a school can help mothers by posting the weekly menus in an easily accessible place.

Parents are also concerned about how much their children eat at school. They question the teacher or the director. On days that the posted menu shows food which the child likes, the mother can relax a little. She can expect that her child will eat an adequate lunch.

At home children may talk about the favorite foods which were served at school. Mothers who wish to serve these foods at home should be given the recipes. There should be no secret recipes in an early childhood education center.

PURCHASING FOOD

The skill of the person who selects and purchases the food will enable the school to get the most out of its food budget. Careful buying reduces waste and increases the quality of meals.

An effective director knows how much food is purchased and used during a given period of time. She should be able to figure the amount of money needed to provide adequate meals for a month, and also know the daily cost per child. Careful records of food purchases and the quantity used must be kept so that this information is available.

Source

Thought must be given to where food is purchased. Food service companies that provide quality food at the lowest cost should be sought. Other considerations in choosing food vendors might include the services they provide. Do they deliver? What is the delivery schedule? Will credit or discounts be given?

Quality

The quality of food to buy should be determined by the use for which it is intended; standards for all food purchases should be developed. Top quality grade may be necessary for some usages. A lesser quality may be completely adequate for another usage. Reading labels and checking grades and certifications are all part of quality determination. In this way, the food that is bought will assure the best meals at a reasonable cost.

	MONDAY	TUESDAY	WEDNESDAY	THURSDAY	FRIDAY
BREAKFAST	1/2 an orange 1/4 cup shredded wheat cereal 3/4 cup milk	1/2 cup tomato juice 2 4"-pancakes 2 Tbsp. applesauce 1/2 tsp. margarine 1/2 cup milk	1/2 cup sliced peaches 1/3 cup oatmeal 3/4 cup milk	1/2 a banana 1/4 cup shredded wheat cereal 3/4 cup milk 1/2 slice toast 1/2 tsp. margarine	1/2 cup orange juice French Toast 1/2 slice bread milk egg powdered sugar 1/2 cup milk
SNACK	1/2 cup milk 2 graham crackers	1/2 slice cheese 4 small whole wheat crackers	1/2 cup yogurt with fruit 2 whole wheat crackers	1/2 slice cheese 1/2 apple	1/2 cup apple juice 2 graham crackers
LUNCH	1/2 cup milk 2 fish sticks 4 carrot sticks 1/2 slice bread 1/2 tsp. margarine 1/3 cup applesauce	1/2 cup milk 1 oz. meat loaf 1/4 cup peas 1/4 baked potato 1/2 tsp. margarine 2" square of spice cake made with w.w. flour	1/2 cup milk 1/2 cup spaghetti 1/4 cup meat sauce 1/4 cup green salad 2 orange wedges	1/2 cup milk 1/2 cup macaroni & cheese 1/4 cup string beans 1/4 cup apple betty w/wheat germ topping	1/2 cup milk 1/2 tuna sandwich 1/4 cup carrot & raisin salad 1/4 cup ice cream
SNACK	Assorted raw vegetables Sour cream dip 1/4 slice whole wheat bread 1/2 tsp. margarine	1/2 cup yogurt with fruit 1 graham cracker	peanut butter sandwich 1/2 cup milk	WW-raisin cookies 1/2 cup milk	1/2 cup milk 1/2 warm tortilla 1/2 tsp. margarine or grated cheese

Fig. 14-3 Sample Menus for a Day Care Center

Quantity

The amount of food purchased at a time should be carefully calculated. The number of children and adults to be served must be counted. The size of the servings and the appropriate container sizes must be determined.

It is helpful to periodically record how much and which kinds of food are not eaten. The next time these particular foods are served, adjustments in the amounts can be made. It is also helpful to keep records of the foods the children like and those they reject. After a period of time, a food that continues to be rejected should be removed from the menu.

Time and Method of Purchase

The time when food is purchased is also an important factor in providing quality at the lowest cost. Perishability, storage space, and seasonal availability must all be taken into consideration. Certain foods such as milk, bread, and fresh produce may have to be purchased daily. Canned or packaged foods may be purchased monthly if storage allows. Only foods that are in season should be included on the menus; seasonal foods are more plentiful and less expensive. Daily papers or weekly food supplements provide this information.

Joint purchasing with one or several other schools may lower the cost of providing good meals for the children. Two schools in the same neighborhood or in an organization may save money by sharing the time and effort involved in shopping; they can also buy in larger quantities. Cases of produce can be bought at central produce markets; a side of meat can be divided. Some vendors may give discounts for very large purchase orders.

SANITATION

All foods served to children must be safe. It is important to feed children nutritious meals. It is equally important that the meals be free of any harmful substances. Nutrition and sanitation must be considered of equal importance in a school for young children.

Being sure that sanitation standards have been met begins before the food is actually purchased. When food is bought, one must be sure that the meat is government inspected and the milk pasteurized. Frozen foods should be bought and kept in their frozen state until ready for use. Fresh produce should be of good quality when bought and thoroughly washed before serving.

All utensils for preparing and serving food must be clean. Cooking pots must be thoroughly washed after use. All serving dishes and glasses must be clean and handled carefully; any damaged or cracked dishes and glasses should be discarded. Water used for washing dishes and utensils should be kept at 170°, and an effective detergent should be used.

Storage facilities and procedures must maintain optimum conditions of sanitation. Food should be stored so that the most recently purchased food is used last. Rotation on the shelf helps to prevent spoilage. Tightly covered containers should be provided for such items as flour, rice, sugar, and cornmeal. This action will prevent infestation in dry foods from insects or damage by rodents. Foods requiring refrigeration should be kept at 40° or below. This prevents growth of harmful bacteria that might cause diseases.

Food handling must be developed to insure that good food is not spoiled during the preparation or serving. Attention must be paid to proper cooking and holding temperatures. Hot foods should reach a temperature of 140°, at least, and be held at that heat until served.

All personnel involved in food service must maintain high standards of health and cleanliness. Clean hands and clean dress cannot be overemphasized. Personnel should be free of colds or other infections. Yearly health examinations should be required.

PREPARING FOOD

The best planned menus will not be successful if the food is not prepared properly. Nutrients must be preserved, and the food must be prepared in such a way that the children will eat it.

Preparation is the most important step in the entire process from menu planning to the time that the food is served. If children do not eat the food, nothing has been gained from all the time, money, and effort that has been spent. Encouraging intake of good food that has been prepared and attractively served is not difficult to achieve. The bonus in well-fed children who enjoy eating is worth the effort. Well-fed children are more likely to benefit from the learning activities provided by the school. Mental and physical alertness depends heavily on good nutrition.

Order of Preparation

Differences in cooking time must be considered in deciding what food is to be prepared first. Careful planning is required to have all foods ready at the same time. Some portions of a menu can be prepared at the end of one day for the next day's meals. Desserts, spaghetti sauce, and meat loaf mix are examples of foods that can be prepared the day before use. Fresh vegetables, eggs, and bacon are prepared shortly before serving the meal.

Those who prepare the meals also must consider how best to save the nutrients. Vegetable dishes should be prepared just before cooking and then cooked only long enough to make them palatable. They should never be prepared early and then left to soak in water. This kind of handling destroys much of the nutritional value of the vegetables.

Fig. 14-4 A nourishing lunch is being prepared.

Food preparation can be made easier by using recipes that have been carefully tested. An experienced cook soon develops a file of familiar successes.

Children's Preferences

During the preparation stage, as well as the planning stage, children's preferences should be considered. It has been said that children have a high awareness of tastes, smell, texture, and color of food. Certain foods that might otherwise be rejected by children can be made more acceptable by proper preparation. For instance, cooking cabbage in milk eliminates its strong odor. Adding a bit of color to foods may make them more interesting. A sprinkling of paprika on cottage cheese or a dab of jelly on vanilla pudding makes them more attractive. Experimentation and thought about how the food will appeal to the children's senses will yield benefits both to the cook and to the children.

The children's ease in handling and eating the food must also be taken into consideration. Food should be served in such a way that the children can manage it themselves. This means that meat should be in child bite-size pieces. Sandwiches should be quartered. Hard-boiled eggs should be shelled and cut in half; oranges and apples are cut into thin slices.

Fig. 14-5 The cook gets some help.

Fig. 14-6 The food is easy to manage.

Food is a major expense in a school that serves meals. It is important that as much benefit as possible is gained from the money and effort spent. The director should encourage the cook to get out of the kitchen at times and into the classrooms while the children eat. This will give the cook a chance to observe the reactions to the food and give her the pleasure of sharing the children's pleasure in good food that is well prepared.

SERVING FOOD

The director of a school for young children should see food service as an integral part of the total program. Mealtimes can provide the opportunity for children to learn a wide variety of concepts and develop a number of skills. Attitudes toward food that will last throughout the child's life may be acquired at this time. It is, therefore, important to plan mealtimes as carefully as other parts of the school program.

The director and staff must be clear about what they are trying to accomplish by serving food at school. In other words, what are their objectives? They must decide whether the only other objective is to provide a balanced diet, or if food service can also be used to help the children develop decision-making abilities, reinforce learning experiences, and increase social skills. Do they also want the children to be aware of foods that are part of the community's ethnic groups?

Food-related goals set up by the staff must be carefully carried out. The length of time set aside for eating may be important in achieving these goals. Staff attitudes may need to be examined and corrected in order to implement goals effectively. Scheduling mealtimes in relation to other learning activities also needs to be considered.

The director and her staff must periodically evaluate how well the food service program meets the goals. If one of the goals is to see that the children eat a balanced diet, the physical setting should be conducive to promoting appetite. Are the tables and chairs comfortable and the dishes attractive? Is the room orderly and pleasantly arranged? Is the air fresh and free from unpleasant odors?

If a goal is to develop decision-making ability, is the food set out in such a way that children can choose? Is the food presented in such a way that the children can serve themselves?

Teachers, director, and cook should periodically evaluate food service together. Are the objectives being achieved? If not, what is the reason? A joint discussion may clarify or change goals, or smooth out problems of implementation.

SUMMARY

What the child eats influences his physical health and growth patterns. Mental development and intellectual ability are also affected.

The director of a school may have to plan menus and supervise the kitchen. A basic knowledge of the food groups is necessary. She must also know the size portion that will provide the child with the proper nutrients.

Meals should be planned according to a knowledge of the foods children like, the facilities, and the equipment available for preparation and serving. The number of personnel available to prepare and serve food must be taken into account. Appetite appeal and the cultural meanings of food should be considered.

Careful food buying reduces waste and increases the quality of meals. Standards for quality should be set. Food should be bought in season. The director might consider joint purchasing with another school as a means to lower cost.

The best planned menus will not be successful if food is improperly prepared. Order

Fig. 14-7 **The lunch table is attractive and the food tastes good.**

and ease of preparation, and children's preferences should be considered. Foods should be presented in such a way that children can eat with ease and enjoyment.

Sanitary standards for preparing and serving foods should be maintained. Storage procedures should assure that foods are free from contamination or spoilage. Personnel involved in preparation and handling of food should be free of disease and must maintain high standards of cleanliness.

The director should consider food service as an integral part of the total program. Mealtimes can provide the opportunity for children to learn concepts and develop a number of skills. Careful implementation of goals must take into consideration the manner in which food is served. Periodic evaluation of food service insures that goals are being met.

STUDENT ACTIVITIES

- Prepare a poster to show the basic food groups. Plan a week's curriculum to teach young children about nutrition.

- Plan a week's menu for the school with which you are associated.

- Visit a school for young children. Ask the director where she purchases food and what factors she has to consider when purchasing food.

- Observe food preparation and serving in a school for young children. Evaluate, based on the information in the text.

- Discuss and compare experiences concerning foods that children like. Make a list of twenty foods that most children like. Compare lists; make one list of foods that all agree most children like.

REVIEW

1. Name four ways in which nutrition affects child development.

2. Name four factors to be considered when purchasing food.

3. Give some guidelines suggested for menu planning.

4. What should be kept in mind when children are served meals and snacks?

5. Name the basic four food groups and give at least three examples of each.

6. Why does proper nutrition play such a critical role in the development of children?

7. What step is the most important in the process of food service from menu planning to the time of actual serving?

8. What is the water temperature which should be maintained for washing dishes?

Unit 15 Planning the Physical Environment

OBJECTIVES

After studying this unit, the student should be able to

- Discuss factors that affect the arrangement of a play environment
- Plan a play environment for young children

Space and the objects in that space are of much greater importance to young children than they are to adults. The two- or three-year-old has only recently become able to move about by himself and has an intense desire to explore his surroundings. Well-planned play areas allow the child to practice a skill until he perfects it and then challenge him to acquire new skills. As his physical agility increases, the child feels a sense of mastery over himself and his environment. This feeling of mastery is essential for coping with later life experiences.

Active involvement in the physical environment also helps the child to acquire knowledge about his world. As he plays with objects he learns about their characteristics. He discovers whether they are hard or soft, big or little, round or square. As he moves himself, he learns concepts such as up and down, high and low, back and forth, in and out, beside and behind. Active play provides opportunities to learn time concepts as well. While waiting for a turn on the swing, the child comes to understand what a *few minutes* means. As he talks with the teacher about the next day's activities, he learns what *tomorrow* means. Finally, active play gives him the opportunity to learn about cause and effect. When he pushes a block building, it falls. When he drops a heavy object into water, it sinks.

A well-planned play environment invites and encourages social interaction with other children. The child learns to share when he must take turns with the bike or at the easel. He learns cooperation when another child's help is needed to lift a heavy board onto a box for climbing. Dramatic play allows him to pretend to be anyone he wishes to be and, thus, to find out how it feels to be that person. He also learns techniques that are needed to get along with other people.

The physical environment, then, is extremely important in determining the kinds of play activities that are suggested or available to the child. Since play is the basis for much learning by the child under the age of five, the environment must be the starting point of the curriculum of any good school for young children.

PLANNING THE ENVIRONMENT

Planning the play environment of a school for young children must be done with a great deal of care and thought. It must take into consideration all of the things that affect what the children do and what they learn there. All play areas of the school should be suited to the goals. Both indoor and outdoor space should reflect what the school wants to accomplish.

Goals

The goals of the program serve as guidelines in planning the physical environment. One of the goals of many programs is to develop the child's ability to care for himself. The environment must be planned so that he can hang up his own coat, wash his hands without help, and get his own play materials. If he must ask a teacher to get what he wants, the goal is not being met.

Another goal might be to further the child's appreciation of his cultural heritage. To meet this goal, the environment must provide a blending of cultures. This can be done by seeing that the dramatic play corner contains items that would be found in his home, and/or the room might be decorated with objects typical of the culture.

Program Types

The play areas of a school should be suited to the program type. A full-day child care center will be planned differently than a half-day school. The day care center will need to provide an area where the children may rest and some space for the storage of cots. There must be a pleasant and adequate area for meals. There must also be space for the children to be by themselves at times during the long day.

It was said earlier that the cooperative school is organized and owned by parents. In this kind of program the rooms will have to be large enough to accommodate the many adults who will participate during the course of the day.

Fig. 15-1 The environment is planned so that the child can care for himself.

Age Level

Play areas should be suited to the age level of the children using them. Different settings are required by children of different ages. A simple, small enclosed space is all that is usually needed for two- and three-year-olds. They often feel insecure if their play space is too large or has too much equipment in it.

As a general rule, four-year-olds need lots of space in which to run, to climb, to dig, and to pretend.

When the age level of the children is mixed, it is necessary to plan the space so that it provides a challenge for all the children, but is safe even for the youngest. There must be a variety of equipment and materials that can be used in different ways by children of diverse ages. As an example, boxes can be used in many ways. The youngest children may crawl inside them. The older children will be able to climb on top of them or pile the boxes even higher. The older children may also use them for dramatic play.

Climate and Weather

The play environment must be planned to suit the climate. In moderate climates, many activities can take place outdoors. Rooms should provide easy access to the playground so that children can go in and out freely. Painting, dramatic play, and blocks can all be done outside. Many of the science learning experiences can take place outside where the children can explore plants, look for bugs, and collect leaves.

When the climate is such that the children have to be inside much of the school year, many activities must take place indoors. Enough space has to be provided inside for climbing, jumping, and running so that excess energy can be used.

Variety

All play areas should provide for different uses and activities. Kritchevsky, Prescott, and Walling write about the classification of play space into units, based on contents in the space. The authors speak of *simple units* that have one obvious use and do not have subparts which enable a child to improvise. (Examples are swings, jungle gyms, rocking horses, and tricycles.) Their *complex unit* has subparts or has two units combined so that children can manipulate and improvise. (Examples are

Fig. 15-2 Boxes may be used in many ways.

Fig. 15-3 Enjoying a Simple Unit

digging equipment and a sandbox.) Also included in this category are simple materials such as art activities that encourage the child to improvise. The authors also describe the *super unit* which has one or more additional play materials next to each other. (Examples are a sandbox with play materials and water; a dough table with tools; and a tunnel with movable climbing boards and boxes.) Space planning should include a variety of units so that children can engage in a wide range of activities.[1]

Organization

Play space should be well organized. There should be sufficient empty space so that children can move around. The empty spaces can also be used to set up new play units. The play areas should be large, but not too large for proper supervision.

Pleasant, well-organized play areas allow children the opportunity to learn and to be creative. A variety of these play spaces offer more choices. They provide the means to develop many different skills.

Safe and adequate play materials should be readily available to the children. In this kind of environment the emphasis can be on learning how to get along with each other and how to develop self-direction.

Changeable Play Units

Whenever possible, play units should be flexible so that a different environment can be made by a few minor adjustments. Barriers that cannot be moved should be used as little as possible. A play area can be outlined by using shelves on wheels. Cupboards on casters can also be moved as needed.

Outdoors, some pieces of equipment such as swings or a jungle gym must be installed

Fig. 15-4 Complex Units

permanently. The placement of these should be planned carefully so there is still ample space for movable and changeable equipment.

Traffic Flow

Planning of space should consider the flow of traffic. The placement of doors and gates determines some of the traffic patterns; placement of equipment will also determine how teachers and children move from one place to another.

Equipment should be placed so that traffic flow does not interfere with activities that require concentration. A reading corner is more likely to be used by the children if it is away from the noise of persons coming and going. Block building can be used more extensively if it is planned for an area that is free from interruption.

The flow of traffic should be planned so that the children's safety is assured. For example, an area near the swings should not be

---

[1]Sybil Kritchevsky and Elizabeth Prescott, with Lee S. Walling, *Planning Environments for Young Children: Physical Space* (Washington, D.C.: National Association for The Education of Young Children), 1969.

used for bike riding; a child on a tricycle may not be watching for a swing and get hurt.

Storage

Adequate storage should be provided in all areas. Teachers and children should be able to get to materials without too much difficulty. Day care programs have the additional problem of finding storage for the children's cots. Adequate storage and ease with which they can be taken out is important to teachers. Day care programs may also need to have space where extra chairs can be stored. More chairs are needed at lunch time. They must then be put away in order to free the space for play.

Materials should be stored near the places where they are to be used. Children will not go very far to get materials they need. If the art materials are a long distance from the table, they are likely not to use them, or they may spill them on the way back to the table. If the cars and animals to be used with blocks are across the room, the children may not think of using them together. If the puzzles are not easily accessible, they will not be used at all.

Proximity

How close one area is to another should be considered in planning. Simple units may be placed together so that a complex or super unit is achieved. Thus, if the sandbox and dramatic play area are together, there may be the possiblity of using them for a cooking activity. If the boxes and boards are near the tricycle area, the children may begin a car wash.

Proximity to the building must be considered in planning the outside area. Often children will not use some pieces of equipment that have been placed a long distance from the building. For instance, they often need the reassurance of closeness to the building when they play in the sandbox. Other equipment needs to be close so that its use can be easily supervised. When the jungle gym is being used, an adult has to be nearby. It should be placed in an area where teachers are most likely to be present.

Fig. 15-5 Indoor Storage Area

Fig. 15-6 Outdoor Storage Area

Health and Safety

When an environment for children is planned, health and safety must be considered. Play areas should be clean and free from any condition that will be injurious. Equipment and building materials should be easy to clean and keep in good repair. In some areas, tile on the floor allows for easier cleaning after some activities. Carpeting on the floor may be best for other areas, but it should be kept clean.

The decision to buy a metal jungle gym is often determined by the fact that it requires little or no maintenance. A wooden one may be more attractive but requires frequent sanding and painting or varnishing.

The sandbox and its enclosure often present a problem. It should be placed in an area where the sun can dry it out after a rain. The enclosure should be chosen with safety in mind. Wood is often used, but it must be kept sanded to avoid splinters. Some sandboxes have plastic or concrete enclosures. Whatever selection is made, the director must be certain there are no sharp corners and that the enclosure is smooth and safe so no bruises or abrasions result from its use.

Children get dirt and paint on the walls. Wall coverings in the building should be attractive and easy to clean, with a finish that is not damaged by frequent cleaning.

Each classroom should have an area set aside for cleaning. The ideal situation would be to have an adult-size sink, and a lower, child-size sink. In this way, the children could help with the cleaning. The adults would also be able to do cleaning chores with ease. If it is not possible to have classroom sinks, a shared adult-size sink in the children's bathroom could be used by two classrooms.

Attractive Simplicity

Play areas should be planned with an eye to beauty. Outdoors, this includes the beauty of nature. Trees, shrubs, and flowers all add to the pleasure that children derive from their environment. A variety of surfaces such as grass, dirt, redwood chips, and sand make the outdoors more interesting to children.

Indoors, simplicity can be beautiful. Young children are soothed by a simple, uncluttered environment. When play areas are cluttered, children often use them in a confused, unorganized way.

The classroom is more pleasant if it has touches of color and is uncluttered. Each teacher should look at the overall picture of her classroom to visualize its lines and colors. For the most part, the classroom for young children has low furniture and cupboards. Most of the lines of the room should be at the child's eye level.

ASSESSMENT OF THE SCHOOL ENVIRONMENT

Few schools have everything that might be considered ideal in their building and yard. Most schools must try to make the best use of less than ideal conditions. Periodic assessment will help the director and staff decide whether

Fig. 15-7 Simplicity and Low Lines

the environment is meeting children's needs and where changes might be made. Several simple procedures are possible to accomplish such an assessment.

First Assessment Procedure

The first assessment procedure uses a list of the goals of the school. For each, the areas of the environment where the goal is met are recorded. Goals used in the following example are taken from unit 5.

Objective 1. The child should be able to initiate, carry through, and take pride in a variety of learning experiences available in the school setting. Areas meeting this objective are listed.

- Indoors: Learning centers
  Art center — choice of activities on shelf
  Dramatic play area
  Book corner with a selection of books
  Music center where child can play records or use an instrument
  Block corner with cars, animals, people

- Outdoors: Movable boxes for climbing and dramatic play
  Several kinds of wheel toys available
  Sandbox with a variety of accessories
  Jungle gym with planks and ladders for changeable additions

Objective 2. The child should begin to understand and accept differences in people, based on ethnic or cultural background. Areas meeting this objective are listed.

- Indoors: Accessories typical of different cultures in dramatic play corner
  Bulletin board with pictures of many different people
  Book corner with books about different cultures
  Cooking area for experiences with different foods

- Outdoors: Accessories typical of different cultures for dramatic play
  Musical instruments from different cultures

Second Assessment Procedure

A second method of assessment is based on the kinds of experiences that a school wishes to provide for children. These may be related to objectives, or they may be determined by the program type or the age level of the children served. For example, a day care center wants to give children opportunities for solitary play. A group of four-year-olds needs a greater variety of activities to challenge their curiosity than a group of three-year-olds. This type of assessment is shown in figure 15-8.

Third Assessment Procedure

The last type of assessment to be discussed is used to determine whether the variety of activities provided is adequate for the number of children using them at any one time. Pieces of equipment or activity areas are listed. Then an estimate of the safe or optimum number of children who can use each is made. A comparison of the number of children in a group or on the playground at one time and the number of play choices available determines the adequacy of the environment.

SUMMARY

Space and objects in that space have more impact on young children than they do on adults. Children are eager to explore and through their explorations develop physical skills, acquire knowledge, and learn how to get along with others.

ASSESSMENT OF EXPERIENCES AVAILABLE TO CHILD	
Experience	**Where Provided**
• Solitary play	• Dramatic play area, book corner, large boxes
• Developing curiosity	• Science corner, bulletin boards, book corner
• Encouraging independence	• Lockers for each child • Bathrooms with low toilets, towel dispensers, mirrors, washcloth hooks, toothbrushes • Selection of materials available on shelves (art, music, science)
• Social interaction	• Attractive dramatic play corner • Games for use at a table • Easels for two children

Fig. 15-8 Assessment of Experiences

ASSESSMENT OF EQUIPMENT AND ACTIVITY AREAS	
Item	**Safe or Optimum Number of Children Able to Use**
Jungle gym	6
Slide	4
Sandbox	8
Boxes, planks (4 each)	8
Bikes (6)	6
Playhouse	4
Rocking boats (2)	4
Water play area	4
Swings (3)	3
Total Outdoor Area	47
Art table	6
Easels	4
Block corner	4
Dramatic play area	3
Book corner	3
Manipulative toys at a table	4
Puzzles	2
Science table	2
Music corner	2
Cooking table	4
Total Indoor Area	34

Fig. 15-9 Assessment of Equipment and Activities

Planning the environment of a school for young children must be done with several considerations in mind. All play areas should be suited to the objectives of the school. The arrangement of the environment should reflect the needs of the program type. Play areas should be appropriate to the age level of the children. A small, protected environment is needed for two-year-olds. Four-year-olds, on the other hand, need more space in which to be active.

The effects of climate must be considered in planning. Moderate climates allow for many activities outdoors; other climates make it necessary to provide for many inside activities.

Beauty of indoor and outdoor space is important. Colors, simple lines, and trees and shrubs are all part of making attractive and pleasant surroundings.

Play areas should have variety and be well organized, yet flexible. This allows for a selection of activities but also leaves free areas.

Flow of traffic, storage, health, and safety must be considered. Play areas should be clean and free from hazardous conditions. Ease of storage and maintenance should be planned.

STUDENT ACTIVITIES

- Make a drawing of a classroom in the school with which you are associated. Place the furniture and equipment as it is now. How would you change it after studying this unit? What are your reasons for the change?

- Visit a school for young children. After observing the playground, discuss its planning in terms of the considerations covered in this unit.

- Draw plans for a school that you would consider ideal.

REVIEW

1. What does a director use as guidelines for planning the play environment of a school? What other factors must be considered?

2. Give examples of a simple, a complex, and a super unit of play space.

3. In what ways does climate affect the planning of the physical environment?

4. Why are space and objects in that space more important to children than to adults?

5. What are some ways to handle traffic patterns in a room?

6. Name some points to consider when planning for storage space.

7. Describe the method of assessment of the school environment that uses objectives as a base.

8. Name the other methods of assessment discussed in this unit.

Unit 16 Maintaining the Physical Environment

OBJECTIVES

After studying this unit, the student should be able to

- Give examples of maintenance problems and solutions
- Develop procedures for proper maintenance of the environment of a school

Any environment that is used by children is subjected to constant wear and tear. Playground equipment wears out and gets broken. Surfaces of walls and floors have paint, clay, and food spilled or smudged on them. Wooden toys and blocks become splintered from much use. Maintenance and upkeep is a constant problem; this is especially true in a day care program that is open for many hours during the day.

TIME

One of the most difficult problems for the director of a school for young children is to find a best time for cleaning and repair. When the school is in session all day, very little cleaning can take place. If the classroom has to be used for lunch and rest, there is no time for proper cleanup; the staff members scarcely have time to clear away lunch before getting the cots down for the rest period.

When children are using the yard all through the day, it is difficult to find time to rake, to water, or to cut the lawn. If this maintenance is done when the children are resting, they may be disturbed by the activity

and kept from sleeping. If it is done when the children are outside, they get in the way.

It is also hard to find time to do all the extra cleaning tasks of the school. When do the storage closets get organized? When is there time to dust off the shelves? When cleaning tasks are left undone or only done at infrequent intervals, they are more extensive and become overwhelming to the person responsible. Teachers who are aware of the importance of an orderly environment make use of opportunities to maintain it whenever possible. A few seconds to straighten out some materials in the supply closet each day can save a lot of time at some later date. A quick dusting of the shelves can be done when the children have removed all the blocks for building. When all of the doll clothes have been taken out of the box, it is easy to sort out those that need washing or mending.

At the beginning of each school year, the director and staff should discuss problems of maintenance and decide upon solutions. They will want to set up a schedule for daily cleaning of the rooms. One afternoon a month might be set aside for extra cleaning tasks. (Needless to say, if this time is scheduled outside of the usual working hours, teachers should be paid for their time.)

Some tasks must be done when the school is not in session, usually in the late afternoon or evenings. A housekeeper or cleaning service must be employed to clean the bathrooms, floors, walls, windows, kitchen, and office. Most directors have found that a part-time cleaning service is the best solution to this problem; two to four times a week is considered adequate. Because this service is often done at night, supervision

Task	Daily	Weekly	Twice Weekly	Monthly	Comments
HOUSEKEEPING SCHEDULE					
Bathrooms					
Toilets sanitized	x				
Washbowls cleaned	x				
Floor mopped	x				
Mirrors cleaned			x		
Towels refilled					As needed
Walls wiped				x	
Classrooms					
Floors wet mopped	x				
Floors waxed				x	
Carpets vacuumed			x		
Wastebaskets					
Emptied	x				
Washed			x		
Windows washed				x	
Stove cleaned				x	
Refrigerator					
Cleaned			x		
Defrosted				x	
Hallways					
Vacuumed		x			
Offices					
Vacuumed		x			
Dusted		x			

Fig. 16-1 Sample Housekeeping Schedule

is difficult. A carefully set up schedule for each task to be completed will help. Figure 16-1 is an example of this kind of schedule.

RESPONSIBILITY FOR MAINTENANCE

The second most difficult problem faced by the director in regard to cleaning and maintenance is deciding who will do it. As the cost of cleaning services increases, the director must consider how much a teacher should be expected to do.

Many teachers feel that cleaning is not part of their job responsibilities and that it takes away from their teaching activities. Some think that because young children are so messy themselves, an orderly environment is not important. A director may have to

point out that children play more constructively and for a longer time when their classroom is orderly. She may also demonstrate that the children enjoy putting their toys away or doing some of the other simple cleaning tasks.

Other teachers accept the premise that a good curriculum begins with the arrangement of the environment and that a sense of order in that environment is important to children. A basic part of the Montessori method concerns predictable order as a part of children's learning. Children are expected to put materials away so that the next child will be able to find them and use them.

Some kinds of maintenance must be done by hired individuals or by a business that

REPAIR AND MAINTENANCE SERVICES				
Name	Address	Telephone	Rate	Comments
Plumbing				
Carpentry				
Painting				
Paving				
Roofing				
Electrical				
Gardening				
General Repairs				
Other				

Fig. 16-2 Sample Repair and Maintenance Services Form

specializes in repair services. These tasks include painting the inside and outside of buildings, replacing floors and roof, resurfacing the driveway and parking area. Outside play equipment may need to be repaired, painted, or replaced. Finding someone to do this kind of work can present a problem. The director must explore various sources available for help. In some schools, parents are willing to take part in scheduled work days.

REPAIR AND REPLACEMENT RECORD					
Item	Repair	Replace	Repaint	Date Requested	Date Completed
Classrooms					
Tables					
Chairs					
Shelves					
Book cabinet					
Hollow blocks					
Floor blocks					
Record player					
Sand table					
Play Yard					
Swings					
Sandbox					
Sand					
Wheel toys					
Planks					
Boxes					
Jungle gym					
Playhouse					
Storage					
Office					
Typewriter					
Duplicator					
Adding machine					
Paper cutter					
Desk					
Chairs					
Bookshelf					
Grounds					
Driveway					
Parking lot					
Walks					
Garden					
Lawn					
Other					

Fig. 16-3 Sample Repair and Replacement Record

Community resources such as youth organizations, senior citizen's groups, or local programs for the handicapped can provide skilled workers. Local colleges or universities often have placement services with workers available. Once reliable services are found, the director should keep a record for easy reference. Figure 16-2 shows one way of recording this information.

When commercial sources such as roofing companies are to be used, the director should be sure to get more than one estimate of cost. Before a decision is made, several businesses should be asked for written estimates of cost, with detailed accounting of the work to be done and the expected date of completion.

RECORDKEEPING

Adequate records are the basis for good upkeep of the equipment and facility. One place to start is with a record of recommended repairs or replacements. This can be a list of all the equipment in the school and can be posted so that any staff member can record needs as they are noticed. If the date of the recommendation and the date of the completion of work are also included, the staff will see that maintenance of the environment is important to the director. If work gets done when requested, staff will be more likely to remain aware of conditions that need repair. Figure 16-3 shows a repair and replacement record.

A file on each piece of equipment should be kept. The file would show date and place of purchase, dates of cleaning, oiling, and repairs, and a description of the repairs made. Warranties and operating manuals for each should also be filed so they can be referred to when needed.

An annual inventory of equipment helps the director plan for future needs. Some equipment gets lost, broken, or worn beyond repair.

EQUIPMENT MAINTENANCE RECORD			

Item _____ Date Purchased _____ Price _____

Purchased from _____

Warranty No. _____ Manufacturer _____

Warranty Expiration date _____

Maintenance Record:

Service Date	Description	By whom	Charge

Fig. 16-4 Sample Equipment Maintenance Record

The annual inventory identifies the equipment that must be replaced. If this information is shared with the staff or if they take part in the inventory, their awareness of the value and need for proper care is increased. When the inventory also includes information concerning depreciation, on items where this is pertinent, it provides a record for tax purposes. Five-by-seven cards can be used to record the information discussed in this paragraph and in the preceding one. Examples are shown in figure 16-4 and figure 16-5. These can be separate cards, or two sides of the same card can be used.

SAFETY

The safety of the children entrusted to their care should be of primary concern to all staff members in a school for young children. A check list of potentially hazardous conditions should be reviewed on a regular basis. For each school, the list is different. Some of the most frequent items to be checked are listed:

- Playground equipment — splinters, breaks, worn parts
- Floors — overwaxing, torn or slippery rugs

- Bathrooms — should be sanitized on a regular schedule
- Kitchens — unclean counters, storage areas, improper storage of perishable items
- Flammable materials — unsafe storage near heat or where it can be reached by the children
- Locks on gates — inadequate or unsafe locks that make it possible for children to wander into the street
- Heavy materials stored on top of shelves — may fall during an earthquake or similar emergency

Every director should know how to cope with emergencies that might occur. For example, she must know how to shut off the water and gas if there is a leak and how to turn off the fire alarm if it rings without cause. Coping with emergencies is made easier if all shut-off valves are clearly and permanently marked. All staff members should also know their locations. A list of emergency telephone numbers — including police, fire department, and utility companies — posted in several places is a necessity. The school's physician on call and the nearest emergency hospital should also be on this list.

EQUIPMENT INVENTORY RECORD			
Item: _____ Date Purchased _____ Price _____			
Dates Inventoried	Accumulated Depreciation	Depreciation Current Year	Insurance Value

Fig. 16-5 Sample Equipment Inventory Record

Many directors find it helpful to learn how to do simple repairs around the school. It is not difficult to replace a washer in a leaky faucet or to tighten the bolts on the tricycles. Simple carpentry and painting tasks can also be done — even by someone who is not skilled. If the interest and time to do these repairs is present, the director can make use of inexperienced help and avoid more extensive and costly maintenance. She may also have a feeling of pride in being able to do these things herself.

SUMMARY

An environment that is used by children is subjected to constant wear and tear. It is difficult to find a best time for maintenance and repairs. It is also hard for the director to decide who should be responsible for maintenance. Many teachers feel that cleaning is not part of their job. It is sometimes difficult to find people who can do the repairs needed.

Adequate records are the basis for efficient upkeep of the equipment and facility. Some of the records that help to make this task easier are

- Housekeeping schedule
- Repair and maintenance services list
- Repair and replacement record
- Equipment maintenance record
- Equipment inventory record

The safety of the children entrusted to their care should be of primary concern to all staff members in a school. There should be a periodic review of a check list of potentially hazardous conditions. In addition, the director should know how to cope with emergencies that occur; all shut-off valves should be clearly marked so that they can be found easily. A list of emergency telephone numbers should be posted in several places in the school. Many directors find it helpful to learn to do simple repairs themselves.

STUDENT ACTIVITIES

- Discuss maintenance procedures used in your school. Are they adequate to maintain a clean, orderly environment?
- List the cleaning tasks that you do daily in your school. Have these been included in the job description for the job you have or are working toward?

REVIEW

1. Why is it so difficult to properly maintain an environment that is used by children all day?

2. What is the most feasible solution to the problem of cleaning bathrooms, walls, floors, the kitchen, and the office?

3. How do teachers usually feel about doing some of the cleaning?

4. List five records that make the tasks of maintenance easier for the director and the staff.

5. List seven potentially hazardous conditions that exist most often in early childhood schools.

6. In what, way does the director learn how to cope with emergencies that might occur in a school?

Unit 17 Health and Social Services

OBJECTIVES

After studying this unit, the student should be able to

- State goals for a health plan in a childhood center
- Discuss ways to implement health goals
- Name available resources for health and social services

The state of a child's health affects his behavior. Every mother knows that when her child is ill, he usually becomes listless and refuses to eat. He may also be irritable and restless during the night.

Teachers, too, see the results of a child's poor health. They notice the child who has limited energy and the child who is unable to concentrate. The sick child may withdraw from group activity or cry easily.

Concern for the health of young children should be a major part of every preschool program. How children grow and how they learn is affected by their total health status. Staff members can recognize a sick child who is not functioning at his best. They should also be able to recognize conditions that may have long-range effects if they are left untreated.

RECORDS

The safety and health of each child in the center may depend on available information. Assessment and maintenance of the child's health necessitate adequate recordkeeping. Each child enrolled in the school should have a file. Information in this file should be checked periodically and always kept current. Infor-

mation to be contained may vary from school to school but the following general categories should be considered.

Health

- **Physician's examination prior to entrance includes**

    General health status
    Any conditions that might interfere with functioning at school
    Immunizations
    Conditions that the school should be aware of such as allergies or seizures

- **Health screening tests or observations**

- **Continuing health care**

    Illnesses, surgery, injuries, current medications

Child Development

- **Information concerning the mother's pregnancy**
- **Developmental history from birth to school entrance (Different schools request different information.)**
- **Profiles done by teachers on a periodic basis**

Family Information

- **Application form** — including residence, place of work of both parents, family members

- **Emergency information** — including persons to contact in case the child is hurt or ill

- **Release for emergency medical treatment**

- **Persons authorized to take child from school**

- **Authorization** — for use of child's photo or voice recording for educational purposes

- **Permission** — to take child on trips away from the school

- **Financial arrangements for payment of tuition**

HEALTH GOALS

Health goals for a preschool program are concerned with improving the health and functioning of individual children. Implementation of the goals affect the health and functioning of the total family unit and community.

General health goals may include:

- Assessing the child's current health status and recommending treatment of existing problems

- Suggesting treatment for conditions that may become progressive

- Identifying and suggesting treatment for conditions that may interfere with how the child functions in school

- Instituting safety measures directed toward preventing conditions that may be hazardous to health

Assessing Current Health Status

When a child first enters a child care center, whether for part of the day or all day, it is important to know the current status of his health. For many children this is a first exposure to other children. For others it is a first experience outside their own home.

In accepting the child for care, the school must also assume responsibility for his health and safety. In day care centers, the school may assume the major part of this responsibility and offer direct services to children and families. Other schools may only see that the family seek the services that are needed.

In order to know what is needed, the school administration must know the child's health status at the time of enrollment. They must know that he has been immunized against communicable diseases. They must have a general idea of his development before he entered school.

Implementation of the first goal begins with a preenrollment physical examination of the child; this requires a report from a licensed physician which includes certification that the child is free from communicable diseases. The report also includes a description of any abnormal conditions and a record of immunizations.

Many schools will also require an interview with the parent to discuss the child's growth and development. The condition of the mother and child during pregnancy and delivery adds to knowledge about the child's health and development. General developmental history such as the age at which he began to walk or to talk will also help. Additional necessary information about allergies, illnesses, hospitalization, and accidents must also be part of his record.

Screening tests to identify any limitations in hearing, sight, or motor coordination may also be required. These tests can be done by nonprofessionals who have been taught how to administer them. There are also community resources for the administration of these tests.

STATE OF CALIFORNIA—HEALTH AND WELFARE AGENCY   DEPARTMENT OF HEALTH

CHILD'S PREADMISSION HEALTH EVALUATION
PHYSICIAN'S REPORT

STATEMENT TO PHYSICIAN

_____ born, _____ is being studied for
(Name of Child)   (Birth Date)

readiness to enter_____ . This day care facility provides a program which extends from
(Name of Day Care Facility)

_____ a.m. to _____ , _____ days a week. The daily activities include vigorous outdoor play, and play with groups

of _____children. The schedule includes morning and afternoon snacks of _____ , a noon meal,

a nap of _____ hours after lunch.

Will you please provide a report on above-named child using the form below?

_____   _____
(Signature of Parent, Guardian, or other Responsible Party)   (Date)

PHYSICIAN'S REPORT

Above-named child   { is not / is }   physically and emotionally able to participate in the day care program described above. Comment: _____

_____

_____

Child's physical conditions requiring special attention in the day care facility: _____

_____

_____

Medication prescribed or special routines which should be included in the day care plan for child's activities:_____

_____

_____

Immunizations given and dates: _____

_____

Test for TB: _____

Does child have any obvious ocular abnormalities? _____

Does vision seem to be adequate in each eye? _____

Date of my most recent examination of child: _____

_____   _____
(Physician's Signature)   (Date)

LIC 701 (7/73)

Fig. 17-1 Sample Preadmission Health Evaluation

STATE OF CALIFORNIA—HEALTH AND WELFARE AGENCY   DEPARTMENT OF HEALTH

CHILD'S PREADMISSION HEALTH HISTORY
PARENT'S REPORT

Name of Child _____ Birth Date _____ Sex _____

Father _____ Age _____ Living in home with child? ☐ Yes ☐ No

Mother _____ Age _____ Living in home with child? ☐ Yes ☐ No

Has child been under regular supervision of a physician? _____

Date of last examination by physician _____

Developmental History

Walked at _____ months. Began talking at _____ months. Toilet training started at _____ months.

Immunizations: Indicate whether given and approximate dates.

DPT 1st ____ 2nd ____ 3rd ____ Booster _____ Booster _____ Poliomyelitis _____

Mumps _____ Rubella _____ Measles _____

Past Illnesses: Check those child has had — give approximate dates.

Chicken Pox _____ Asthma _____ Rheumatic Fever _____

Ten-Day Measles (Rubeola) _____ Hay Fever _____ Diabetes _____

Three-Day "German" Measles (Rubella) _____ Epilepsy _____

Whooping Cough _____ Mumps _____ Poliomyelitis _____

Other serious or severe illnesses or accidents:

_____

Does child have frequent colds? _____ How many in last year? _____

Any allergies that staff should be aware of: _____

_____

Daily Routines

What time does child get up? _____ Go to bed? _____

Does child sleep during the day? _____ When? _____ How long? _____

Sleep well? _____

(OVER)

LIC 702 (6/75)   D OSP

Fig. 17-2 Sample Preadmission Health History

Eating: Usual hours _____

Diet pattern: Breakfast _____

                   Noon Meal _____

                   Evening Meal _____

Any food dislikes? _____

Eating problems? _____

Toilet habits: Bowel movements regular?_____ Usual time?_____

Word used for bowel movement? _____ Urination? _____

Parent's evaluation of child's health: _____

_____

_____

_____

Parent's evaluation of child's personality: _____

_____

How does the child get along with parents, brothers and sisters, other children? _____

_____

Has the child had group play experiences? _____

_____

Does the child have any special problems - fears? _____

_____

Plan for care when child is ill: _____

_____

Reason for requesting day care placement: _____

_____

                                 Signature of Parent: _____

                                          Date: _____

Fig. 17-2 Sample Preadmission Health History (continued)

Observations by teachers are also extremely useful in discovering a child's health problems. The teacher is in a position to observe the child for many hours during the week. She may be able to detect poor coordination or hyperactivity. She may recognize a possible hearing or vision impairment. She should notice behavior such as extreme tiredness or withdrawal from the group.

Treating Progressive Conditions

Certain health conditions will become progressively worse if left untreated. These conditions can have lasting and irreversible effects upon a child's health and ability to function. Examples are excessive tooth decay which could result in the loss of permanent teeth. Strabismus (crossed eyes) results in poor vision if left untreated. Malnutrition may cause permanent disturbance to the child's physical growth pattern. Behavior problems may affect learning and may become increasingly more difficult to treat successfully as the child grows older.

Some publicly funded preschool programs have comprehensive health care. Sometimes physicians may be called upon to spend a certain number of hours each week at the schools. One of their functions may be to identify and recommend treatment of conditions that are progressive. Schools which do not provide this service will refer families to private physicians or to clinics.

Some dentists volunteer their time or render services at a reduced rate. They examine children's teeth and may take care of any caries (decay). In many communities, dental schools offer services to families at reduced rates.

Nutritionists may play an important part in the health program of schools. They are able to help in diet planning and may also work with the physician and family to alleviate conditions of malnutrition. The nutritionist

Fig. 17-3 **The nurse gets developmental information.**

should be encouraged to help in planning for health needs of the children.

Psychologists or psychiatrists can also offer valuable services to the school. They are able to determine probable causes of learning disabilities. They may be able to assess behavioral disorders to determine if intervention is necessary. Working with parents and staff is also an important part of their involvement with the children.

Social services are necessary in some schools for young children. Social workers help parents and children with the problems of adjusting to school. Social workers provide counseling to families about problems with siblings (brothers and sisters) of the school child and may help families to find services recommended by other health personnel.

Not all centers can offer the comprehensive services outlined here. When money cannot be budgeted for extensive health care services, the school sees its responsibility as identifying the need for health care and referring the family for the service. The referral may be made to the child's own physician or to a community resource.

Identifying Learning Problems

Some health problems severely limit the child's ability to learn or to take advantage of the curriculum of the school. Many of these can be treated more easily and more quickly in early childhood. If left untreated, the child's total school experience may be affected.

Visual and hearing conditions certainly affect the child's ability to learn. If he is unable to see well, he may not develop the ability to discriminate objects or shapes. This will have a profound effect upon his ability to read. If he cannot hear, his speech may be affected.   He may have difficulty understanding directions or learning how to pronounce words. He may withdraw from contact with others.

The child with mental retardation or minimal brain damage may sometimes be helped if the condition is diagnosed and treated during early childhood. With proper supervision and guidance, a retarded child may begin to develop his capabilities. He may be able to learn to care for himself and to better perform the things he can do. It is possible for a child with minimal brain damage to exercise the use of other areas of the brain. If coordination is affected, for instance, special exercises may be prescribed to improve muscle control.   If there are perceptual problems, intensive prescribed work may help to overcome them. The physician and family should work closely with the director and staff.

Some children may need help with speech difficulties. The rate at which children develop speech varies greatly; clarity of speech also shows wide variation. However, in some cases, it becomes evident during the early school years that time will not eliminate problems. Poor muscle tone or malformations of the mouth may indicate that the child must be trained to speak correctly.

Behavior problems in the young, preschool child may also call for intervention. Extreme aggression or withdrawal and problems with eating, sleeping, or elimination are some examples.

Preventing Future Problems

Each school should employ measures that help to prevent future health problems for the children and their families. Providing a safe environment helps to decrease the possibility of endangering a child's health.

Policies and procedures should be established to insure a safe and sanitary environment for children and staff. All classrooms and equipment must be planned and maintained with safety in mind. The total environment of the school must be clean and free from unsanitary conditions. The staff must be trained to be alert to proper supervision to prevent accidents.

Each school should establish procedures for handling possible disasters that would affect the safety of all the children. Traffic patterns for evacuating the building in case of fire should be well known by every staff member.   Periodic drills help both children and staff to be familiar with the procedure. In various areas of the country, disasters such as earthquakes, tornadoes, or floods may have to be anticipated and planned for.

Local and state laws which apply to safety are discussed in more detail in unit 23.   Before employment, all staff members should be required to have a physical examination, including a chest X ray. Most schools require all employees to have a yearly examination also.   All staff members should be encouraged to maintain high standards of personal health.   This means that teachers should stay home when they are ill. It also means that all employees of the center must be concerned with cleanliness in their personal habits and their dress.

Everyone working with children should know how to administer first aid and be able to meet emergencies that might occur in a group of children. Bleeding, choking, burns, and head injuries are some examples of these emergencies.   Teachers should know what to do when they occur. They should also know what not to do; complications often arise from the mishandling of a situation. Communities offer first aid courses; excellent manuals are available.

A procedure for handling accidents should be established by the school and known by every staff member. The telephone number and address of the nearest hospital must be easily available. A release from the parents for emergency care is kept in each child's file.

School policy should require that parents are called when accidents occur, even those that are minor. The parents will be less anxious about injuries if they have been told about them before they come to get their children. For injuries that are more serious, the parents may have to decide if they feel treatment is necessary. The children's records should include the telephone number of a relative or family friend in case neither parent can be reached.

Policies concerning inspection and exclusion of children who are ill should be established by the administration. Whenever a child complains of not feeling well, he should be

SUGGESTED SCHEDULE	2 months	4 months	6 months	1 year	15 months	1½ years	4-6 years	14-16 years	Adults	Elderly (over 65) & Chronically Ill	COMMENTS
DIPHTHERIA-TETANUS-PERTUSSIS	✓	✓	✓			✓	✓				
POLIO	✓	✓				✓	✓				Not for adults living in the U.S. unless actively exposed
MEASLES					✓						Little danger of getting measles after fifteen
TB TEST				✓					✓		No need to repeat more than twice if test results are negative
RUBELLA (German Measles)					✓						A woman of childbearing age can be tested for immunity
MUMPS					✓						Also recommended for pre-pubertal males if not already immune
TETANUS-DIPHTHERIA								✓			And every ten years afterward
INFLUENZA										✓	Once a year

Fig. 17-4 Recommended Schedule for Active Immunization and Tuberculin Testing of Normal Infants and Children

examined by the nurse or another qualified person. If there are signs of illness, he should not be allowed to stay at school. However, a few schools provide care for children with mild illnesses.

Preventive measures will also include a schedule for immunizations. Administration and staff should know if the school child and other children in the family have been protected against communicable diseases.

Generally speaking, children from one to four years of age should have been immunized against diphtheria, tetanus, pertussis (whooping cough), measles, rubella (German measles), and polio — certainly, by the time they enter first grade. The mumps vaccine is now being added to the immunization schedule, and some states still require smallpox vaccination. A booster of combined immunization called DTP (diphtheria, tetanus, pertussis) is often given at 4 to 6 years of age; a triple booster of the oral Sabin vaccine may be given also at this time. According to U.S. Center for Disease Control, surveys show that there is an "alarming trend of declining immunization levels." It has been estimated that up to 10 million children between the ages of one and four are not protected against one or more of the major diseases which can be prevented.

Personnel in the child care centers should immediately contact their local health departments for further information when it is found that a child has not received immunization shots. This information should be given to the parents; follow-up must be done. An immunization schedule currently recommended is shown in figure 17-4.

Family health problems should also be the concern of the school. A mother who is chronically ill cannot properly care for the child. A sibling with untreated behavior problems may seriously affect the younger child. Other family health problems include nutrition, family planning, care for aged members, and prenatal care.

Health education is an important part of the child care programs. Health education and prevention of disease should be directed at the entire family, not just the child who is enrolled. Children can be taught the basics of good health in the school and in the family. They can learn to brush their teeth, wash, and eat properly. They can learn the value of sleep and rest. They can also be taught to protect themselves from injury. Safety hazards should be emphasized to and by the entire staff.

Staff members who are interested in the children with whom they interact can see

Fig. 17-5 Children learn to brush their teeth properly.

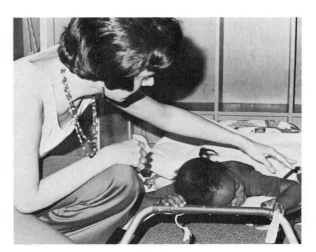

Fig. 17-6 In day care centers, rest time is needed.

signs of possible impairment: the child who squints and peers too closely at pictures and books, the child who cocks his head to one side so he can hear better, the child who sneezes and breathes with difficulty when a plant or flower is examined. These observations may serve as a basis for visual, hearing, and allergy referrals. Future emotional problems may be avoided when a physical disorder is found and treated.

UTILIZING COMMUNITY RESOURCES

A comprehensive health care program for young children and their families involves many different people and many different health fields. Planning should be done jointly by the school and community agencies so that quality services are available at the least expense. The school program should not duplicate services that are readily available in the nearby community.

Individuals as Resources

The staff and administration can involve professional people and professional associations in their plan for an effective school health program. Some examples of these resources are listed:

- Nurses
- Physicians
- Dentists
- Child psychiatrists
- Optometrists
- Medical technologists and clinical laboratories
- Mental health counselors
- Speech and hearing therapists
- Psychologists
- County and state medical societies
- Local, regional, and state health officers

- Pediatricians and pediatric nurse practitioners

Publicly funded schools generally have easy access to this extensive variety of services; small schools or private schools may have to find ways to obtain them. Sometimes two or more schools may plan their health programs together and use consultant help. Parents should also be involved in the health plan for the school since they have the final responsibility for the child.

Agencies and Organizations

A comprehensive health care program for young children and their families will also involve agencies and organizations. These can be the source of funds to support the services. They can also be called upon to provide the direct services.

Each community has different resources, but the director will find it helpful to investigate the following as possible sources of funds and services.

- City, county, and state health departments
- School health programs
- Clinics
- Neighborhood health centers
- Child health centers
- Dental service agencies
- State crippled children's programs
- Medicaid
- Insurance and prepaid plans

Some associations help children with specific handicaps. Sources of funds for health services may be the following agencies.

- Family service organizations
- Civic clubs, women's clubs, and PTA
- Church associations

- Associations for retarded children
- Crippled children's associations
- Tuberculosis associations
- Mental health associations
- Visiting nurse associations

When administration, parents, and staff are committed to good health for the children, they will find that there are extensive resources available.

SUMMARY

Because poor health has an immediate effect upon a child, concern for health should be a part of every program for young children. Health goals should assess the child's present status and treat conditions that interfere with school functioning. The administration must establish safety measures to avoid hazards to the child's future health.

Assessing the health status begins with an examination by the family physician before enrollment. Screening tests to identify limitations in hearing, sight, and coordination may be required. The developmental history may be obtained from the parents. Observations by teachers also provide valuable information.

The administration will follow up on conditions that might become worse if left untreated such as dental caries, strabismus, malnutrition, and behavior problems. The services of health personnel can be used. The school budget may provide for these services. They may also be obtained through community resources.

Some conditions such as visual and hearing loss may interfere with the child's ability to learn. Speech difficulties may require special training. Some behavior problems may be treated more easily during the early years.

Policies and procedures that help to provide a safe and sanitary environment should be established. There should be a known and established procedure for handling any accidents or injuries to children. Staff members should be knowledgeable in first aid. Morning inspection, immunizations requirements, and health education are part of the plan for preventing disease by maintaining health.

A comprehensive health care program for young children involves many different health fields and personnel. In order to provide the highest quality services, all available services of community agencies, organizations, and people should be utilized.

STUDENT ACTIVITIES

- Visit the health department in your community. What services are available to children? What are the requirements for using these services?
- Look in your telephone book under the listings for physicians. How many pediatricians are there?
- Find out the location of the emergency hospital nearest to the school with which you are associated. Is the telephone number posted in the school office? Are taxi telephone numbers posted? Do you know the most direct route to get to the hospital?

REVIEW

1. Name at least three health goals for a program in schools for young children.

2. Why is it important for the director to see that these goals are implemented?

3. Name two health conditions that will become progressively worse if left untreated.

4. Who may assess behavioral disorders in the child?

5. How can the director and staff members meet school emergencies?

6. Why should it be necessary to have a knowledge about routine immunizations?

7. What immunizations should a child have by the time he is four years old?

8. What sources may be contacted for up-to-date information about control of disease?

9. Name three examples of behavior that might call for referrals.

10. What are some community resources for health and social services? What are some individual resources?

Unit 18 Volunteers

OBJECTIVES

After studying this unit, the student should be able to

- Name factors to consider when planning a volunteer program
- List sources for recruiting volunteers
- Explain the role of the coordinator of volunteers

Many schools use unpaid people to perform staff functions. Publicly funded schools often require participation by volunteers. Community day care centers use volunteer help as a way to gain greater community support; some schools use it to decrease the cost of operation.

PLANNING FOR VOLUNTEER SERVICES

Board members, the director, the staff, and parents all should be involved in determining the role of the volunteer before a program for volunteers is started. It is not enough just to decide to use volunteer help to gain support or cut costs. All persons involved must feel that volunteers can really be of value to the school.

After the decision to use volunteer services is made, the functions of the school operation are examined. Decision is then made on what functions the volunteers could perform, depending on their background. All jobs should be considered, from administration to maintenance.

Thinking should also be directed toward new ways in which volunteers could add to the program or services. Many volunteers have had extensive background and experience. Some may be unemployed college graduates, retired business men and women, parents, and retired teachers. Their suggestions can help with curriculum development. Planning and carrying out the redecoration of the building might be another volunteer assignment.

The Volunteer Coordinator

When the concept of using volunteer services has been accepted, a coordinator is appointed. This person may be a staff member whose job can be redefined. In some schools, the budget will allow for a separate position; often, the director must assume the responsibility of coordinating the volunteer program. When the volunteer service has been used for a long period of time, it may be possible to select one of the volunteers as coordinator.

The importance of having one person responsible for volunteer services cannot be overemphasized. The coordinator can also function as supervisor of volunteers. Volunteers are unpaid and sometimes untrained. In order for the contribution of their time to be meaningful to them, they need to receive something in return. They must feel that someone knows they are there and working hard. They need to feel they are learning something and that their efforts are appreciated.

RECRUITING VOLUNTEERS

How the coordinator accomplishes the task of finding volunteers varies with the size of the school. In a small organization, volunteers are often found among persons known to the staff, parents, or board members. Larger organizations, that may need a greater number of volunteers, may have to use broader recruiting techniques.

Senior citizen groups are a good source of volunteer help. Often, elderly persons in a community want to do something constructive with their time. Many are ideally suited to offering mothering relationships to children in day care centers. Retired men can often add to the program of a school through use of skills they learned while working.

The local high school or junior high school may be another source for volunteers. Young people often want to learn more about child care and offer to help after school. Some high schools have child development programs that allow their students released time to

spend in nearby early childhood schools. These young people can bring vitality and interest to the children and can be a great help to the staff.

Nearby colleges or universities can also be a source of volunteers. The student service organizations or clubs may be pledged to work with young children. Future teachers often gain additional experience through this kind of activity while they are completing their training.

The neighborhood in which the school is situated is also a source for volunteers. Often residents have walked by the school and have seen the children. They may already have some knowledge of the school's program. Publicity in a local newspaper or direct door-to-door publicity may find persons who are interested. A notice on the door or fence of the school may also be seen by the local residents.

If the city has a volunteer bureau, listing the need with this bureau is another way to reach large numbers of people. Wide publicity may be required if large numbers of

Fig. 18-1 A Senior Citizen Volunteer

Fig. 18-2 A college student works with a small group of children.

volunteers are sought. Newspapers with wide circulation may consent to carry an article about the school and its need for volunteers. An advertisement can also be placed in the paper.

Any recruiting appeals or materials should be kept positive in tone. Reference should not be made to poor or underprivileged children. The feelings of the parents of the children in the school should always be remembered. Recruiting information should emphasize what the center is doing, and offer the prospective volunteer an opportunity to share in the work of the school.

SCREENING VOLUNTEERS

It is not necessary to accept all persons who wish to volunteer their time. It should be made clear to every applicant that there is a screening process. Screening will help to make the experience more meaningful to each volunteer accepted by matching the person to a job. Applicants who are not chosen can be helped to find other places to use their abilities.

A written application for volunteers is recommended. The following information should be included on the application.

Name, address, telephone number
Educational background
Interests and hobbies
Car, license, insurance coverage
Special training (dance, music, art, for example)
Work experience
Kinds of volunteer work desired

Each volunteer applicant should be interviewed by the coordinator or staff member in charge of volunteers. The interview is directed primarily to the applicant's interests and abilities; ways should be explored to use these in the school setting.

If the volunteer wishes to work with the children, his or her suitability to do so must

be considered. Questions concerning why the person wishes to work with children will be helpful. The health and physical stamina of an elderly person must also be considered. The prospective volunteer may visit the classroom for a short period; observation by the coordinator will yield information about the volunteer's effectiveness with children.

When volunteers have been chosen, a regular schedule should be agreed upon. If the school is going to depend upon the services of the volunteers, it will be necessary for the volunteers to understand the importance of keeping their commitment; this is particularly important when assigned to work with children. Children may adjust more easily to the presence of many different adults if they know that each will be there at definite times.

Volunteers who are to work with children should also be assigned to one group and one teacher. It is too difficult for an untrained person to learn to work with several teachers and large numbers of children.

Fig. 18-3 A volunteer should become part of a group.

ORIENTATION OF VOLUNTEERS

Before volunteers begin their work assignment, they should attend an orientation. An orientation period may be only one day or it may extend over a week.

Orientation should be a joint effort of those persons responsible for the operation of the school. Where appropriate, this means that board members as well as staff and parents will plan and conduct the orientation sessions. Orientation can be a means for staff to develop their skills for working with adults. It can also help board members and parents to clarify their knowledge about the school.

Orientation should cover all aspects of the school operation so that the volunteer gains an understanding of the school. Persons doing office work should know what happens in the classrooms so that routine work will become meaningful to them. A tour around the facility or to other facilities might be included.

Allow time for introductions of all those present. Unscheduled time should be allowed for informal talking so that people can get to know each other. Time should also be allowed for the volunteer to ask questions.

Orientation should cover some general topics as shown.

- Organizational matters: the structure of the school, staff members, children's groups
- Educational matters: program objectives and how they are implemented
- Developmental information: ages of the children, general information about the children, and what to expect from them
- Responsibilities of volunteers: general expectations, schedules, and assignments in written form
- Supervision of volunteers: who will supervise, who will evaluate, who should be consulted when there are problems

HANDBOOK FOR VOLUNTEERS

A handbook of information needed by volunteers will make it easier for both coordinator and volunteers. In addition to the topics covered in orientation, the following might be included.

- Rules and regulations
- Sample time sheets and instructions for signing in and out
- Sample of evaluation forms
- Suggestions for activities to do with the children
- Suggestions for ways of dealing with common incidents with the children
- Safety rules for the children and the staff
- Rules for field trips or excursions
- DOs and DON'Ts for working with the children

This information should be kept short and to the point. Volunteers cannot be expected to spend many hours studying the material.

Continued on-the-job training should be planned for volunteers. Part of their scheduled time could be devoted to attending workshops, films, discussions, or visits to other schools. Persons working with children will benefit from a workshop in children's art materials, or science experiences. Persons involved in fund-raising activities could benefit from a discussion with a professional fund raiser. Films that are used for teacher training may be suitable for volunteers. Discussions with staff members add to the skills and knowledge of volunteers.

SUPERVISION OF VOLUNTEERS

The same principles of good supervision that apply to staff also apply to supervision of volunteers. The coordinator must see that each volunteer knows exactly what is expected.

Fig. 18-4 Supervision helps the volunteer to develop further skills.

The specific tasks to be performed should be made clear. The limits of the volunteer's job should also be clear. Times and schedules must be available in written form.

When new tasks are assigned, the volunteer must be shown how to perform the task. When a task is mastered, the volunteer is free to perform the task with minimal supervision.

As with staff members, the volunteers' abilities should be recognized and their limitations understood. Achievements should be praised. The relationship between the staff and the volunteers should be such that the volunteers feel they contribute to the program. The supervisor should approach volunteers as though they were coworkers; they should not be treated as privileged members simply because they are not being paid.

EVALUATION OF VOLUNTEERS

Evaluation of the use of volunteers should be in two parts. First, the volunteers themselves and the jobs they perform should

be evaluated. Second, the volunteers should have an opportunity to evaluate the volunteer corps and the use that the school makes of their time.

Evaluation of volunteers is similar to the evaluation of staff members. The supervisor should make periodic observations of the volunteers performing their jobs. Written evaluations may be made. A review of the observation and written evaluation is made in conference with each volunteer. Plans should be made jointly to help each person develop further skills as needed.

Periodic meetings are to be held with all volunteers. Problems can be discussed at this time. Plans for the development of skills as a group can also be discussed. Individual weaknesses are not discussed at this time.

RECOGNITION OF VOLUNTEERS

Some method of formal recognition of volunteer services should be implemented by the school. A certificate of merit may be designed and used for this purpose.

One-time service by individuals or groups may be followed by a letter of thanks or a token gift. Someone who has done something special for or with the children might enjoy a picture made by the children.

A party for the volunteers is another way to show appreciation for their services. This could be the kind of event that includes the children, such as a weekend picnic, or it might be a more formal affair such as a dinner for adults only. Some schools have developed a merit system that awards a pin to volunteers completing a specified number of hours of service.

RECORDS OF VOLUNTEER PROGRAM

An effective volunteer program may need to develop records. This is more likely to be done in a large organization. Records insure continuity of the program with noted changes in coordinator, volunteers, and staff. Records also make it easier for volunteers to understand the importance of their contribution to the school. It helps to know how many volunteer hours have been contributed during the year and what duties were performed. Records may also provide information for other centers who may wish to start a volunteer service.

Records of the volunteer program should include some or all of the points listed:

- Overall plan and objectives
- Kinds of work open to volunteers
- Lists of groups, agencies, or other sources for recruiting volunteers
- Applications for volunteer work
- Starting dates and termination dates for each volunteer
- Jobs filled by volunteers and by whom
- Notes of orientation sessions
- Evaluations of volunteers
- Evaluations of the program
- Minutes of meetings concerning the service
- Record of awards given for service
- Correspondence relating to the program

Use of volunteer services requires investment of time; however, this time may yield extensive returns to the school.

SUMMARY

Many schools use unpaid persons to perform staff functions. Board members, the directors, the parents, and the staff should all be involved in determining the role of the volunteer before they implement a volunteer corps.

When the concept of using volunteers has been accepted, a coordinator should be appointed. The director may assume this responsibility, or it may be a budgeted, separate position.

The method of recruiting volunteers is determined by the number needed. In a small school, volunteers can be found among persons known to staff, parents, or board members. If larger numbers are needed, the coordinator must go to other sources: senior citizen groups, local high schools, nearby colleges or universities, neighborhood around the school, or newspaper articles. A screening process should be set up similar to that used for staff positions.

Orientation for volunteers should be planned and include information about the children's program.

A manual for volunteers and continued on-the-job training may also be a part of the volunteer program. The manual will include material covered in the orientation, rules for volunteers, time sheets, and samples of evaluation forms.

Supervision and evaluation of volunteers is important. Recognition of volunteer services should be included. A certificate, a party, or a merit pin are ways that schools can show their appreciation to the volunteers.

An effective volunteer program has records to show and insure continuity of the program; changes in coordinator, volunteers, and staff are indicated. The use of volunteers should yield extensive returns to any school willing to make an investment of time.

STUDENT ACTIVITIES

- Visit a school that uses volunteer help. Observe and record what the volunteers do.
- Discuss the role of the director as coordinator of volunteers.
- Role play an interview with a prospective volunteer.

REVIEW

1. What general factors must be considered in planning a program for volunteer help?

2. How does one go about recruiting volunteer assistance?

3. What general topics are covered in the orientation of a volunteer?

4. How does screening volunteers help the program?

5. Name three ways to provide on-the-job training for volunteers.

6. Name some items which should be included in a handbook for volunteers.

7. Of what value is a handbook of information?

8. How should volunteers be treated?

Unit 19 Student Teachers

OBJECTIVES

After studying this unit, the student should be able to

- Describe the role of the director with student teachers
- List the criteria for choosing a supervising teacher
- Discuss student reactions to the teaching experience

Many private colleges, public community colleges, and universities offer a curriculum in child development. As part of the requirement for a certificate or degree, the student must spend a specified amount of time in practical experience with young children.

Although some colleges or universities have a laboratory school in which students do practice teaching, many do not. In some, the demand for practice-teaching placements cannot be filled in the laboratory school on campus. Therefore, early childhood schools in the nearby vicinity are often used for placement of student teachers. Because of this, directors of private or public preschools may have the opportunity to work with student teachers. They may also have the benefit of a professional relationship with the college or university through the faculty member designated as advisor of student teachers. This person makes regular visits to the school to meet with the staff and to observe student teachers.

CHARACTERISTICS OF STUDENT TEACHERS

Student teachers, like volunteers, are unpaid. How they differ from volunteers should be understood by those who work with student teachers.

Student teachers have had some educational background and contact with children before they reach the practice teaching experience. They will have had courses in child development and in curriculum. They may have had a separate course in the observation of children.

Student teachers are receiving college credit for the teaching experience. This presupposes a serious commitment to the assignment and completion of a required number of hours within a specified period of time. Many of the responsibilities of teaching are to be assumed by student teachers. Students want to experience every aspect of teaching they can include in the time allowed.

Because the practice teaching experience is evaluated, student teachers know that their careers may depend upon how well the practice teaching is done. This situation can create a great deal of anxiety for them.

With the current emphasis on early childhood education, persons of all ages are entering the teaching field. Recognition of the characteristics of student teachers brings about better understanding and cooperation.

Many student teachers are in their early twenties; some of them may have had younger brothers and sisters. Age and experience place these young students of early childhood education somewhere between adolescence and adulthood in their own development. They will probably still be developing the kind of mature behavior and responses required of a teacher. On the other hand, their youth enables them to enjoy and appreciate the activities of the school.

Some student teachers may be young men. Today's male college students are not afraid to enter a field previously thought to be for women; they have found they can be successful in working with young children. They can offer some important experiences and relationships to young children. Men are particularly important in schools where many of the children do not have a father in the home.

The older woman student who has had children of her own brings maturity and experience. She can form effective relationships with children; she also knows what to expect of children at each age level. Often she shows ability to cope with problems that might upset a younger student teacher.

ROLE OF THE DIRECTOR

The role of the director in student teaching is very important. It is the director who must make the experience work for the school, the supervising teacher, the student, and the college or university.

The director must recognize that accepting students for practice teaching requires an investment of time and energy. The teacher to whom the student is assigned must spend time with the student almost every day. The director must be prepared to show recognition of the teacher's efforts in some way. Increased salary is one way. Relief from some other responsibilities might be another. The

teacher must be assured that the director is available for support or help when needed.

Some teachers may not be ready or feel capable of working with student teachers. The director must respect a teacher's wish not to have a student. She should, however, discuss the reasons in confidence and with understanding.

The director notifies the teacher well in advance of the time when a student is to be placed in the classroom. The teacher should have plenty of time to prepare herself and the children for the introduction of the student teacher.

A college which offers a degree in early childhood education may appoint an advisor or supervisor to coordinate the student's practice teaching with the college program. When the college has such a person on its staff, the director and teacher who will be the student's master teacher meet with the college advisor to outline the expectations for the student. Sometimes the college may have a handbook describing the desired outcomes; if so, there must be time for a thorough discussion of the handbook as well as a free exchange of ideas and goals.

Fig. 19-1 Student teacher, director, and college advisor discuss student teaching.

The role of the advisor should be clearly understood by both the director and the teacher. The teacher needs to know when the advisor will visit, what she will be observing, and how involved she will be with the students.

The director works closely with the college in order to place the student with the appropriate master teacher. Student and teacher should be matched so that conflicts in personality and teaching style can be avoided.

During the placement period of the student, the director must be available to all those concerned with the student. It has been mentioned that she must be available to support the teacher. She must also be available to talk with the college advisor when problems or questions arise. There may be times when it is she who can be most helpful to the student.

The director should participate in meetings or workshops scheduled by the college. Often these are provided to help community schools learn more about the total curriculum. Meetings also provide the opportunity to learn more about making the student's teaching experience meaningful for all concerned.

CHOOSING A MASTER TEACHER

In community schools where all teachers may not work with student teachers, the director must use her knowledge to determine which teachers are capable of guiding students. As stated previously, the first consideration should be the teacher's willingness. No teacher should be forced to accept a student unless she wants to; neither would benefit from a relationship such as this.

The second criterion is the teacher's willingness to share. She must be able to share her knowledge, materials, and time. Most important of all, she must be willing to share her relationship to the children with the student.

Third, the teacher must have enough self-confidence so she can accept questioning

Fig. 19-2 The master teacher and the student discuss a child's behavior.

or differences of opinion from a student. Because they have had courses in curriculum and methods of teaching, many students have their own ideas about teaching style. They should be able to question why an experienced teacher does things differently; they also need the opportunity to test theoretical knowledge against experience.

Fourth, the master teacher must be the kind of person who can allow other adults to make mistakes. She does this gracefully and without interference. Many teachers can make this allowance for children but are intolerant of adults. Sometimes, teachers step into a situation too quickly and do not allow enough time for the student to learn how to deal with it.

Fifth, the master teacher should be encouraging. She should be able to express confidence that the student will learn. Often reassurance that the ability to teach does not happen overnight is helpful. The ability to laugh with the student about what went wrong may decrease tension and encourage the student to improve teaching methods.

Sixth, the master teacher must be a good model for the student to observe. She must be capable of interacting effectively with children. She must be knowledgeable in curriculum planning and able to carry out learning experiences for the children.

ORIENTATION OF STUDENT TEACHERS

The student, master teacher, director, and college advisor should meet for an orientation period before the student begins practice teaching. The orientation consists of information about the early childhood center and about college requirements. Discussion would cover such topics as organization of the childhood center, goals and objectives, characteristics of the group the student is to teach, student responsibilities, and details of assignments, evaluation, and counseling procedures. Information about the children is given at this time, also.

Students are told about the goals of the school. They are given a copy of the school's objectives and should be informed of the ways in which these objectives are implemented.

Each student should have an opportunity to meet with the master teacher to get specific information about the assigned group. Because students are to become professionals, they may be allowed more detailed information about the children they will work with than would be given to volunteers. This action, of course, is at the discretion of the director and is based on school policy.

Information about the college or university is the second part of the orientation. Students and staff must know details of the assignment, such as the number of hours, the number of weeks, and the procedure for reporting illnesses and absences.

Students and staff need to know what student responsibilities are. If lesson plans are to be expected, they should be discussed and related forms distributed. The kinds of learning experiences which the student must plan and participate in should be clear to all.

Grading or evaluation methods should also be clarified by the college supervisor. The evaluation form should be given to staff and students for comments and questions. The date when evaluations are due should also be stated.

Counseling and student conferences should be outlined at this time. Usually a student first contacts the master teacher to discuss problems that arise about her teaching experience. The advisor at the college may be the next source. The director is an additional source of help or information. If necessary, the teacher, student, director, and advisor may find it necessary to discuss a problem together.

RESPONSIBILITIES OF THE MASTER TEACHER

The master teacher is the key person when students are placed in community schools. It is the master teacher who sees the student every day; it is she who helps the student to develop the skills of teaching. It is the master teacher who gets to know the student better than either the college supervisor or the director.

It is the responsibility, then, of the master teacher to create a climate in which each student with whom she works can develop to the maximum of his or her ability. Some practical suggestions for the master teacher may be helpful:

- The master teacher should become familiar with whatever information is available concerning the student. A student file containing biographical information, academic background, and experience should be available through the college or university.

- The student should be introduced to the children, parents, and other staff members. In general, the student should be treated like a colleague.

- An opportunity should be provided for the student to become familiar with the total school environment and the room assignments.

- Long-range and short-range goals for the class should be discussed with the student.

- The master teacher and the student should plan together for the student's gradual assumption of teaching responsibilities.

- The student should have an opportunity to observe the master teacher before taking over any part of the program.

- The master teacher should pace the assumption of teaching responsibilities according to the student's readiness to do so. This implies a sensitivity to the student's abilities and feelings. It also implies knowing when to wait and when to accelerate the student's involvement.

- The master teacher may convey to the student that failure can be a way of learning, and should create a climate in which the student can feel confident to try again.

- The master teacher allows for experimentation. Students often bring a fresh approach to the classroom by trying their own ideas.

- Time should be scheduled on a regular basis for student conferences. Time to evaluate and discuss what happened every day is most helpful. If this is not possible, then two or three time periods a week should be set aside.

Fig. 19-3 The student teacher has planned an interesting lesson.

- All professional materials and resources should be made available to the student.

- An evaluation of the student's performance is to be made midway in the practice period. This allows time for improvement in any areas that need it.

- The master teacher should maintain continual communication with the college advisor and the director concerning the student's progress.

REACTIONS OF STUDENT TEACHERS

A director who is actively involved with student teachers should be familiar with the feelings that are part of practice teaching. Sometimes, those who have been working with children for many years forget what it was like to be inexperienced or to be a student teacher. Meetings with staff teachers for the purpose of discussing these points enable teachers to be more effective with students.

Students are often afraid they will not be able to control undesirable behavior in the children. They are not sure that they can follow through when they must discipline children and, when dealing with aggression, feel they may somehow hurt the child.

Evaluation of Student Teaching

Student _____   Supervising
Teacher _____

Date of Placement _____   School _____

Teaching Skills

Outstanding   Above Ave.   Ave.   Below Ave.

1. Ability to recognize and provide for health
    and safety of children
    _____

2. Ability to organize learning materials
    _____

3. Ability to relate academic learning to
    practical aspects of teaching
    _____

4. Ability to encourage children's creative
    ability in

    art
    _____

    music
    _____

5. Ability to develop good working relation-
    ships with other staff members
    _____

6. Ability to act independently when faced
    with responsibility
    _____

Personal Characteristics

7. Warm, natural and friendly contacts
    with children
    _____

8. Friendly contacts with parents of
    children
    _____

9. Expresses a desire to learn
    _____

10. Is able to accept criticism
    _____

Final Grade in Course _____

Other Pertinent Comments:

Signed _____
            Supervising Teacher

Date _____

Fig. 19-4 Form for Evaluation of Student Teaching

Fig. 19-5 A student teacher interacts with a child.

Fig. 19-6 Student teachers often feel all they do is clean up.

Students are unsure of the limits of their role in the classroom. During the practice teaching period, they may assume responsibility for the teaching; yet they do not have the authority that goes with the teacher's position. The question of how far they can go in making changes in the environment or atmosphere of a classroom causes student concern.

Students may be afraid that the children will not like them; when the children do not respond immediately to the student teacher, it is often interpreted as dislike. The same is true if the children refuse a student-prepared activity.

Students may feel uneasy when they do not know how to do something. Curriculum courses may have taught them the importance of finger paints, but not how to make them. When confronted with this gap in their knowledge, they may feel they will be considered inadequate if they have to ask the master teacher for help.

Some students are frightened by the unpredictable things that happen during a day of working with children. A well-planned day may be disrupted completely because of something that upsets the children. An inexperienced student may find it difficult to spontaneously change plans to adapt to the upset.

Some students feel that they are exploited by the master teacher. If the teacher pushes the student into assuming too many responsibilities too soon, it may be perceived by the student as laziness on the part of the teacher. The student may feel that she does the work while the teacher takes it easy.

A student may feel that the teacher has found the right way of teaching through experience. There is often the feeling that certain words will solve a problem with a child, or that there is a right way to present a lesson so that the children will want to participate. The students may feel frustrated and sometimes become angry if the teacher cannot give them this information. They may feel that the teacher knows but is withholding the information. The inexperienced student teacher fails to realize that there may be many alternatives in all situations involved in teaching young children.

The chairs, tables, and other furniture in a school room for young children are scaled to the children. Students often feel awkward moving about in the child-size environment.

Students sometimes identify more closely with the feelings of the children than with adult feelings. They may become angry when the teacher disciplines a child; they may feel upset at the way a mother treats her child.

When first confronted with the intensity of their anger at a child, students may become afraid of their emotions in relation to children. They may feel they can never become good teachers. They may also be afraid of liking some children too much. They know that the relationship with the children is limited in time, and that parting from them will be painful.

Because students are being graded, there is a tremendous pressure to perform well. Students often feel that the master teacher is watching and judging every word and act. They think every mistake or lapse must surely be seen and criticized by the teacher.

Recognizing her own feelings will help the student teacher to speed the process of becoming a teacher. Learning to work with young children effectively takes a long time and is sometimes painful as well as rewarding. There are many things for a student teacher to learn in a situation that cannot always be controlled.

Fig. 19-7 Affection develops between the child and the student teacher.

getting college credit for their work in the school and are being graded or evaluated. Although they are often young people in their early twenties, older men and women are also interested in early childhood education.

The director recognizes that students require an investment of time and energy. She should be available to students and to teachers when problems arise. Participation in workshops offered by the college will help the director to provide an optimum experience for students and be kept aware of current trends in child care.

The director will make it easier for teachers if she notifies them well in advance of the time the student will begin practice teaching. The director should understand the role of the college advisor and work closely with her and the master teacher. Master teachers must be chosen carefully by the director based upon their abilities to work with others.

An orientation precedes the placement in order to provide information about the school and about the college requirements. The

SUMMARY

Directors of public or private early childhood schools may have an opportunity to work with student teachers.

Student teachers have some characteristics that should be understood by the director. They have had some background and, possibly, experience with children. They are students, teaching staff, director, and college advisor should participate in the orientation.

A director who has student teachers in her school should be aware of the feelings that are part of practice teaching. Concerns about control, the limits of their role, and fears about the children's reactions are typical of student teachers. Some students also feel inadequate or exploited.

The master teacher is the person who sees the student every day and gets to know the student better than anyone else. It is the master teacher's responsibility to create an environment in which each student can develop to the maximum of his or her ability. The director must be knowledgeable about the problems of teacher and student; she must be available for guidance whenever it is needed.

STUDENT ACTIVITIES

- Discuss your own experiences as a student teacher. How did your reactions compare with those discussed in the text?

- Observe a master teacher. What functions does she perform in relation to the practice teaching of the student?

- Talk to the director of a community school which is used for practice teaching. How does she see her role with the students?

REVIEW

1. What two factors must be considered by the director who accepts students for practice teaching?

2. What is the first criterion for choosing a master teacher?

3. Besides the staff and children, to whom should the student teacher be introduced?

4. What must a master teacher be able to share with the student teacher?

5. Name two items which should be included as part of an orientation to practice teaching.

6. Who is to plan for the gradual assumption of teaching responsibilities?

7. When should the student teacher's performance be first evaluated?

8. What role does the master teacher assume for the student?

Section 5

PARENTS AND THE COMMUNITY

Unit 20 Parent Involvement

OBJECTIVES

After studying this unit, the student should be able to

- Name factors to consider in determining degree of parental involvement
- Describe parental roles in preschool education
- Describe ways to encourage participation

Traditionally, parents have been responsible for rearing children; and the schools, for educating them. In recent years this belief has been seriously challenged both by professionals and by parents.

CHANGING ROLE OF THE TEACHER

Teachers in schools for young children can no longer consider only the child. Education and training of teachers must include an understanding of parents and their attitudes toward raising children. Teachers must learn how to work with parents to care for and educate children. Experiences must be provided so that teachers can learn to respect and use the abilities of parents.

Teachers should understand how family life and structure are affected when parents become involved in the school community. The impact of the ideas discussed and learned at the childhood education center may change ideas about raising children.

Involving parents in the activities of the school and the education of their children will change the traditional role of the teacher. It is up to the administrator and staff to learn to use involvement of parents in the early educa-

tion of children for the benefit of both the school and the family.

PARENT INVOLVEMENT

Research has shown that parents have a tremendous influence on what children learn long before they go to school. Parental influence also affects the child's ability to make use of the learning experiences offered by the school. Parents are now recognized as the child's first teacher.

Many of those who took part in the early cooperative schools found that involvement in the education of their young children had benefits they had not expected. The parents found they learned a great deal about their own child and gained a general knowledge of child development. They found comfort in knowing that other parents have the same kinds of problems in raising their children. They learned that, in fact, some problems are a normal part of growing up. They found that the school community became a social unit as well as an educational one. A few parents found that they gained a basic training that made it possible for them to become teachers when their own children were older.

At the height of the civil rights movement of the 1960s and during the formation of Project Head Start in 1965, parents demanded a more active role in the education of their children. Some of the demands came from general criticism of the schools. More specifically, criticism was aimed at the failure of education to understand the needs of minority children, and at the lack of response on the part of schools and legislators in meeting their needs.

Early attempts to involve parents in Head Start were difficult both for the parents and for the schools. Parents felt insecure in the presence of teachers who supposedly had so much more knowledge about children than they did. Teachers were afraid to involve parents in the school for fear that they would take over. Many of the early Head Start programs used the services of parents on advisory councils or in other ways outside the classroom.

In successful Head Start programs, parents and professionals now appear to be truly working together. Parents have an important part in determining what their children should be learning. Parents function as aides in the classroom helping the teachers with all the children. Parents are also taught how to enhance learning through activities provided in the home.

The increased number of day care programs on the national scene has further changed the picture. The professional staff and the parents must work together because the children spend most of their waking hours in school. The mother is concerned about her child and wants to have some control over what happens to him during the day. The teacher needs the mother's help to learn more about the child. The mother and teacher must share the responsibility for determining

Fig. 20-1   Mother and child are involved in this activity.

Fig. 20-2 Mother and teacher share direct responsibility for the child's growth.

the best environment for the child's physical, social, and intellectual growth.

Nonprofit schools have used parents for fund raising, recruitment, and public relations. However, the attitude was often there that the educational aspects of the school should be left to the staff. Now, the staff members are finding that parents have many skills that they are willing to share with the school in order to enrich the program.

Even proprietary schools have found that parents are willing to take part in many ways. Parents who have a profession sometimes offer their skills for consultations; others use their abilities to provide enrichment for the curriculum. Parents who are pleased with the education of their children are usually willing to help the school broaden its recruitment activities.

The kind and extent of parent involvement in a school depends on the program. Some programs mandate parent involvement in the funding or administrative guidelines. The kind and extent of the involvement is specifically stated and only minimal variation is allowed.

The kind and extent of parent involvement in programs where there is no specific agreement will depend upon the philosophy and attitudes of the staff. In early childhood centers where the director and teachers accept the importance of active partnership with parents, parent involvement can be broad and almost unlimited.

PARENTAL ROLES

Parents may be involved in a school in several different ways. They may participate in policy-making activities, play a supportive role, function as aides in the classroom, or be trained as teachers of their own children at home.

As policy-makers, parents may be asked to take part in planning a new program and in determining objectives. They may be asked to participate in some operational aspects such as hiring and evaluating staff. They may also plan activities for parent education.

The rationale for involving parents in these kinds of activities stems from the belief that people feel a commitment to

decisions in which they have had a part. In order for children to fully benefit from their school experience, the parents must believe that the experience is right. Also, many publicly funded programs depend upon active community support for continued renewal of their funds.

Further rationale for involving parents comes from a belief that development of decision-making skills will help the parents in other aspects of their lives. Learning that their input can influence the school community encourages self-growth and participation in activities outside the school environment.

Some policy-making functions are listed:

- Being members of an advisory council or committee
- Representing parents on a board of trustees
- Determining policies concerning finances and personnel

A parent may perform a supportive role, unrelated to the academic functions of the school:

- Clerical duties may be performed.
- Parents may organize work days to provide maintenance for the school.
- Parents may plan and carry out fund raising.
- Parents may be responsible for social activities of the school.
- Parents can help each other by organizing social affairs, car pools, and baby-sitting service.

The purpose of a supportive role for parents is to fill a mutual need; the school and parents both want to provide a good program. Financially the school may need the unpaid services that parents can render.

The supportive role may also enable some parents to begin involvement at a level where they feel comfortable. Not everyone is ready or willing to invest as much time and energy as it may take for the policy-making role or to be an aide in the classroom.

When they work as aides, parents must learn some of the duties of a teacher and how to help in the classroom. As aides, the parent may do the following:

- Perform tasks as assigned by the teacher, such as helping with large group activities or working with individual children

- Prepare materials, arrange the environment, and keep records on children's progress

- Supervise small groups of children at certain times during the day

In some programs, the participation of parents as teacher aides is a career development component. Head Start and many day care centers train mothers for jobs in schools for young children.

Parents may be trained to become better teachers of their own children. This may be seen as either in addition to or in place of the child's school experience:

- The parent learns the value of a variety of learning experiences to further the child's development.

- The parent is helped to make use of the common materials that are found in the home.

In this role, the parent is both a teacher and a learner. It is assumed that the mother already has the ability to teach her own child. However, guidance, counseling, and practice with the professionals in childhood education will help her to develop her child's fullest potential.

Kinds of Involvement

Each school and each community is different. The appropriate kind of parent involvement must be determined if it is to be effective.

Factors to be considered are (1) the number of working mothers, (2) ethnic group values, (3) stability of the community, (4) size of the community, and (5) physical setting of the school.

The number of working mothers in a school is one factor that determines the kind of parent involvement. Obviously, in a day care school where all of the parents are working, few parents could be used as teacher aides. It is possible that some parents might work part-time or have flexible schedules that would allow them to take part in this way. However, most parents are not able to do this. Therefore, the working hours of parents must determine the ways in which they can be involved in the school.

Some ways in which the working parent can be involved in the education of the child are suggested:

- Participate in decision-making processes

- Provide a supportive role by doing work for the school at home or after work hours

- Be involved in training as teachers of their own children

However, the director and staff of the school must realize that a mother or father who works a full week may have little time or energy left. The parent who has to spend a large part of the time earning a living and keeping the family together has little time to spare.

The ethnic group values of the parents in the school must be considered in determining the kind of involvement:

- Is it acceptable for the mother to be involved in school decisions and activities, or must the father be included?

- Is the school seen as the absolute responsibility of the professionals?

- Do the families see the school and the home as completely separate?

The stability or mobility of the community from which the school draws its population may also determine the kind of parent involvement:

- If the population is highly transient, involvement that takes a long period to develop will not be possible.

- In a stable community, time can be allowed for parents to develop decision-making skills and teaching skills.

The size of the community from which the school draws its children will determine the kind of parent involvement:

- If children are bussed to school from distant areas, it may be very difficult to arrange ways to involve parents.

- A school located within walking distance may become a center for many kinds of activities.

The physical setting of the school may also affect the degree of parent involvement:

- If the school can afford the luxury of space where parents can meet on an informal and on a scheduled basis, parent involvement becomes easier. Setting aside an area for parents conveys the idea that the school is their school as well as that of the children.

ENCOURAGING PARTICIPATION

The process of involving parents in the education of their children has some built-in obstacles. First, parents and teachers often have ideas about each other that make it difficult for them to work together. The parent may see the teacher as knowledgeable and critical of parents and may feel unwelcome and unskilled in the school environment. The teacher may feel that the parent does not want any help and expects the teacher to change the child. The teacher may feel completely unwelcome in the home environment.

Fig. 20-3 This father is involved.

Some teachers may be untrained in working with parents; this contributes to the difficulty of involving parents. Teachers are often unaware of the feelings of parents about their children. Some teacher education programs fail to help the beginning teacher understand community attitudes about child raising.

Parent participation in a school is built on the relationship of the parent with the people in the school. One teacher may be quite successful in involving parents because of her own personality. Other teachers can learn ways in which to bring about a commitment from parents.

The first step in bringing about parent involvement is the initial contact with the parents. Other points to consider are providing incentives and sustaining interest.

Initial Contact

First impressions of a school and its staff may determine whether parents feel welcome and able to be involved. Some schools have found that initial contacts are best made through having mother and child come to the school during or after school hours. The teacher can have a chance to talk to both the mother and child in the school setting.

Fig. 20-4 The child and family explore the school environment.

Other schools arrange a visit to the home as the form of initial contact. The visit must be scheduled ahead of time by telephone or a written note. Care must be taken to see that the formalities of this visit fit into the customs of the community. For instance, in Mexican-American families where the father is the recognized authority, the home visit may take place at a time when the father can be present. In some communities, it may not be possible to arrange the home visit until a relationship has been established between parent and school.

Some programs may decide that initial contact with parents is best managed through an "open house." Parents have an opportunity to see the school and meet the staff; they also may wish to attend with other parents whom they already know. This kind of social event can be followed by a home visit in order to encourage further involvement by parents.

Parents must feel they have a place in the school. This means the staff must be aware that every contact with parents is important. Teachers must be as responsive to the parents as to the child; a few words of greeting when the child arrives are important. At the end of the day, a brief chat between parent and teacher may also be arranged; it helps the

Fig. 20-5 The parent and teacher relax and talk.

parent to ease back into the role of being an active parent again. These actions show parents that the school and the teachers are interested in them as well as in the children.

Parents will feel more welcome if they have physical space in the school. A lounge area for parents may be an important part of the school building. Here, parents can talk to each other. Here, a parent who has been working all day can rest for a few quiet moments before picking up the child. Provision for this kind of space has been found to be invaluable in day care programs.

Parents feel more a part of the school if they are kept informed of the school and community events that affect their families. A bulletin board in the lounge can be used to post notices concerning parent meetings, community lectures, fund raising events, books of interest to parents, or any other pertinent information. This could also be the place to post the weekly lunch menu as suggested in unit 14. In addition to the bulletin board, a newsletter prepared by the staff or the parents can be helpful in keeping parents informed.

Incentives

The most important incentive is the parents' interest in their children. Parents want their children to be successful in school. Parents also want to know more about child-rearing. Incentives must be offered and nurtured in order to bring about a commitment from parents.

Few programs can offer pay for parent participation. In some publicly funded programs there is provision for expense money such as transportation or babysitting costs. When participation is seen as job training, there may be consideration of minimal pay.

Several incentives for parent participation are listed:

- In a school which is sponsored by a business or corporation, mothers are allowed paid time away from the job to visit or help at the school.

- In a day care center, participation can be encouraged by arranging dinner meetings right after school. Care for the children can be provided while the parents participate.

Sustaining Interest

Parents' interest must be sustained once their involvement is accomplished. Feedback information from the school about the children's progress helps parents see the value of their work in the classroom or at home. Frequent recognition of the parents' contributions in the classroom or their work with their children at home also helps to sustain interest.

A mother's interest will be sustained if she can see her own personal growth. In many programs, contact with the school is the first time that the mother has attempted any activity outside the home. If she can feel successful and useful in this capacity, it will enhance her feeling of worth. She may then be able to broaden her outlook to include other kinds of community activities.

Social relationships which are developed through parent involvement are also important in sustaining interest. For single parents, the school relationships built around friendships between children may be an important part of their lives. Relationships with other adults offer the single parent something more than a child-centered world.

Some programs sustain parent involvement through activities geared to adult needs and unrelated to children. Sewing classes, classes in nutrition, and classes in family finance have been successful. If these activities take place at the school, there is the additional advantage of showing parents that they, too, have a place in the school. Other activities such as trips to museums or theaters may broaden the parents' experiences and enhance friendships.

Records of Parent Involvement

Records should be kept to show the extent of parent involvement in a school. In some publicly funded programs, this is necessary in order to obtain continued funding. In other programs documentation can be used to evaluate the extent and kinds of parent involvement and to determine where changes should be made.

- Lists of committee members should be current.

- Minutes of meetings should be written.

- Attendance at committee and board meetings should be kept.

- Copies of resolutions made at meetings should be available for all parents in the school.

- Correspondence pertaining to parent activities should be copied and filed.

- Evaluations of parent involvement should be recorded.

- Information regarding any citations or awards to parents should be kept.

SUMMARY

Most schools find that active involvement of parents in the school has been successful both for the school and for the parents. Parents may be involved on a policy-making level, they may play a supportive role, they may function as aides in the classroom, or they may improve their skills as teachers of their own children at home.

The degree of parent involvement must be determined for each school. The number of working mothers is one factor that determines the kind of participation. Ethnic group values, the physical setting of the school, stability or mobility of families, and the size of the community also affect parent involvement.

Parent participation in a school is built on the relationships of the parent with the people in the school. The first step in bringing about parent involvement comes with the initial contact with the family. Incentives must be offered to bring about a commitment from parents.

A parent's interest must continue after involvement is accomplished. Information concerning the child's progress and recognition of personal growth help the mother to feel that her contributions are worthwhile. Social relationships developed through parent involvement are also important. Some programs hold parent interest through activities which are designed to meet adult needs and are unrelated to children.

STUDENT ACTIVITIES

- Discuss the degree of parent involvement that would be appropriate for the school with which you are associated. What factors are important in determining this?
- Talk to several parents in a Head Start program in your community about what they do. How do they feel about it? Present your findings to the class.

REVIEW

1. Name two early events that gave rise to a more active role for parents in the education of young children.
2. Name the four roles parents may play when involved in their children's early education.
3. Why should parents be involved in the school program?
4. Name some examples of activities provided by those in the supportive role.
5. Name five factors to consider when administration has determined to have parents involved in the school program.
6. Name three steps to encourage participation by the parents, and discuss their beneficial application.
7. Were early attempts to involve parents in Head Start programs successful? Explain the reasons for your answer.
8. What factor is the most important incentive for parents to participate?

Unit 21 Parent Education

OBJECTIVES

After completing this unit, the student should be able to

- Discuss parents' and teachers' feelings about the child's school experience
- State goals for a parent education program
- Plan an effective parent education activity

The director of a school for young children determines the degree to which parent education is effective. It is she who sets the tone for the staff-parent relationship.

The director must hire teachers who can work with parents as well as with children. This means that when she interviews prospective teachers, she explores their background and their experience with adults. She should know how they relate to adults, if they have had opportunities to work with parents in other jobs, and how they feel about involving parents in the education of their children.

The director must provide time for her staff to work with parents. She provides time within the working day for the teacher to telephone parents. She knows the value of parent conferences. She provides opportunities for staff to participate in planning parent education meetings or workshops.

The director sees that office space or lounge space is provided for conferences and meetings. Although conferences can be held in a classroom, they are usually more effective when they are held in a comfortable lounge or office.

The director must share the responsibility for working with parents. This means that she will offer help and guidance when the teacher needs it. She may participate in some conferences with parents. She may also conduct some parts of the parent education program.

Fig. 21-1 The director shares the responsibility of working with parents.

The director must provide leadership to her staff in setting objectives for the parent education program of the school. She helps the staff to determine what objectives are appropriate for the school and community — objectives that establish a partnership for educating and rearing children.

The staff must be aware of the feelings and attitudes that present obstacles to an effective parent education program. The director can help them to understand the feelings that parents may have toward the teacher and the school; she listens to her staff and helps them to understand their own feelings toward parents.

PARENTS' FEELINGS

When a child goes to school for the first time, it marks an important milestone in the life of the family. It signifies that the child is growing up. It also means that he is taking his first step into the outside world. He is taking a step toward independence from the family.

The mother who decides to enroll her child in an early childhood center may have some conflicts about it. She may want him to go to school because she recognizes the benefits. She may also realize that this will mean giving up some of her own closeness with the child. He will now have a life that she can only share to some extent.

The mother who enrolls her child in a full-day program at a day care center may feel guilty because she has to work and let others take care of her child. She may also feel sad that she has to miss so much of her child's growing years.

When children come to school for the first time, some mothers feel uneasy about having other people judge their children. They want others to think they have done a good job of raising them.

Some parents have strong feelings about certain kinds of behavior in their own child or in other children. They may not like to see children hitting each other, for instance. They may be uncomfortable or angered by the behavior. Their own child may already have learned other ways to express anger and they fear the child will revert to "hitting."

A parent may feel threatened by the teacher. A fear that the child will like the teacher better or will compare the mother unfavorably with the teacher may be present. Some children say that they wish the teacher were their mommy. Mothers fail to realize that this is only a child's way of saying that he likes the teacher.

Parents may misunderstand changes that take place in the child after he has been in school. The child may become more assertive, may use bad language, or may be more demanding. Sometimes, parents attribute the changes to bad habits that the child learned in school. They do not realize that these behaviors might have developed without school attendance and may be due to normal child development.

Fig. 21-2 **A mother may find it difficult to leave her child in the care of others.**

Parents may relive some of their own school experiences when their child begins school. If their own school experience was happy, they may expect the same for their child. If they did not like school, they may convey this attitude to the child without realizing it.

TEACHERS' FEELINGS

If a teacher is a great deal younger than the parents or has no children of her own, she may feel that parents do not respect her ability. She may expect that they will feel she lacks knowledge and experience with children.

Differences in cultural backgrounds also make it difficult for teachers to understand parents and their children. In some cultures, the family expectations for the child may be quite different from what the teacher has learned to expect because of her education and experience. It might also be very different from her own life experiences. She may find it hard, for instance, to understand when a parent tells her to spank a child to make him obey.

Teachers too may have ambivalent feelings about certain kinds of behavior. For example, the teacher may get upset when she finds out that the child is punished at home for not eating all of the food on his plate.

Some teachers may be confused about the kind of relationship that is proper with parents. They want to be liked by parents and want to get to know parents. It takes patience, skill, and open communication to form a professional, yet friendly relationship.

GOALS FOR PARENT EDUCATION

The following general goals for parents can serve as a guide toward setting up objectives for parent education.

Establish a partnership with the family for the education and care of the child. The attitude that it is a partnership must be conveyed by every staff member in the school. This begins when the parent first comes into the school and talks to a secretary or director. It is especially important to convey this attitude during the period when the child and parent are getting adjusted to school attendance.

Help parents to recognize and respect their own abilities. Most parents do a good job of raising their children. Often, however, they feel inadequate. An important part of parent education is to help them to recognize their own strengths and to trust their own feelings about what is best for the child.

Provide parents with factual information about child development. Many parents have had limited experience with young children and may feel that some of the things their children do are unusual. A knowledge of child development will help them to view behavior as stages that children pass through.

Explain reasons for the school curriculum and planned activities. Parents should know why certain kinds of activities and materials are provided. They should understand why the teacher presents the materials in a specific way. They need to understand the value of free play and what is gained by group participation.

Help parents understand the ways that children can learn. Parents believe that learning is taking place in situations where the instructor is teaching. They may not remember or realize that children are actively learning while they are playing. Children learn in different ways. Parents can be encouraged to recognize experiences at home that can be meaningful.

Introduce the parents to the wide variety of educational materials and experiences. The family can be helped to make use of readily available materials for the child's learning experiences. Guidance as to the sources and values of toys, books, paper supplies, puzzles, and other aids such as how-to-do-it books and games should be given. The appropriate materials for the child's age level is recommended to encourage creativity and self-growth.

ACTIVITIES

A good parent education program will provide a wide variety of activities and methods from which parents can learn. Some of these are planned and structured; others occur spontaneously. An exciting and effective program uses many or all of the following methods.

One of the first opportunities for a parent to learn in the school setting is the orientation meeting. This is usually held for new parents at the beginning of a school year. It provides a time for staff and parents to have a chance to meet each other. This is also a time when information important to parents can be communicated. Some of the purposes of an orientation meeting are listed:

- Welcome new parents
- Introduce staff

Fig. 21-3 The school provides many experiences that lead to learning to read.

- Explain purposes and goals of the school
- Describe essential aspects of the curriculum
- Acquaint parents with rules about clothing, home toys, snacks
- Describe methods of introducing child into classroom
- Allow for questions from parents
- Set the tone welcoming parents into all parts of the school program

Some schools have found that it is helpful to record some of the information given at an orientation meeting. For example, a slide presentation covering the curriculum might be made to be shown at this meeting as well as to be viewed by parents unable to attend. A taped presentation of the purposes and goals of the school could also be made to be heard at a later time by parents unable to attend. It is also helpful if some of the material presented at the meeting is available in printed form so that parents can read it at their leisure.

Observation is an important avenue for learning. Parents can see how the school activities are conducted and can see the interactions between the teacher and the children.

Observations can be casual and unscheduled. Each time a mother is in a classroom she has an opportunity to observe. If a school has one-way screens into the classrooms, parents have many opportunities to observe.

The author's experience in a school where each classroom could be viewed through a one-way screen showed the value of this arrangement. It was found to be particularly helpful during the child's initial adjustment to school. The mother could see that the child stopped crying soon after she left. She could also see how the teacher helped or comforted the child.

The mothers in this school also watched later in the day at "pick-up time," this was usually lunchtime for the children. The parent could see what the child was eating and how well he ate with the others.

The one-way screen has an additional advantage; a mother can observe the activities, unseen by her child. Many children react quite differently when their mother is in the room. They may cry and refuse to take part in the play activities. If the mother has no other opportunity to observe, she may feel this is what goes on all the time; she may question the value of the school program and its management.

If provision for casual observation is part of the school environment and program, the director must be aware of the impact upon parents. At times, the mother may observe something that she does not understand or like. The director can be helpful by making herself available when parents are observing so that she can answer questions or discuss the parents' concerns.

Scheduled observations also help parents learn. Their attention can be directed to specific kinds of behavior or parts of the curriculum. They might also be asked to observe the ways that the teacher manages activities or children.

A discussion following the observation will help to reinforce learning. If a group of parents observe at the same time, each may have seen different things. Sharing and comparing observations can be an exciting way to learn.

Group discussions with other parents is another important parent education activity. The opportunity to share experiences and feelings common to all parents is invaluable. Parents may learn that their child is not so different from other children. They may learn that it is not uncommon to sometimes have conflicting feelings about children.

Group discussion can also provide an opportunity to talk about each child's classroom. Parents can gain knowledge of the developmental level of children. They can understand the rationale for the curriculum of the class. They can learn ways the teacher is effective with the children.

Lectures or panels are additional teaching methods. Persons who are expert in a particular field may be asked to speak to a meeting of all the parents in the school. Care should be taken to find an interesting speaker. Nothing can be so deadly to a parent education

Fig. 21-4 Observation through a One-way Screen

Fig. 21-5 A Parent-Teacher Discussion Group

program as a long, dull speech. After sitting through a two-hour lecture by a poor speaker, some parents may feel that the entire parent education program will be of no value.

Lecture topics should be chosen with care. Some topics may create anxiety in parents rather than convey knowledge. Controversial topics can sometimes be conducive to learning, if handled skillfully.

Films, slides, and tapes help parents learn. Many good films geared to parents of young children are available. Films should always be previewed by the staff or director before being shown; preparation for a good discussion can follow.

Films made at the school can be used to illustrate the kinds of activities and materials used there. For this purpose, 8mm film is satisfactory and not too expensive. It is widely used, easily available, and rapidly processed.

Slides and tapes can also be used to supply knowledge. Slides can show materials and equipment; they can also portray important aspects of the environment. Tapes are often used to illustrate language development and to develop further discussions of music and storytelling activities. Care should be taken to protect the families involved in the films, slides, and tapes. Nothing should be shown that will cause anyone to be embarrassed or criticized.

Workshop participation can offer education about the curriculum. Parents may actually participate by doing the same things that the children do, such as painting, woodworking, building with blocks, and participating in music activities.

A workshop in which parents can make learning materials for their children can have a two-fold benefit: (1) they have made something useful for their child, and (2) they will

have learned the potential for further use of materials to further the child's development.

Parents can learn through participation in the classroom. Some parents have special skills or interests that can be shared on a short term or occasional basis. The child will benefit from this close relationship between the school and his family. The parent will gain from being able to enrich the curriculum of the school.

Some schools use parents as aides in the classroom, providing extensive opportunities for them to learn. Parent participation is required in cooperative schools. In others, parents may be given tuition credit for assisting. In order to fulfill the functions of an aide effectively, the parents should be given some initial as well as ongoing training sessions. They need to understand the goals of the school and how these are carried out in the curriculum. They need to develop techniques for interacting with children. They should increase their knowledge of child development.

Saturday or holiday sessions of a school provide opportunities for fathers to participate. Many schools schedule this kind of activity at least once a year in order to allow the fathers an equal chance to learn about the program and share an experience with their children.

All communications with a parent have an educational potential. A telephone call when a child is sick may improve the relationship between the teacher and the mother; the mother feels that the teacher cares about her child. It gives the teacher the opportunity to help the mother deal with anxiety over the child's illness.

Daily contacts between the parent and the teacher are also important. The way the teacher answers the mother's questions about what the child ate or what he did at school establishes a basis for educating the parent. If the teacher knows what the child ate or did, the mother will feel that her child is noticed. If the answers satisfy the mother, she can place more trust in the school.

Conferences are probably the most profitable way that a school can help parents learn. This is a time when the teacher and parent can talk about the child's progress and development. This is also a time when problems that come up at home or at school can be discussed.

Conferences are most effective when the following guidelines are used.

- The content of the conference should be thought out beforehand.
- The conference should be started and ended with a positive tone.
- The parent should be encouraged to discuss concerns or ask questions. It is important for the teacher to listen to the parent.
- The teacher should avoid making the parent feel anxious or guilty. (Only rarely is this necessary in order to get the family to seek help for the child.)
- Parents should be encouraged to find their own solutions to problems.
- Parents look to the teacher as an authority, but the teacher should not be afraid to say that she does not have all the answers.
- The conference should be free from interruptions.
- The time should be adequate to discuss the topics planned for, but should not drag on when the discussion is completed. (Sometimes it is helpful to leave a conference topic unresolved and to schedule a second discussion after each has had time to think about it.)
- Whenever possible, a conference should be ended with a summary of what has been discussed. A time for reevaluation may be set.

Information for parents can be conveyed through a parent library, a newsletter, or a bulletin board. Many parents like to increase their knowledge through reading. The school can help by having books available for parents to borrow. If the purchase of books cannot be included in the school budget, lists of books available at the local library can be offered. A newsletter can keep parents informed of events at the school and can also be a method for helping parents learn more about curriculum or child development. An article written by the director or by a teacher or one reproduced from another source can be used. A bulletin board is a handy place for many kinds of information for parents. Here, too, interesting articles can be posted, notices of coming events, suggestions for recreational activities, or ideas for play materials for children at home can be seen by parents.

SUMMARY

The director of a school for young children influences the effectiveness of parent education by:

- Hiring teachers experienced in working with adults
- Providing time and space for parent activities
- Offering help and guidance when a teacher needs it
- Providing leadership to staff in setting objectives for parent education
- Being aware of the feelings and attitudes that teachers and parents have toward each other

Goals for parent education are:

- Establish a partnership with the family for the education and care of the child
- Help parents to recognize and respect their own abilities

- Provide parents with factual information about child development
- Explain reasons for the school curriculum and planned activities
- Help parents understand the ways that children can learn

A good parent education program provides a wide variety of activities and methods from which parents can learn. Some of these are planned and some occur spontaneously.

Parent education activities that are most frequently used are

- Orientation meeting
- Observation
- Group discussions
- Lectures and panels
- Films, slides, and tapes
- Workshops
- Parent participation as aides
- Communications with parent
- Conferences
- Parent library, newsletter, or bulletin board

STUDENT ACTIVITIES

- Plan a parent education activity for your school. Use an evaluation questionnaire to determine its effectiveness.
- Talk to a director of a school in your community. What are the goals of the school for parent education? How do they compare with those listed in this unit?

REVIEW

1. How does the director determine the effectiveness of the parent education program?
2. Discuss parents' feelings about their children's first school experience.
3. Discuss the feelings that teachers may have toward parents.
4. Briefly state the goals for parent education discussed in this unit.
5. List five purposes of a parent orientation meeting.
6. List the ten parent education activities discussed in this unit.
7. Discuss ways to conduct effective parent conferences.

Unit 22 Interpreting the School to the Public

OBJECTIVES

After studying this unit, the student should be able to

- Discuss areas to consider when planning a public relations program
- Discuss the kinds of public relations a school can engage in
- Describe information to be included in a school brochure

Very young children are not required by law to go to school. Their parents decide to put them in school. Even the parents who work and enroll the child in day care have a choice. They can hire a baby-sitter and keep the child at home, or the child can be cared for by a relative. Also, the child could go to family day care. Instead, the parents decide that a school for young children will be best.

How do parents decide what school to select for their child? Some make a choice based on cost and convenience. If the school has a reasonable tuition and is close to home

Fig. 22-1 The openness of the director's office welcomes parents and visitors.

or work, the parent may not look any further. Some parents are looking for a particular kind of educational program for the child. Others hear about a school through neighbors or friends.

People in the community must be alerted to the existence of the school for young children. Public relations and advertising are involved in the process. The administration of a school that has a waiting list must recognize the importance of its public image. The waiting list is there because people heard about the school.

The director needs to know what steps to take to acquaint the public with the school and create a good image of the school in the community. When planning a public relations program, she has several broad areas of concern to keep in mind: (1) the appearance of the building and grounds, (2) telephone inquiries, (3) visitor control, (4) brochures, (5) open house, and (6) community activities.

APPEARANCE OF THE SCHOOL

The outside appearance of the school is the first thing that will be noticed. This includes the building and the grounds. Often staff members do not see things that a stranger might see. Every director should occasionally approach her school and enter, trying to look at it objectively, as a stranger might. It will help her to correct those things that can and should be changed.

The building and school entrances are important. Although the director may be able to do nothing about the architecture of the building, she can make other changes. She can select paint colors that are pleasing to the eye and see that necessary repairs, however minor, are made. The school can be made more attractive by adding plants and shrubs around it. Maintenance of the building and grounds must be a priority item. Is the entrance a place that appears to welcome parents and children? Is it clean and attractive? Are there places to sit down inside?

The play yard is often noticed by people driving or walking by. The kind of equipment that is in the yard will convey a message about the school. Is the equipment pretty but not very useful to children? Is the equipment shabby or has it been well cared for? There should be enough materials and equipment, but there should also be some open spaces for play.

The kind of activities that go on outside will also tell people about the school. As they walk by, do people see children who are involved in play or do they notice children who have nothing to do but get into trouble?

What teachers do outside may also tell something about the school. Are teachers talking to each other or interacting with the children? Are teachers a distance away from the children, or are they sitting nearby?

Of course, what the children and the teachers do outside will be determined by the objectives of the school, not by public relations. The director and the staff should

be aware, however, of the image they create by what they do outside.

TELEPHONE INQUIRIES

As the first step in deciding about a school, many parents telephone to find out about the cost, how old children need to be, the hours, and similar items. Therefore, the telephone becomes a primary instrument for public relations.

The person who is selected to answer the telephone must be tactful and knowledgeable. The director should be available to answer inquiries from parents. If a secretary is hired to perform this function, she should be chosen with great care.

When parents call, they often ask to speak to the director. Is the director easily available or is she too busy? If she is not available at that moment, can she be counted on to return the call? A parent may get discouraged if telephone calls are not returned.

The manner in which questions are answered tells a lot about the school. Does

Fig. 22-2 The secretary is important to good public relations.

the person answering the phone have a pleasant voice and seem ready to give as much information as is needed? Is the conversation hurried or leisurely? If the caller has to wait, is it a long or a short time?

What kind of information is given over the telephone? Is the caller given enough or too little? Sometimes it is better to give some information on the phone and then mail the written material.

The school should have a procedure for handling telephone inquiries. There should be a form for recording the name, address, and telephone number of parents who inquire about the school. They can then be sent a packet of information. The packet should include an application for enrollment.

VISITOR CONTROL

Some schools do not allow visitors. The rationale is that it disturbs what is going on in the classrooms. Other schools feel that the parents should visit and see the program before enrolling the child.

A set procedure makes handling visitors easier for the school. Visits by individuals should be scheduled whenever possible. If the director knows when visitors are expected, she can allow time. Setting aside one or two days each week for visits by a group may also be easier. When parents or teachers call, they can be informed of the usual visiting days; Tuesdays and Thursdays are often found to fit into the program.

Group discussion is also an effective way of handling questions which visitors may have. After a short orientation about the school, they may go into the classrooms to observe. A discussion can be scheduled at the end of the observation period. This provides an opportunity to share observations and ask questions. If a group of students or teachers wish to visit, it probably is best to schedule separate days for parents and for teachers, as the interests and questions will be different.

The director should be the person to greet visitors and lead the discussion. It should not be left to a secretary or someone who is not familiar with the program of the school. It is possible that teachers might share in this responsibility as part of the staff development program; the director would have to substitute in the classroom at that time.

The length of time allowed for group visits should be carefully planned. About thirty minutes is the average time for observation in the classroom. Another hour may be allowed for the discussions before and after the observation. Visits by individuals can be shorter.

When visitors are brought into the classroom, they should be introduced to the teacher. (The teacher should also have been told about the visit beforehand.) The visitor is given a place to sit, away from the center of

Fig. 22-3 The director should be available to greet visitors.

activities. If more than one visitor is in the classroom at a time, they should be asked not to talk to each other while they are in the classroom.

Visits to the classroom should be scheduled when program activities are actually taking place; they should not be scheduled for periods when transition is going on since there tends to be confusion at that time. Also, visitors will not learn much about the educational and social benefits from watching children eat or rest.

The director can help the parent to understand the program by pointing out the kinds of things to observe. She may suggest that the parent watch for interaction that goes on between the children or teacher and children. She may direct attention to the number and kind of activities that will be going on. She may ask the parent to watch for the opportunities that the children have to learn.

Discussions after a visit will also help to focus on the program of the school. The director can ask what has been observed. Observations can be discussed in terms of the program of the school.

BROCHURE

A brochure is a convenient way of telling people about a school. It can be sent out in response to a telephone call. It can be given to a parent who stops by the school. It can be distributed at professional meetings or community organizations.

The effectiveness of the brochure depends on how carefully it is prepared. A poor brochure is worse than none at all. A well-done brochure can be extremely effective in publicizing the school. Often there are staff members who can help with the preparation. This may be a time to call on parent volunteers who have special talents.

When designing a brochure, the director will want to consider carefully what the bro-chure is to convey about the school. What image should it present? Colors, pictures, and text will all tell the story.

The information in the brochure should be clear and brief. Many people do not read a brochure carefully. The written information should be done in such a manner that the essential material is easily available when the brochure is skimmed by the reader.

The brochure should contain all the necessary information. It should be of a size that can be mailed conveniently without extra postage.

The kind of paper used should be heavy enough so that is has a good "feel." It should be strong enough to withstand handling when mailed. Some brochures can be mailed without an envelope if the paper is chosen carefully; this saves cost.

Cost of the brochure must be considered. The kind of paper used will determine much of the cost; adding pictures adds to the cost. Different printing processes, also, will affect the cost. Keeping the cost low is to be considered, but should not be done at the expense of conveying a poor image of the school. It would be better to print a good brochure for limited distribution than print unlimited numbers of a poor brochure.

Information that should be included in a brochure is listed:

- Name, address, and telephone number of the school

- Sponsorship of the school

- Hours that the school is in session — Days of the week and months of the year might also be included.

- Procedure for enrollment of children — If new enrollments are taken only at the beginning of a school year, include a statement to this effect.

- Ages of the children served

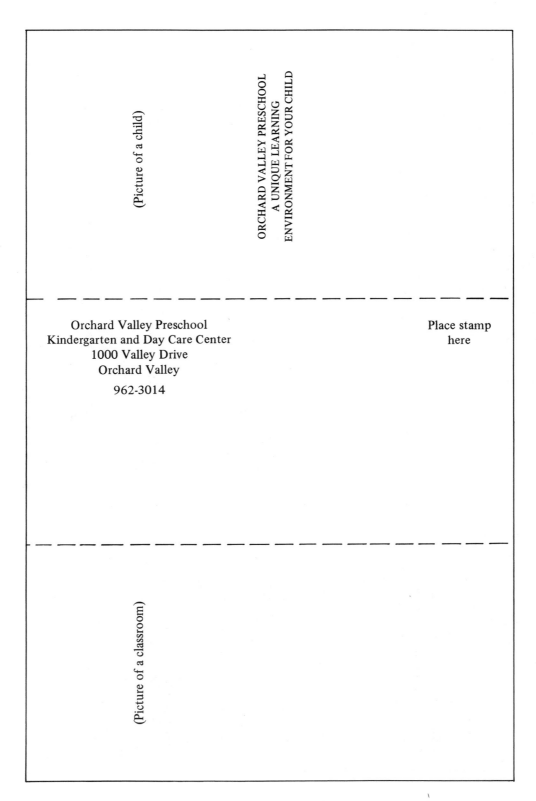

Fig. 22-4 Sample Brochure

ORCHARD VALLEY PRESCHOOL — ONE OF FIVE EDUCATIONAL ACHIEVEMENT CORPORATION SCHOOLS

Program—

Orchard Valley Preschool offers a balanced program of group and individual activities. Classrooms are arranged with interest centers and are designed to foster all aspects of a child's development — emotional, physical, social, and intellectual. Literature, science, math, cooking, prereading readiness, music, art, and language activities are part of the program.

Children are encouraged to initiate and participate in free play experiences, alone or with other children. Special materials are provided in the classroom for this purpose and the playground is designed to stimulate imaginative play.

Health and nutrition are also emphasized in the daily curriculum. Children take responsibility for personal hygiene, learn about safety, and are taught to make appropriate food choices for optimum nutrition.

Enrollment

New enrollments are accepted in January and in August or when openings are available. Application must be made in person. For an appointment, please call:

Mrs. Mary Anton
962-3014

A $15.00 Registration is charged at the time of enrollment.

Ages

Children may be enrolled between the ages of three years and six years.

Fees

Preschool	*9:00-12:00 AM*	
M-F	5 days/wk	$ 65/mo
MWF	3 days/wk	$ 45/mo
T-Th	2 days/wk	$ 35/mo
Kindergarten	*9:00-12:00 AM*	
M-F	5 days/wk	$ 70/mo
Day Care	*7:00 AM-6:00 PM*	
	5 days/wk	$165/mo
	3 days/wk	$130/mo
	2 days/wk	$ 95/mo

(Picture of a child)

(Picture of a child)

Orchard Valley Preschool is a member of Preschool Owners Association.

Fig. 22-4 Sample Brochure (Continued)

- Tuition and other fees (for example, application fee)

- Statement of the philosophy of the school — This should be stated in terms that everyone can understand.

- Short description of the program of the school

- Statement of the benefits of the school

- A brief description of the educational program for parents

- Name of the person to contact for enrollment

- Affiliations or associations to which the school belongs

OPEN HOUSE

An open house can be used to tell prospective parents and the community about a school. A day or evening is set aside when the school is open for visitors to come in and see the facility and the program. A well-planned open house can dramatically display the school. As many staff members as possible should be involved in planning and participation.

Classrooms with displays such as children's art work will demonstrate the creative aspects of the school. Displays of selected

materials show the kinds of activities from which children can learn. Block buildings made by the children, pictures, and storybooks will also tell about the program.

The room arrangement shows how it can be used by the children. If there is a doll corner, it can be set attractively. A story corner can be prepared as though children were expected. A table might be set for snacktime to show that nutrition is an important part of the program.

Slides or films of the children and their activities can be shown in one of the rooms. The pictures are chosen carefully and a thoughtful narration may accompany them.

A room might be designated to allow visitors to use some of the materials that the children use; art materials, puzzles, clay and other manipulative or science materials may be provided.

If the school has a one-way observation screen, the activities that would normally take place could be seen in progress. This, of course, is only possible if the open house is held in the daytime. Visitors would have a

Fig. 22-5 Children's work tells about the school curriculum.

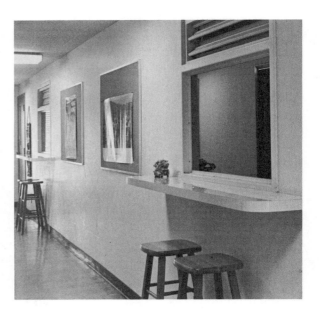

Fig. 22-6 One-way observation screens make it possible for visitors to see classroom activities.

chance to observe and then participate in a discussion.

An open house should give the visitors time to talk to staff members and ask questions. Refreshments may be served to allow for informal conversations. A guest book could be available at this time also. Those signing the guest book can be added to the school's mailing list.

A brochure should be available to hand out to the visitors. If the school has not been able to afford a brochure, a one-page statement can be prepared. It should contain a paragraph explaining the school philosophy and goals. The school name, address, and telephone number of the administrator is included.

Publicizing an open house is sometimes a problem. If a record has been kept of all telephone inquiries, individual notices can be sent; they can also be sent to community organizations and agencies. Neighborhood newspapers can be contacted to include an article about the school. A notice can be placed at the entrance of the school, and posters can be displayed in nearby businesses.

COMMUNITY ACTIVITIES

The director can make the school better known by participating in community activities or by bringing the community into the school. Some schools are actually planned to serve as a community center. Others become community centers because of the services provided.

Participation in professional meetings, conferences, and workshops is one way to be active in the community. Each time a staff member attends one of these, there is an opportunity to talk to other teachers and directors about the school and its objectives.

School displays are a part of some professional conferences. These displays can be of special programs, materials, or teaching methods. They may show equipment designed

or built by staff members. Any school that has something special to share with others can use display opportunities for publicity.

Publication of articles or books was mentioned as part of staff development. Staff should be encouraged to write about the special features of the school or their ideas about teaching.

All directors can find ways to bring people from the community into the school. Services for parents, older people, and older children are all of interest. Lectures, films, and discussions on raising children may be attended by parents in the school and in the neighborhood. Rummage sales, art shows, and book sales attract people of all ages. Saturday art classes and recreational activities for older brothers and sisters of the children could be offered.

Fund-raising events should be planned to publicize the school as well as to raise money for its operation. The format and publicity should provide an opportunity to tell the public about the school. Events held at the school will further help to familiarize people with the school.

The director should be constantly aware of any possibilities for newspaper, television, and radio coverage for events at the school. Getting news coverage may take some personal contact with people in the news field or help from someone who knows the school. Whenever something interesting or unusual takes place, a news release can be sent out. A news release does not take much effort to type and send. It may bring worthwhile results.

Although few directors want to put publicity as a primary job responsibility, they must be aware of the many opportunities that are available. With a little effort and time, the school can become well known in its community. This is important for the growth of the school and as a force in bringing better education to children.

SUMMARY

The director of a school needs to be aware of how the public learns about her school. She must do everything she can to create a good image of the school in the community.

The outside appearance of the school is the first thing that may be noticed. This includes the building itself, the entrance, the play yard and the activities that go on there, and what teachers do outside. These all relay information about the school.

The telephone is a primary instrument for public relations since most parents first call a school to ask questions. Who answers the telephone and how questions are answered must be considered by the director. The kinds of information given and whether the director is available also create impressions of the school. The procedure for handling phone calls should be such that follow-up information can be sent.

Visits should be scheduled. Group discussions are an effective way of handling questions about the school.

A brochure is a convenient way of telling people about a school. The effectiveness of the brochure depends on how carefully it is prepared.

There are other ways to tell the public about a school. An open house can be planned to display the school program and facilities. Slides or films may be shown, and demonstrations presented. Materials can be available for use by the visitors. Observation of children in a classroom is also an effective way of telling about the school.

Staff participation in community activities, professional meetings, conferences, and workshops provide the opportunity to tell others about the school. Publication of articles and books should also be encouraged. Services for parents, older people, and older children are of interest. Fund-raising events also bring the public into the school.

Although few directors would put publicity as a primary job responsibility, each is aware of the many opportunities that are available. With a little effort, the school can become well known in the community.

STUDENT ACTIVITIES

- Obtain brochures from three different schools in your community or area. Compare and evaluate them.
- Discuss ways that your school makes itself known. Have you found methods that are not discussed in the text?
- Write a two-paragraph news release about a recent event at your school.

REVIEW

1. Name six general points to consider when planning public relations.
2. In the preparation of a brochure, what major factor determines the cost?
3. Name four ways in which an open house can tell the community about the school.
4. The text lists twelve kinds of information that should be included in a brochure. Name nine of them.
5. How can the outside of a school building be made more attractive to the public?

Section 6

LEGAL RESPONSIBILITIES AND PROFESSIONAL GROWTH

Unit 23 Laws and Regulations

OBJECTIVES

After studying this unit, the student should be able to

- Name regulations to consider when planning and evaluating a school for young children
- Identify the general categories of laws which pertain to children
- Define some questions to be considered in the regulation of schools for young children

The United States has witnessed changing attitudes toward having young children cared for and educated in groups. More and more women are choosing to work in order to support their families, to supplement the family

Fig. 23-1 It's fun to play and learn at the same time.

income, or for personal reasons. Parents and educators recognize that children are ready and eager to learn long before they enter the elementary schools. Early childhood education centers offer an opportunity for children to participate in learning experiences at this early age.

ISSUES RELATED TO REGULATION

As more children are cared for and educated away from home, the need for regulation becomes necessary. Rules and regulations governing schools for young children may be seen as the exercise of public responsibility for private facilities. Regulations are also used to enforce minimum standards for the protection of children attending private schools. Control and accountability of public funds used in the operation of schools for young children is another reason for rules and regulations.

Increasing numbers of publicly funded programs have been started in the last few years. Hopefully, more programs will be funded in the future. This, of course, depends on federal and state legislation.

Levels of Government

The question of which level of government should regulate schools for young children is an important issue. All levels of government are involved in various ways. City or county regulations may determine where a school can be operated. State departments of health, welfare or education may determine the guidelines for licensing. Federal agencies may write the guidelines for administering or funding certain kinds of programs. Often regulations from all levels are overlapping or conflicting. This makes it difficult for schools to meet the specifications.

Setting the Standards

Should regulations be formulated to set minimum standards or encourage something better? It is sometimes assumed that unless regulations set minimum standards only some persons subject to those regulations will be faced with a hardship. In practice some schools do no more than meet the minimum standards. Other schools design programs that meet the minimum standards, but also add much more.

Who should set the standards for regulation is another important issue. Should governmental agencies be responsible for setting appropriate standards? Should a community be responsible because of its greater knowledge of the needs of families living in that community? Should the users of the service (the parents of the children) set the standards since they are most directly affected?

Licensing

Licensing has traditionally dealt first with the facility in order to insure the safety of the children. There is some confusion concerning what the "facility" is. Is it just the building and grounds or does it include people, services, and programs? Licensing in some states now includes requirements for staff qualifications and teacher/child ratio. Federal and state guidelines may also include requirements for health services, social service, sanitation, and nutrition.

Who should be regulated? Is licensing required for private and public programs? Is licensing for both large and small schools? Does it apply to family day care? Private schools sometimes find themselves financially unable to meet standards that are designed for programs that receive large sums from public sources.

Quality of Program

Quality of program is another issue that needs to be explored. Before minimum standards can be set, a determination of requirements for a quality program must be made. There is also the question of whether one kind of program is suitable for all children. A quality program for one group may not be considered a quality program for another group of children.

Fig. 23-2 A Small Group of Children Making Collages

Monitoring Regulations

The problem of monitoring any kind of regulation system is difficult to solve. Monitoring of guidelines set by a federal agency is extremely complicated. It is also costly to provide regional offices and staff. Local or community agencies have a better opportunity to visit schools under their jurisdiction to determine if regulations are being met. In practice, however, monitoring has not been as effective as it should be. Different persons serving as monitors who visit the schools often interpret the guidelines differently. Therefore, the requirements for implementation vary from school to school.

Clarity of Guidelines

The language in which regulations are written is another concern. There are those who feel that regulations should be broad and general; the licensing staff can then use their own judgment to interpret them in individual circumstances. Others feel that regulations should be quite specific and written clearly so everyone can understand them. This would make it possible for those subject to licensing to know exactly what they are supposed to do.

KINDS OF REGULATIONS

Specific regulations vary from state to state. This text can present only generalizations about some of the regulations that a school might have to meet. The owner, director, or anyone involved in setting up a school for young children should contact the appropriate agencies to get the information for their state or locality. Usually the departments of health, education, and housing will supply the required information.

Zoning

In urban communities, the first regulation a school may be faced with is zoning.

Cities and towns can establish codes that restrict the use of land within their jurisdiction. A school may be allowed to operate in one area of the city or town, but not in another. Some cities restrict early childhood centers to areas reserved for commercial use; others restrict them to residential areas. The local zoning commission should be contacted before any property is purchased or leased.

Licensing Requirements

Most early childhood centers and other schools for young children must have a license issued by a state agency. In most states, licensing is accomplished through some branch of the social services department. In others, the department of education, public health, or child welfare may have the responsibility.

Licensing requirements deal first with the physical requirements of the site to be licensed. Most states require thirty-five square feet of indoor space and seventy-five to one hundred square feet of outdoor space per child. Requirements for window area, the number of

Fig. 23-3 **Zoning codes place the early childhood school on a busy street.**

toilets, and the kind of heating may also be included.

Recommendations for teacher/child ratio at different age levels may also be included. In some states, program content and quality is considered for licensing. Some licensing laws also cover teacher qualifications.

Fire Safety and Sanitation

Public safety laws and public health laws serve as the statutory base for another form of regulation of schools for young children. Schools must meet fire safety and sanitation requirements in order to receive a permit to operate the program. These requirements are imposed to protect the children from an unsafe physical environment.

Requirements may include the specification that the space be on the ground level. An adequate fire alarm system must be provided and adequate sprinklers installed. Each room must have two exits. Other specifications are directed to the adequacy of sanitary conditions in the kitchen and bathrooms. The state department of health may be contacted for specific information.

Building Codes

If a new building is being provided for the school, building codes must be met. Inspections and approval may be required by local and/or state building departments. The inspection covers electrical safety, plumbing, and general building construction.

Transportation

When transportation is provided for the children, another form of regulation must be met. The state motor vehicle department sets regulations for any bus that carries children. These requirements include identifying the vehicle as a school bus, the use of certain types of lights, and transporting only a certain number of children at any one time.

Qualified Staff

In public education, credentialing of staff is a form of regulating the kind and

Fig. 23-4 The school bus must meet regulations.

Fig. 23-5 This young man enjoys working with preschoolers.

quality of programs for young children. Credentials are issued by a state department of education upon the completion of the required program of study. Attempts are being made to more clearly define requirements for a credential that will qualify a person to teach in a day care or preschool program.

Professionals in early childhood education have been reluctant to adopt the same kind of credential qualifications that exist for other sectors of public education. Elementary and secondary credentials have been, by tradition, based on subject matter. In other words, the teacher was primarily expected to have an extensive knowledge of the subjects that would be taught. A limited number of courses would deal with understanding child development or would offer actual experiences with children.

Teachers of young children feel that it is more important to be able to understand the child and his development. Teaching of subject matter is important, but helping the child develop his full potential as a person is the primary purpose of early childhood education. Changes in the educational system and the trend toward a more open structure in classroom environments have caused teachers and institutions of learning to examine current requirements for credentials. Attempts are being made to design a credential that will qualify a person to teach in day care programs, various types of preschool programs, and in the early elementary grades.

State and Federal Control

Programs that are publicly funded and publicly operated may be subject to regulations that are not applicable to private schools. Schools that are administered by a public agency are subject to control through administrative procedures and restrictions outlined by the state legislature. For example, some states have early childhood education programs administered under the state social services department. Administrative guidelines are compiled by the department for the purpose of achieving quality control. Budget requirements, qualification and number of staff, and program content may be covered. Service components of the program may also be covered by the guidelines.

Another form of control of publicly funded programs is achieved through the Federal Interagency Requirements. These guidelines were compiled by an interdepartmental group from federal agencies. They serve as a means to insure quality services for children regardless of what federal agency was the funding source.

Federal Interagency Guidelines cover many parts of the operations of a program for children. Comprehensive social, health, and nutritional services must be offered. Parents must have an extensive participation in planning the program for the children and in determining overall policies of the school. Limits are set on the size of the groups of children. The teacher/child ratio is very specific: 1:5 for three-year-olds, 1:7 for four- and five-year-olds, and 1:10 for children over six years of age. All educational activities for the children must be under the direction and supervision of a person who has had early childhood education. Staff must participate in a continuous inservice training.

Monitoring of programs subject to Federal Interagency Requirements is often difficult. A project may be receiving money from several sources and, as a result, be subject to several sets of requirements. The federal monitor has difficulty in determining the extent of compliance. Also, the federal monitor may not be familiar with local conditions and may not understand the need for slight variations in interpretation of the guidelines. Some programs, because of their location in areas distant from the federal offices, may not be able to receive much help, and little monitoring may take place.

EMPLOYMENT LAWS

Conditions of employment, particularly of women, are regulated in most states by a state labor code, administered by a department of industrial relations. Regulations may be specified concerning the number of working hours per day and per week that are allowed. Minimum wages may be specified, with additional information concerning wages for learners or student workers. Usually, a provision of time is stated for meals and rest periods. The type of facilities necessary may also be covered including a room and couch for rest, toilet facilities, and washing basins.

Some states provide workmen's compensation and/or disability insurance. Requirements and benefits are specified in the state unemployment insurance code. Payment is made to an employee during absence from work because of an injury or a prolonged illness. The amount of the payment is based on the wages the employee earned during the highest quarter of the benefit year. The cost of this insurance is shared by both the employer and the employee.

Under Title VII of the Civil Rights Act, and subsequent laws, an employer cannot discharge or refuse to hire any individual because of sex. It is also unlawful to "limit, segregate or classify his employees in any way which would deprive or tend to deprive any individual of employment opportunities."

Since schools for young children have traditionally been staffed by women, this law does not open an employment field to women. One of the things the law has done is to force a reexamination of other laws related to the employment of women. For instance, state laws relating to maximum number of working hours and rest periods

are being tested in many states. Also, another important side effect is that this law has begun to open the field of early childhood education to men.

The Federal Equal Pay Act specifies that no employer can pay different wages for equal jobs to men and women except under certain specified conditions. This provision is part of the Federal Fair Labor Standard Act. It also provides that it should not conflict with any federal or state law or municipal ordinance establishing a minimum wage or a maximum work week. Where state laws require a higher minimum wage for one sex engaged in a particular job, the federal law requires that the same wage be paid to the opposite sex engaged in the same job.

These laws are currently being tested in the courts to determine further refinements of interpretation. Their impact upon the employment of both women and men will be extensive in the future.

In addition to nondiscrimination in jobs, a second category to be familiar with involves the employment of minors. There are statutes that specify the age at which minors can begin to work. There may be restrictions upon the number of hours they may work. There may

Fig. 23-6 Many schools employ high school students as assistants.

be restrictions on the kinds of occupations that the minor can engage in. Many schools employ young people as assistants after school hours or during summers. It is important to be familiar with laws pertaining to employment of young persons.

LAWS AFFECTING CHILDREN

Laws pertaining to minors are important to the operation of a school for young children. Some of the laws directly affect the treatment of children in the care of someone other than their parents. Other laws relate to education of children and to parental responsibility. Because of the variations in the laws from one state to another, this text can only summarize the categories of laws that pertain to children.

Treatment of Children

The first important category concerns the treatment of children. No person may commit sexual acts upon or in the presence of children. Many other acts are prohibited, such as annoying, molesting, selling drugs or alcohol to, or involving a minor in criminal acts. Any person convicted of any of these crimes may be refused employment by a school.

Child Abuse or Injury

Another category of law concerns abuse of or injury to a child. Neither the parent nor another person may willfully injure a child. In the case of abuse by the parent, the child may be removed from parental custody. When injury or death is caused by a wrongful act or by neglect, a parent can sue. Implications for the owner or operator of a school are clear. Abuse of a child by a parent is unlawful and should be reported. Abuse or neglect of a child by someone other than the parent is also unlawful.

Parental Responsibility

Responsibility of parents for the acts of their children is another area involving legal action. Some states now have laws putting the responsibility for willful and criminal acts of children upon the parents. In some cases, parents are financially liable for damage to a school. These laws make parents liable for injury to another person if it can be proved that the parents provided their child with a dangerous implement. Although preschool personnel may not be involved in enforcement of these statutes at the school, it is important to be aware of the implications.

Child Education

The state education or administrative codes outline requirements for compulsory attendance at school and the age of admissions to school. The director of a school for young children should be familiar with reasons for exemption from education and with provisions for the education of physically or mentally handicapped children.

Many schools for young children prepare children for continuing education to the elementary level. Therefore, it is important to

Fig. 23-7 The early childhood center prepares children for continuing education.

know state requirements and prohibitions in curriculum areas.

Employment of Minors

As stated earlier, there are statutes which specify the age at which minors can begin to work, the number of hours, the kinds of occupations, and other factors. The child labor laws are quite specific and can be easily obtained from the state department of labor.

In short, administrators, directors, and others interested in the operation of schools for young children should contact the local and state sources for information pertaining to their community's regulations and laws. The local library, college or university may be helpful; the state departments of health provide excellent referrals when necessary. The director must know about the regulations and laws. She has legal and moral responsibilities.

SUMMARY

As more women work outside the home, more children are being cared for in group situations. Laws and regulations governing those programs are necessary to insure the safety of the children. They are also necessary to insure wise use of public funds for early childhood education programs.

There are some important issues related to the regulation of schools for young children:

- Which level of government should regulate schools?

- Who should set the standards for regulation?

- What should be regulated?

- What is covered by licensing?
- Quality of program?
- How can programs be monitored effectively?
- Should regulations be written in broad, general language or be very specific?
- Should regulations set minimum standards or encourage something better? Both new and ongoing schools are subject to many kinds of regulation.
- Zoning requirements
- Licensing requirements
- Fire safety and sanitation requirements
- Building codes
- Regulations for bus transportation
- Credentials of staff
- Administrative procedures and restrictions
- Federal Interagency Requirements

Laws relating to employment are important to the operation of early childhood education programs. Two important laws with wide implications are listed.

- Title VII of the 1964 Civil Rights Act
- Federal Equal Pay Act

It is also important for the director of a school to be familiar with the laws pertaining to:

- The treatment of children
- Abuse or injury to the child
- The responsibility of parents for the acts of their children
- The education of children
- The employment of minors

STUDENT ACTIVITIES

- Research the regulations governing early childhood education programs in your state.
- Discuss any problems that the school with which you are associated has had concerning laws and regulations.

- Visit a school which is funded differently from your school. Describe the methods of regulating and monitoring this program.

REVIEW

1. Name two important laws which deal with employment of personnel in schools for young children.

2. Why were Federal Interagency Requirements formulated?

3. What are some of the issues to be considered in reference to the regulation of schools for young children?

4. Why is there a feeling that regulations should be written in a broad, general manner?

5. How do the Civil Rights Act (Title VII) and the Federal Equal Pay Act differ in the major emphasis?

6. Name the general categories of laws pertaining to minors.

7. Name some regulations to be considered when planning a new school.

Unit 24 Organizations, Agencies, and Publications

OBJECTIVES

After studying this unit, the student should be able to

- Discuss the purposes of professional organizations
- List some organizations for teachers of young children
- Recognize the publications of the professional organizations

It is the responsibility of the director of an early childhood education center to be informed of the organizations that are working toward better education for children. She may choose to be active in only one or two, according to her interests and time. Even though she may not be able to participate in others, she can be knowledgeable about their purposes. She keeps her staff informed and makes the publications available for their use.

Professional organizations usually keep their members informed about legislative action that affects children. The director may also wish to maintain contact with the legislative representative for the school district; mailings from the legislator will help to keep the staff informed.

Some states have organizations that have been formed specifically for the purpose of political action. The director and her staff should consider the value of belonging to these political organizations. They can certainly be aware of the current political issues concerning early childhood education. Political action can be achieved through profes-

sional organizations, political organizations, or local elections.

Teaching is a profession requiring extensive knowledge and varied skills. Becoming a good teacher takes all of one's life. It begins with one's own childhood experiences and continues through the years in school. It goes on during the countless daily experiences with children in the classroom.

Early childhood teachers have always considered themselves professionals. Persons outside the field, however, have been slow to accept them as teachers. For years, early childhood education has been perceived as merely baby-sitting. The public image of early childhood teachers is now changing.

Active early childhood organizations have been instrumental in bringing about this change. They have bombarded the public with information about early childhood education. They have lobbied in state and federal legislatures in order to bring about recognition. They have solicited new members. They have sponsored workshops and conferences so that teachers can share ideas.

PURPOSES OF PROFESSIONAL ORGANIZATIONS

Having seen the results of pressure groups, most teachers of young children recognize the importance of belonging to professional organizations. Organizations for these teachers of early childhood education now have thousands of members throughout the United States. Organizations for elementary teachers often have programs for teachers of early childhood education, also.

Public Relations Campaigns

Professional organizations have the ability to launch massive public relation campaigns. A national organization, such as National Association for the Education of Young Children, with branches throughout the United States, can disseminate information to an extensive public. They have the means to print pamphlets. They have the contacts to get articles into newspapers and magazines. They may have the ability to get radio or television coverage. All of these media influence public thinking.

Improvement of Working Conditions

Professional organizations have long been used to upgrade working conditions of those in the profession. Negotiations over salaries and fringe benefits have been successful. These professional groups have also been influential in changing teacher/child ratios in the classroom.

Job Placement

Conferences and newsletters sponsored by professional organizations offer job placement services to teachers. New teachers who are seeking a first job often find a wider range of options through the organization. Teachers seeking changes in jobs know whom to contact and where to go for help.

Research

Some professional organizations sponsor research on child development and teaching. Some set aside funds for this purpose. Others seek funds from foundations and government to carry out research. The findings are then published in the magazine of the organization.

Continuing Education

Teacher organizations provide many kinds of activities designed to further the continuing education of their members. Workshops and conferences serve this purpose. Magazines, newsletters, pamphlets, and books published by the organization keep teachers knowledgeable about developments in their field. Some may offer consultation services to schools for curriculum planning, staff development, or parent education.

Common Goals

Professional organizations provide the opportunity for persons from related fields to work together toward common goals. Social workers, doctors, psychologists, and nutritionists may be active with teachers. They all have a common interest in the welfare and education of children.

Political Action

Political action has become an important function of many organizations. They maintain contact with legislators and stay informed about proposed laws affecting children. Many sponsor letter writing campaigns to legislative representatives when crucial issues are to be voted on. Some may even suggest or help to write new laws. They keep their membership informed about current and proposed legislative action.

Social Activities

Many teachers feel isolated because they spend so much time in a classroom with children. During the working day there is little time to talk to other adults. Conferences, meetings, and workshops bring teachers together. Dinners, picnics, and tours also provide the opportunity to meet others.

NATIONAL ORGANIZATIONS

Early childhood education is a fast growing field. New knowledge is discovered and shared each year. New ideas are frequently discussed among those involved in education. New opportunitites for teachers are being created.

All those interested in the education of young children have a responsibility to themselves and to the profession to be informed. In addition to being knowledgeable, each should accept a responsibility for shaping the future of early childhood education. Teachers, directors, and parents must be active in determining what happens to schools and to children. It is hoped that the following information about organizations and agencies concerned with young children will provide a framework for participation.

Although there are many state and local organizations for teachers, the following summary includes only those that have national scope. Each may have regional chapters, but are under the sponsorship of a nationwide organization. The information on each of the groups discussed was obtained from the Encyclopedia of Associations, Vol. 1, National Organizations of the United States, Edition 7. This is published by Gale Research Company in Detroit, Michigan.

NATIONAL CONGRESS OF PARENTS AND TEACHERS (PTA)

National office: 700 North Rush Street
Chicago, Illinois 60611

Founded: 1897

Purpose: Broad aim is to develop among community institutions and agencies a type of cooperation that will preserve the American way of life. Its work encompasses parent education and teacher education. This organization has been active in influencing laws affecting children and schools and has waged public relations campaigns to educate the public concerning good education. In 1969, PTA promoted a nationwide campaign for the expansion of early childhood educational programs. They have encouraged the formation of preschool PTAs and preschool sections in order to further influence what happens to children.

Publications: PTA Magazine, 10 times a year
National Parent Teacher
National Congress Bulletin

NATIONAL ASSOCIATION FOR THE EDUCATION OF YOUNG CHILDREN (NAEYC)

National office: 1834 Connecticut Avenue, N.W.
Washington, D.C. 20009

Founded: 1931

Purpose: Broad aims are to serve and to act on behalf of young children, with primary focus on the provision of educational services and resources. To accomplish this, the organization works to increase the competence of teachers of young children. Its members publish informative materials and assist individuals and groups to learn more effective ways in influencing legislation related to children. They strive to accomplish a commitment by this nation to provide a good beginning life for every child.

Publications: Young Children, bimonthly

ASSOCIATION FOR CHILDHOOD EDUCATION INTERNATIONAL (ACEI)

National office: 3615 Wisconsin Avenue, N.W.
Washington, D.C. 20016

Founded: 1931

Purpose: Teachers, parents and other adults interested in promoting good educational practices work for the well-being of all children. This organization is active in promoting continued professional growth of teachers. Members work to bring about active cooperation among all groups concerned with children in the school, home, and community. They inform the public of the needs of children and the ways in which the school program can meet these needs. The association encourages professionalism through awards of fellowships each year. The national office maintains a library of 1500 volumes on child development, early childhood education and elementary education.

Publications: Childhood Education, 8 copies per year
A.C.E.I. Yearbook, annually
Bulletins on equipment, bibliographies

DAY CARE AND CHILD DEVELOPMENT COUNCIL OF AMERICA (DCCDCA)

National office: 1012 14th Street, N.W.
Washington, D.C. 20005

Founded: 1960

Purpose: To generate broader public understanding of and support for quality services for children. DCCDCA functions as a national information center about such services. Consultant services on program planning, fund-raising, and organizational techniques are available.

This organization is active in influencing legislation concerning schools and children and maintains close contact with the federal legislature. Local and regional groups are helped to organize for state legislative activities. Its goal is to see creation in every community of a comprehensive system of daytime service programs. These services would help children develop their full human potential: intellectually, physically, emotionally, and socially.

Publications: Voice for Children, monthly
Action for Children, bimonthly
Pamphlets, bulletins, books on child development and education

NATIONAL EDUCATION ASSOCIATION (NEA)

National office: 1201 16th Street, N.W.
Washington, D.C. 20036

Founded: 1857

Purpose: To bring about unity among elementary, secondary, and college teachers, principals, administrators, counselors, and others interested in American education. Recently, the organization added a committee on elementary-kindergarten nursery education. The members strive towards teacher governance of the profession; they believe that teachers know what is best for teachers and education. They are currently concerned with the concept of accountability and believe that accountability is the joint responsibility of administrators, school boards, the public, and teachers. They see the professional teacher as an active participant in all aspects of education.

Publications: Today's Education, 9 copies per year
NEA Reporter, 8 copies per year
Research Bulletin, quarterly
NEA Handbook, annual

PARENT COOPERATIVE PRESCHOOL INTERNATIONAL (PCPI)

National office: P.O. Box 40123
Indianapolis, Indiana 46240

Founded: 1960

Purpose: To serve those interested in preschool education in nonprofit schools for young children operated by parents on a cooperative basis. The organization provides information pertaining to parent cooperatives and encourages the exchange of ideas among member schools. The membership promotes desirable standards for program practices and conditions and encourages continuing education for teachers and directors. Legislation related to the education and well-being of children and families is studied and information distributed.

Publications: PCPI Journal, 3 times a year
Directory of Parent Cooperative Preschools, annual
Bibliographies and bulletins on publicity, organization, teacher hiring, safety, and starting a cooperative

CHILD STUDY ASSOCIATION OF AMERICA (CSAA)

National office: 9 East 89th Street
New York, New York 10028

Founded: 1888

Purpose: To promote family mental health. The organization conducts training programs for professional, paraprofessionals, and parents interested in early childhood education. Workshops and conferences for educators and social workers involved in early childhood education are held. Books on child development are reviewed and annotated lists are published. Books for children are reviewed.

Publications: Children's Books of the Year, annual
Recommended Reading About Children and Family Life
Extensive pamphlets and books for parents and educators

SOCIETY FOR RESEARCH IN CHILD DEVELOPMENT (SRCD)

National office: University of Chicago
                    5801 Ellis Avenue
                    Chicago, Illinois 60637

Founded: 1933

Purpose: To further research in all areas of child development. It is an interdisciplinary society including anatomists, anthropologists, dentists, educators, pediatricians, psychologists, etc.

Publications: **Child Development, quarterly**
                 Child Development Abstracts and Bibliography, 3 per year
                 Review of Research in Child Development

OTHER SOURCES OF INFORMATION FOR TEACHERS AND DIRECTORS

Space does not allow for review of all the numerous organizations that provide services for persons interested in early childhood education.

A guide to additional sources of information, however, will allow each school to pursue further help as needed.

American Council of Education
1785 Massachusetts Avenue, N.W.
Washington, D.C. 20036

Appalachian Regional Commission
1666 Connecticut Avenue, N.W.
Washington, D.C. 20235

Bank Street College of Education
610 West 112th Street
New York, New York 10025

Black Child Development Institute, Inc.
1028 Connecticut Avenue, N.W.
Suite 514
Washington, D.C. 20036

Child Development Associate Consortium, Inc.
7315 Wisconsin Avenue, N.W.
Washington, D.C. 20014

Child Welfare League of America, Inc.
67 Irving Place
New York, New York 10003

Dr. Martin Luther King Family Center
124 North Hoyne Avenue, Apt. 113
Chicago, Illinois 60612

ERIC (Educational Resource Information Center/
    Early Childhood Education)
University of Illinois at Urbana-Champaign
805 West Pennsylvania Avenue
Urbana, Illinois 61801

ERIC Information Retrieval Center on the
    Disadvantaged
Teachers College
Columbia University
New York, New York 10027

The Merrill-Palmer Institute of Human Development and Family Life
71 East Ferry Avenue
Detroit, Michigan 48202

Pacific Oaks College
714 West California Boulevard
Pasadena, California 91105

Play Schools Association
120 West 57th Street
New York, New York 10019

U.S. Department of Health, Education, and
    Welfare
Office of Child Development
Washington, D.C. 20201

Children's Bureau
P.O. Box 1182
Washington, D.C. 20013

Child Development Service Bureau
400 Sixth Street, S.W.
Washington, D.C. 20201

Women's Bureau
U.S. Department of Labor
Washington, D.C. 20201

Office of Education
Washington, D.C. 20202

SUMMARY

Many teachers belong to organizations concerned with early childhood education. It is the responsibility of the director to encourage participation and to keep her staff informed. She may choose to be active in only one or two, depending upon her time and interests. She can know about other organizations and can subscribe to their publications.

Organizations in some states have been formed specifically for the purpose of political action. The director and her staff may choose to belong to this type of organization. Political action is among the purposes of many organizations that were originally established for other reasons.

Large organizations have the means to launch massive public relations campaigns. They also have the power of numbers needed to bring about an upgrading of working conditions for teachers.

Conferences and newsletters sponsored by professional organizations offer job placement services to teachers. Many sponsor research on child development and teaching. Others provide many kinds of activities designed to further the continuing education of their members.

Organizations provide the opportunity for persons from related fields to work together toward common goals. Social workers, doctors, teachers, and others concerned with the welfare of children can share their common interests. Social activities, too, are an important part of many organizations.

Political action has become an important function of many organizations; contact with legislators is maintained; letter writing campaigns help to make new laws. The membership is kept informed about proposed legislation and results of organized action.

All those interested in the education of young children have a responsibility to themselves and to the profession to be informed. In addition to being knowledgeable, each must accept a responsibility for shaping the future of early childhood education.

STUDENT ACTIVITIES

- Investigate which professional organizations are active in your community. Determine how many members belong to these local groups.
- Discuss ways the school with which you are associated has used the resources of a professional organization.
- Attend a workshop or conference offered by one of the local organizations. Report on the purposes of the workshop or conference and its effectiveness.

REVIEW

A. Indicate the name of the organizations that are represented by the letters:
1. DCCDCA
2. PCPI
3. NAEYC
4. SRCD
5. NEA

B.   Match the publication with the organization.

1. National Parent Teacher
2. Young Children
3. Today's Education
4. Voice for Children
5. Childhood Education
6. Children's Books of the Year

a. National Association for the Education of Young Children
b. Association for Childhood Education International
c. Day Care and Child Development Council of America
d. National Congress of Parents and Teachers
e. National Education Association
f. Child Study Association of America

C.   Name some purposes of the professional organizations.

D.   Explain why persons from related fields can benefit by belonging to a professional organization.

E.   Explain how political involvement may help the cause of early childhood education.

BIBLIOGRAPHY

Auerbach, Aline B. *Parents Learn Through Discussion: Principles and Practices of Parent Group Discussion.* New York: John Wiley & Sons, 1968.

Bloom, Benjamin S., et al. *Taxonomy of Educational Objectives; Handbook I, Cognitive Domain.* New York: David McKay, 1969.

Bloom, Benjamin S., et al. *Taxonomy of Behavioral Objectives; Handbook II, Affective Domain.* New York: David McKay, 1969.

Butler, Annie L. *Early Childhood Education: Planning and Administering Programs.* New York: D. Van Nostrand Co., 1974.

Evans, E. B.; B. Shub; and M. Weinstein. *How to Plan, Develop, and Operate a Day Care Center.* Boston: Beacon Press, 1971.

Friedberg, M. Paul. *Playgrounds for City Children.* Washington, D.C.: Association for Childhood Education International, 1969.

Frost, J. L. and B. L. Klein. *Children's Play and Playgrounds.* Boston: Allyn and Bacon, Inc., 1979.

Gilley, Jeanne Mack. *Early Childhood Development and Education.* Albany, N.Y.: Delmar Publishers, 1980.

Hildebrand, Verna. *Introduction to Early Childhood Education.* New York: Macmillan, 1971.

Kritchevsky, S. and E. Prescott with L. S. Walling. *Planning Environments for Young Children: Physical Space.* Washington, D.C.: National Association for the Education of Young Children, 1969.

Landreth, Catherine. *Preschool Learning and Teaching.* New York: Harper and Row Publishers, 1972.

Mager, Robert F. *Preparing Instructional Objectives.* Belmont, CA: Fearon Publishers, 1975.

Mallum, Mary A., ed. *Curriculum Guide — Goals and Growth Experiences for the Early Years.* Hawthorne, CA: Cohee Enterprises, 1971.

Martin, Beatrice D. *Teaching Young Children.* Albany, N.Y.: Delmar Publishers, 1975.

Massoglia, Elinor T. *Early Childhood Education in the Home.* Albany, N.Y.: Delmar Publishers, 1977.

Morgan, Gwen G. *Regulation of Early Childhood Programs.* Washington, D.C.: Day Care and Child Development Council of America, Inc., 1973.

National Organizations of the United States, Encyclopedia of Associations, Vol. 1, Detroit: Gale Research Company.

Nedler, S. and O. D. McAfee. *Working With Parents.* Belmont, CA: Wadsworth Publishing Co., 1979.

Nixon, R. H. and C. L. Nixon. *Introduction to Early Childhood Education*. New York: Random House, 1971.

"NLN Supports Major Drive to Immunize Preschool Children," *National League for Nursing News*. 22:6, July-August, 1974.

Pickarts, E. and G. Fargo, *Parent Education: Toward Parental Competence*. Englewood Cliffs, New Jersey: Prentice-Hall, Inc., 1971.

Pitcher, E., et al. *Helping Young Children Learn*. Columbus: Charles E. Merrill Publishing Co., 1974.

Read, Katherine. *The Nursery School, A Human Relationships Laboratory*, 5th ed. Philadelphia: W. B. Saunders Company, 1971.

Readings in Early Childhood Education, Annual Editions. Guilford, Connecticut: Dushkin Publishing Group, Inc.

Reinesch, E. H. and R. E. Minear, Jr., M.D. *Health of the Preschool Child*. New York: John Wiley & Sons, 1978.

Sciarra, Dorothy J. *Developing and Administering A Child Care Center*. Boston: Houghton Mifflin Company, 1978.

Tyler, Ralph W. *Basic Principles of Curriculum and Instruction*. Illinois: University of Chicago Press, 1970.

Ward, M. R., Jr. *California Juvenile Laws*. Los Angeles: Legal Book Corporation, 1970.

Wiles, K. and J. T. Lovell. *Supervision for Better Schools*, 4th ed. New York: Prentice-Hall, 1975.

Zigler, Edward. "A New Child Care Profession — The Child Development Advocate." *Young Children*, 29:2, 1971.

An Annotated Bibliography For Child and Family Development Programs. DHEW Publication Number (OHDS) 78-31118.

Food Buying Guide and Recipes. Washington, D.C.: Project Head Start, Office of Economic Opportunity.

Food for Groups of Young Children Cared For During the Day. Hille, Hellen M., Washington, D.C.: Department of Health, Education and Welfare.

Kitchen Equipment Guide For Child Service Institutions. Washington, D.C.: United States Department of Agriculture.

A Menu Planning Guide for Breakfast at School. Washington, D.C.: United States Department of Agriculture (FNS-7).

A Menu Planning Guide for Type A School Lunches. Washington, D.C.: United States Department of Agriculture (PA-719).

North, A. Frederick, Jr., M.D. *Day Care Health Services: A Guide for Project Directors and Health Personnel*. Washington, D.C.: HEW, Office of Child Development, Bulletin No. 72-4.

Nutrition, Better Eating for a Head Start, Washington, D.C.: Project Head Start, Office of Economic Opportunity.

Parker, Ronald and Laura L. Dittman, ed. *Staff Training*. Day Care Bulletin No. 5 (OCD 72-23), Office of Child Development, 1971. DHEW PUBLICATION No. 72-23. U.S. Department of Health, Education and Welfare, Washington, D.C.

ACKNOWLEDGMENTS

The author wishes to thank the following individuals for their assistance.

Nat Charnley

Donald W. Click

Helen Condon

Dolores Deutsch

Shirley Garber

Allene Goldman

Kit Kollenberg

Lee Murray

Terri Spingath

Docia Zavitkovsky

Cooperation by the administrators, teachers, staff members and parents of these educational institutions is deeply appreciated.

Charnley Johelen School, Santa Monica

Lincoln Child Development Center, Santa Monica

Los Angeles Valley College

McKinley Children's Center, Santa Monica

Moorpark College

Ocean Park Children's Center

Santa Monica College

Santa Monica Montessori School

The help and cooperation of the following individuals and early childhood centers in obtaining new photographs for the second edition are greatly appreciated.

Arbor Hill Day Care Center; Albany, N.Y.

Pineview Community Church Day Care Center; Albany, N.Y.

John Black

Justin DuPont

Gail Ellison

Karyl Gatteno

Jack Lasek (Jack 'L Photos)

Joseph Tardi Associates

The staff at Delmar Publishers Inc.

Sponsoring Editor — Barbara Mohan

Source Editor — Elinor Gunnerson

Consulting Editor — Jeanne Machado

During the Fall Semester of the 1974–75 school year, this instructional material was classroom tested at

Los Angeles Valley College, Van Nuys, California, Dept. of Home Economics (Child Development Courses)

Santa Monica College, Santa Monica, California, Dept. of Child Development

Revisions for this second edition of the text have been tested at Moorpark College, Moorpark, California.

INDEX